PLANNING AND THE POLITICAL MARKET

PLANNING AND THE POLITICAL MARKET

Public Choice and the Politics of Government Failure

MARK PENNINGTON

THE ATHLONE PRESS

LONDON & NEW BRUNSWICK, NJ

First published in 2000 by
THE ATHLONE PRESS
1 Park Drive, London NW11 7SG
and New Brunswick, New Jersey

British Library Cataloguing in Publication Data
A catalogue record for this book is available from the British Library

ISBN 0 485 00406 2 HB
0 485 00606 5 PB

Library of Congress Cataloging-in-Publication Data
Pennington, Mark.
  Planning and the political market : public choice and the politics of government failure/
Mark Pennington.
    p. cm.
Includes bibliographical references.
ISBN 0-485-00406-2 (cloth : alk. paper)–ISBN 0-485-00606-5 (pbk. : alk. paper)
  1. Social choice–Great Britain. 2. Land use–Great Britain–Planning. 3. Pressure
groups–Great Britain. I. Title.

HB846.8.P46 2000
333.73'17'0941–dc21   00-031308

Distributed in The United States, Canada and South America by
Transaction Publishers
390 Campus Drive
Somerset, New Jersey 08873

Typeset in Garamond by
Aarontype Limited, Easton, Bristol
Printed and bound in Great Britain by
MFP Design & Print, Stretford, Manchester

For my mother

CONTENTS

LIST OF FIGURES

LIST OF TABLES

LIST OF ACRONYMS

AAS	Assisted Areas Scheme
ALURE	Alternative Land Use and the Rural Economy
AONB	Area of Outstanding Natural Beauty
BEC	Building Employers Confederation
CAP	Common Agricultural Policy
CC	Countryside Commission
CIPFA	Chartered Institute for Public Finance and Accounting
CLA	Country Landowners Association
CPOS	County Planning Officers Society
CPRE	Council for the Protection of Rural England
DAS	Development Area Status
DoE	Department of the Environment
DoT	Department of Transport
DETR	Department of the Environment, Transport and the Regions
DPOS	District Planning Officers Society
DSS	Department of Social Security
DTI	Department of Trade and Industry
EN	English Nature
ESA	Environmentally Sensitive Area
EU	European Union
FMB	Federation of Master Builders
FoE	Friends of the Earth
HBF	House Builders Federation
HMIP	Her Majesty's Inspectorate of Pollution
MAFF	Ministry of Agriculture Fisheries and Food
MPOS	Metropolitan Planning Officers Society
NCC	Nature Conservancy Council
NFU	National Farmers Union
NHBC	National Housing and Building Council
PPG	Planning Policy Guidance
RICS	Royal Institute of Chartered Surveyors
RSG	Revenue Support Grant
RSNC	Royal Society for Nature Conservation
RSPB	Royal Society for the Protection of Birds

RTPI   Royal Town Planning Institute
SPZ   Simplified Planning Zone
SSA   Standard Spending Assessment
SSSI   Site of Special Scientific Interest
TCPA   Town and Country Planning Association
UDC   Urban Development Corporation
VBSG   Volume Builders Study Group
YOC   Young Ornithologists Club

ACKNOWLEDGEMENTS

There are a number of people I would like to thank for their help with the prep-aration of this book. The journals *Environmental Politics* (Frank Cass: London) and *Government and Policy* (Pion Press: London) for their kind permission to reproduce some material contained in Chapters 4 and 5. The staff and students in the Department of Geography and Environment at the London School of Economics for helping me to enjoy some of the best years of my life. Andrew Patterson and Dan Graham for invaluable computer assistance and undying tolerance of my technophobic tendencies. My friends at LSE, especially Iris Hauswirth, Catarina Cardoso and Gustav Visser; Vicky Rea. The staff in the Department of Politics at Queen Mary and Westfield College, University of London, for providing a supportive and friendly environment in which to complete the final manuscript. Hugh Ward and Phillip Allmendinger for some friendly, but penetrating comments; John and Christine Blundell; the Institute for Humane Studies and the Earhart Foundation, without whose financial support this book would not have been possible; Tristan Palmer and all those at the Athlone Press; and Yvonne Rydin for her help and encouragement – in spite of the views expressed within. Special thanks go to Gerard Roscoe for all his love and help in Up Holland.

1

PLANNING AND THE
POLITICAL MARKET
The Rise of Public Choice Theory

INTRODUCTION

Following the 1992 Earth Summit, considerable attention has focused on the potential of land use planning to deliver the improvements in environmental quality, that are now demanded by electorates throughout the industrialised world. In the wake of a period when political discourse was unsympathetic to the case for more government regulation, land use planning appears to have regained legitimacy by staking a claim to the environmental agenda. Advocates of planning argue that the roots of environmental problems lie in the chronic inability of the market system to reflect the value placed on environmental resources by society as a whole. On the one hand, planning is thought to be essential to the supply of 'public goods', which it is alleged would not be provided by the free market (Simmie, 1993; Blowers, 1994; DoE, 1994; Thornley, 1994). On the other hand, planning is said to provide an important vehicle for the 'empowerment' of individuals and communities through a process of democratic participation in environmental decision-making (Forester, 1989; Jacobs, 1992; Healey, 1997).

In Britain, the land use planning system has for many years been associated with public concerns over environmental quality and democratic participation. The 1947 Town and Country Planning Act nationalised the right to develop land and introduced what remains one of the most comprehensive systems of land use regulation in the modern world. This legislation set the scene for the various statutory designations, including Green Belts and Areas of Outstanding Natural Beauty, that have since become such characteristic features of British environmental policy. Subsequent legislation, contained in the 1968 Town and Country Planning Act, enshrined the principles of public participation in the practice of planning. And, more recently, the twin themes of environmental protection and democratic accountability have been reflected in a raft of government policy statements that outline an enhanced role for the planning system in the pursuit of 'sustainable development' (DETR, 1998).

This apparent enthusiasm for planning, however, does not always appear to be warranted by the practical experience of government land use policies as experienced in Britain and throughout the industrialised world. More specifically, it is not clear how land use planning is supposed to alleviate environmental problems, when it has been argued that many of these problems are often the result of previous planning schemes. In the British case, for example, the chronic congestion and air pollution that blight many towns and cities have increasingly been attributed to land use policies that may have encouraged development at excessively high densities (Herington, 1984, 1990; Evans, 1988, 1991). In the United States, by contrast, there is evidence to suggest that the problems associated with low density urban sprawl owe as much, if not more, to the structure of zoning laws than they do to the inadequacies of the free market in land (Fischel, 1985; Gordan and Richardson, 1997). The record of agricultural subsidy programmes, in both Europe and in the United States would certainly appear to suggest that state intervention, far from providing a cure for environmental problems, is often the cause of the disease (Bowers and Cheshire, 1983; Pennington, 1996). Neither is it clear how land use planning can hope to become a model of democratic participation and empowerment for the disadvantaged, when many of its' advocates have themselves recognised that the reality is often synonymous with special interest capture and chronic bureaucratisation. Nearly every study in Britain and the United States has concluded that the operation of land use planning, far from helping the worst off, has redistributed wealth from the poor to the middle class (Hall, et al. 1973; Frieden, 1979; Fischel, 1985; Herington, 1984; Simmie, 1993).

In the light of such experience, this book argues that the contemporary enthusiasm for planning may be misplaced. Drawing on evidence from Britain and other western democracies, the book uses public choice theory to explore the practice of land use planning as a case study of 'government failure'. Public choice theory examines the role of economic incentives within the 'political market place' of planning and by exploring the institutional structures of liberal democracy, questions the merits of government regulation. The purposes of the book, therefore, are twofold. First, the book aims to provide a new analytical framework that can explain why land use planning has failed to live up to expectations in the past and why it is likely to do so again in the future. Second, the text builds on this positive framework to generate a normative agenda for institutional reform. More specifically, it argues that whilst the market system is prone to numerous 'imperfections', the evidence of 'government failure' suggests a powerful case for relying to a much greater extent on property rights solutions and 'imperfect' market processes as an alternative to the regulatory state.

This introductory chapter sketches out the institutional focus of the book, examining the central questions of 'market failure', 'government failure' and the theoretical case for planning intervention in the market for land. Drawing on the insights of public choice theory, the analysis suggests that the contemporary environmental policy literature may be over-optimistic of the capacity for planning to correct deficiencies in the market system. It then proceeds to review existing attempts to explain the political and institutional dynamics of planning and illustrates how a public choice perspective on the 'political market' may provide a more appropriate form of analysis. Finally, the chapter outlines the empirical focus of the book and sketches the structure of the chapters that follow.

PUBLIC CHOICE THEORY, INDIVIDUAL ACTION AND THE IMPORTANCE OF INSTITUTIONS

Public choice theory or the economic theory of politics represents an attempt to apply economic modes of reasoning to the analysis of collective choice and democratic decision-making. Following the seminal works of writers such as James Buchanan, Gordon Tullock and Mancur Olson, public choice theory analyses the institutional conditions (the property rights) under which economic decisions are made. More specifically, public choice and especially the so called Virginia School, helps to clarify how economic incentive structures differ between institutions characterised by private property rights operating through the marketplace and state-owned or state-regulated property operating through the 'political market' of representative government.

The starting point of public choice analysis is the rational individual and her motivations and beliefs. From the perspective of public choice theory, even where individual action takes place in a collective setting such as an interest group or the state, the individual actor must always be the focus of concern. As Buchanan and Tullock (1962, p. 13) put it, collective action is nothing more than, 'the action of individuals when they choose to accomplish purposes collectively rather than individually.' Institutions such as the state, therefore, are 'nothing more than the set of processes, the machine, which allows such collective action to take place (Ibid.).'

If individual agents form the core of the public choice paradigm, the following set of assumptions about their behaviour provide the building blocks for a theory of economic and political processes:

- Individuals are predominantly self-interested – they choose how to act on the basis of achieving their personal goals, material or non-material.
- In pursuit of these goals agents act as 'maximisers' who seek the biggest possible benefits and the least costs in their decisions.
- Individuals order their preferences transitively. The condition of rationality implies that if an individual prefers a to b, and b to c, she will also prefer a to c.
- The chosen course of individual action will be affected by changes in the structure of costs and benefits at 'the margin'. The marginal principle implies that ceteris paribus, any increase in the cost of an action will decrease the likelihood of that action, taking place.
- Information is a 'cost' – the more time spent on information gathering the less will be available for alternative courses of action. As the cost of information rises, the more likely it is that individuals will be less than perfectly informed about their decisions.

Building on these primary assumptions, public choice theory analyses how institutional arrangements may affect the pattern of individual incentives. Individual action always takes place in a specific institutional context and the different economic incentive structures which people face under different regimes may fundamentally affect the content of their behaviour and the outcomes derived from the decision-making process. *Ceteris paribus*, institutions that allow individuals to reap the rewards and to bear the costs of their actions and which transmit information about these decisions, may be advantageous from the viewpoint of the individual and society. Where institutional defects allow costs to be passed on to others, where wealth is not affected by the quality of decisions made and where there is a lack of information, efficient resource allocation[1] is less likely to result (Buchanan and Tullock, 1962; Libecap, 1989; Eggertsson, 1990; North, 1990; Kasper and Streit, 1998). Within this context, one of the major achievements of public choice theory has been to provide a framework that can be used to evaluate the relative merits of government and market decision-making. This book uses a public choice approach to examine the merits of government intervention in the form of land use planning. More specifically, can the information and incentives that are generated by the 'political market' of planning be relied upon to correct deficiencies in the market system? And, if they cannot, what type of institutional arrangements might be better suited to the crucial task of improving environmental quality?

THE THEORETICAL CASE FOR PLANNING

Drawing on neo-classical welfare economics, advocates of planning often judge the performance of markets by the *Pareto* standard. A pareto optimal allocation of resources is said to be achieved where 'there can be no other arrangement which will leave someone better off, without worsening the position of others' (Musgrave and Musgrave, 1980, p. 67). The conditions for the attainment of this standard within the free market are perfect information, perfect competition (large numbers of buyers and sellers in the market, none of whom can affect market prices) and the absence of externalities. *If* such conditions prevail, it is widely accepted that the market provides an efficient mechanism to indicate the relative scarcity of goods and services, the value of inputs used in producing such services and the foregone opportunity costs of utilising the inputs (Pearce et al., 1989; Turner et al., 1994). Because the profitability of a project is determined by the price consumers are willing to pay, the operation of the market ensures that both producers and consumers face the full opportunity costs of their actions. Consumers pay directly for the resources they use, are informed by prices of the relative value placed on resources by other individuals and have an incentive to monitor alternative suppliers in order to make the best possible choice. Similarly, the price system and the institution of private property allow entrepreneurs who satisfy consumer preferences to reap the rewards of so doing.

Within the literature of environmental policy, the theoretical case for land use planning is based on the view that the market system 'fails' the institutional test in the environmental sphere, because private decision-makers are *not* held properly to account for the consequences of their actions. Following the classic work of Pigou (1920), the most frequently cited cause of 'market failure' is the presence of external benefits and costs that may not be reflected in private transactions. Externalities exist when the results of an action, be they positive or negative, are *not* visited upon the decision-maker. The creation of an attractive landscape through the adoption of traditional farming methods is a good example of a *positive* externality. A farmer may receive no payment for the external benefits resulting from her action and so in the absence of government regulation, may have little incentive to produce 'landscape goods' in quantities that accord with a pareto optimal level. By contrast, the construction of urban developments on green-field sites is often considered a *negative* externality. Consumers of new buildings and construction companies may not take into account the loss of open spaces resulting from their actions and in the absence of land use planning these developments may be 'overproduced' in the market. The introduction of planning controls, therefore, such as the designation of Green Belts is considered essential to the task of managing such externalities and maintaining environmental quality.

Related to the concept of externalities are two qualities characteristic of many environmental goods: non-excludability and non-rivalrous consumption. Non-excludability occurs when the producer of a good is unable to keep non-payers from its consumption, non-rivalrous consumption, when the marginal cost to a seller of providing a good to an additional consumer is zero. Goods exhibiting both these characteristics are known as *collective goods* and according to welfare economics may be 'under-produced' unless there is a system of land use planning. Scenic views are often cited as an example – it is difficult to exclude non-payers from the benefits of a view and one person's consumption of the view does not detract from the consumption of others. *Public goods*, by contrast, exhibit non-rivalrous consumption but the exclusion of non-payers *is* possible. From the perspective of welfare economics, the operation of the free market may result in an inefficient exclusion of potential consumers from these goods. Statutory land use designations such as National Parks and Areas of Outstanding Natural Beauty, therefore, are deemed necessary to safeguard environmental amenities and to ensure an adequate level of public access to the attractions of the countryside.

In addition to the problems of externalities and collective/public goods, markets are also considered prone to a number of other important deficiencies. Producers and consumers may lack sufficient information to be aware of the environmental consequences of their actions; the dominance of the profit motive in private markets may lead individuals to maximise the short-term use of environmental resources to the neglect of longer-term interests; and markets may be distorted by the presence of private monopoly power. Combined with the pervasive existence of environmental externalities these departures from the perfectly competitive conditions, that would otherwise generate a welfare maximising pareto optimum, are considered to provide a prima facie case for government intervention. This reasoning provides much of the intellectual rationale for the renewed advocacy of land use planning as a tool in the pursuit of greater environmental quality. By limiting externalities, ensuring the provision of collective/public goods and correcting for other imbalances within the market system, it is argued that planning can 'improve' on the 'imperfect' allocation of resources that would result from a situation of *laissez faire*.

If the theoretical case for land use planning is based on the common assumption that markets are responsible for resource misallocation and environmental degradation, there are two rather different conceptions of the way that planning should respond to these instances of market failure. On the one hand, theorists in the rationalist/procedural tradition of planning tend to see the regulation of markets as an essentially 'technocratic' activity, with the planner assuming the role of an objective, professional expert (Faludi, 1973). Advocates of 'participatory' or 'collaborative' planning, on the other hand, reject this technocratic approach, arguing instead for an explicitly political conception of the process of planning. Associated predominantly with the 'New Left', theorists in this tradition conceive of planning as an exercise in radical participatory democracy (Forester, 1989; Jacobs, 1992; Healey, 1997).

Within the rationalist tradition, the planner is viewed as an impartial arbiter of public preferences, who balances the environmental costs and benefits of decisions not reflected by the market, in order to maximise 'social welfare' (Harrison, 1977; Pearce et al., 1989; Turner et al., 1994). As such, planning is seen as a quasi-scientific process, which operates to a large extent outside of the political process. The role of the planner, therefore, is to 'correct' for market failures by assigning values (monetary or otherwise) to environmental goods, through a range of 'neutral' evaluation techniques such as social cost/benefit analysis. Collaborative planning theory, by contrast, argues that as an alternative to technocratic procedures, members of the public should themselves set the priorities of planning via the democratic political process. Through 'citizens juries' and other public forums individuals should engage with one another in a process of democratic dialogue in order to arrive at a common conception of the 'public interest'. In this model the role of the planner is to facilitate a process of democratic 'consensus-building' in environmental decision-making.

PLANNING AND THE NIRVANA FALLACY

It is largely as a response to the market failure rationale for planning, in both its technocratic and democratic forms, that recent years have witnessed the rise of public choice theory. Public choice authors and especially those of the so-called Virginia school (see, for example Buchanan 1969, 1975, 1986, 1987) argue that the identification of 'market failures' is *not* a sufficient condition to justify government intervention. More specifically, if the economic case for land use planning (technocratic or democratic) is to be made, then it must first be established that planners can obtain the necessary information to know how to 'correct' for market failures. And second, that they have sufficient personal incentives to act on the basis of this information (Buchanan, 1969, 1986; Anderson and Leal, 1991). If these conditions cannot be met, then it is to commit the *nirvana fallacy* to suggest that the alternative to 'imperfect markets' is a government immune from similar, if not more serious, institutional failings (Demsetz, 1969). It is the contention of this book that much debate over the future role of land use planning in Britain and other western democracies may have been subject to a version of the nirvana fallacy.

The Virginia school of public choice theory draws on the works of Hayek (1945, 1948, 1960, 1982, 1988) and the Austrian school of economics (Kirzner, 1973, 1985, 1992; Lavoie, 1985; Cordato, 1992), to argue that there may, in fact, be no way for planners to obtain the information that would be necessary to 'correct' for market 'inefficiencies' (Buchanan, 1986).[2] According to this perspective, markets may well be 'imperfect' institutions but they may still offer important advantages over the governmental alternative.

The Austrian school or Hayekian case for using markets rests on their purported characteristics as decentralised discovery mechanisms and conveyors of information, the results of which cannot easily be replicated by government planners. In any society, the economic problem is to harmonise the pattern of production so that the composition of total output is appropriate to the resources and wants of the population. Because at any time the number of socially desirable projects greatly exceeds the capacity of available resources, a mechanism is required to decide *which* of these projects has the greatest priority and *which* individuals should be involved in their production. In a liberal society, there is typically no social consensus about values and thus the way in which resources should be collectively disposed. Moreover, in the unlikely event that a consensus on values could somehow be achieved, it is even less likely that there will be a consensus on *how* to realise such values. Within this context, private property rights, market competition and the account of profit and loss, are considered to provide a socially useful way of discovering, which of the multitudinous possibilities for resource use are most in accord with consumer valuations and which of all the potential production techniques are in the best position to satisfy these demands.

As Buchanan (1969) argues, because the values individuals attach to resources are *subjective*, an outside observer cannot easily know them. Consequently, it is only when people decide to exchange one thing for another – an amount of money for a scenic view, for example – that *relative* weights can be assigned to their preferences through the generation of market prices. In turn, it is the generation of these prices that indicates to producers the relative urgency of consumer wants and the producer's success or failure in fulfilling them. (Kirzner, 1973, 1985, 1992, 1997; Lavoie 1985; Cordato, 1992). Although the technocratic methods of cost/benefit analysis may allow economists to make guesses with respect to consumer valuations, it is only through a process of market exchange and the rejection of available alternatives that individual preferences are actually revealed. Seen from this perspective, in the absence of a market, where exchangeable property rights are assigned to individuals and firms, planners lack the feedback provided by market prices and the signals of profit and loss and there is no effective way for them to know *how much* or *what type* of environmental protection is actually desired. This Hayekian critique of planning is, of course, most forceful when explaining the failures of attempts to plan the entire economy, but its conclusions apply *mutatis mutandis* to lesser measures of government intervention, especially when these attempt to suppress the operation of the market.

The informational problem of planning noted above is not, as often thought simply a calculational problem that might be solved through improvements in technology, such as the development of computer simulations that could theoretically 'solve' the equations matching supply with demand (an error committed by the 'market socialist' school – see Roemer, 1994). On the contrary, in many cases the relevant information that would be needed for effective government planning is not objectively *given* in advance (as in orthodox neo-classical and so called market socialist models), but must be *discovered* through a process of trial and error. The data necessary for planning decisions is often *not* the knowledge of basic facts that can easily be quantified into statistics; it is local knowledge expressed in the subjective hunches and tacit insights of entrepreneurs, tried and tested through the account of profit and loss and the generation of prices (Hayek, 1945; Polanyi, 1951; Kirzner, 1973, 1985, 1992, 1997; Lavoie, 1985). This information is, by its very nature, dispersed throughout society and cannot easily be obtained by a central co-ordinating authority. Perfect information is impossible in any institutional setting, but the profit seeking activities of dispersed individuals and firms operating in the market, may mobilise *more* information and thus facilitate a *degree* of co-ordination, *which would not be possible under a centrally planned alternative.* Of course, some useful information, such as historical data on land use trends, prices and population patterns, may be made available to planners in a centralised form. Different people will, however, interpret the economic and environmental implications of this data in different ways. In the absence of a competitive market process, which can test the subjective judgements of different decision-makers and match these to consumer preferences through the account of profit and loss, it remains the case that there is no direct way for planners to evaluate the quality of their decisions and to learn from their mistakes (Lavoie, 1985; Littlechild, 1986; Cordato, 1992; Pennington, 1999).

The informational problems discussed above may not appear quite so severe, if, as often suggested by 'New Left' theorists, planning should take place at the 'local community' scale. The economies and environments of different 'local communities' are, however, inextricably linked to one another, so the Hayekian analysis is relevant again when one asks how co-ordination is to be achieved *between* the disparate and perhaps inconsistent plans of these *different local communities?* If the goals and values of different communities are not themselves to be co-ordinated through the market, then at some point recourse must be made to a form of 'central planning' in order to 'integrate' these otherwise disparate agendas. It is, however, precisely this kind of planning which the Austrian/Hayekian account suggests is unlikely to succeed. In the absence of market generated prices there is no way for planners to know how to prioritise the allocation of resources *between communities*. Consequently, any attempt to achieve 'strategic co-ordination' must require some *central* political authority to make subjective planning decisions, a position which would seem radically at odds with the supposed goal of 'empowering' local communities.

The Hayekian analysis, therefore, suggests that the theoretical rationale for planning may be flawed. All attempts to attach values (monetary or otherwise) to goods that are not actually traded in a genuine market and to calculate the 'social costs' of environmental decisions may be arbitrary, reflecting the *subjective* valuations of the planners concerned. If the decision-making procedure is inefficient or inaccurate and 'too much' or 'too little' land is allocated for environmental conservation or economic development, then there is no direct feedback mechanism for the planner comparable to the potential for financial loss and bankruptcy experienced in the market. In the absence of market prices there is no easy way for planners, whether the technocratic 'experts' of welfare economics or the 'citizens juries' of the 'New Left', to know the *intensity* of other peoples values and thus what the specific content of the public good actually is. In these circumstances, any attempt to 'plan' may resort to the subjective judgement of the planner or to relatively crude measures of social preferences, such as majority voting, which do not take into account the variation of individual valuations. Markets, on the other hand, are, from a Hayekian perspective, evolutionary processes where knowledge of public preferences is continually discovered through a process of entrepreneurial trial and error (Kirzner, 1973, 1985, 1992, 1997). It is the existence of entrepreneurial profits and losses, which prompts other individuals to *learn* about opportunities, evaluating the appropriateness of previous decisions and correcting erroneous ones. Profits and losses provide a useful, if imperfect way of ensuring the reallocation of resources away from those who make consistently bad decisions and towards those who exhibit greater foresight in matching production to the pattern of public demand.

It should be noted at this juncture that for the market process to work effectively does *not* require the 'perfect competition' depicted in neo-classical textbooks, but rather the rivalrous activities of firms trying to obtain profits by offering *better opportunities than are currently available*. 'Super normal' or 'monopoly' profits exist because change occurs, reaction takes time and because each entrepreneur is uniquely different in assessing and reacting to the new situation. The entrepreneurial reward is to receive a temporary excess of price over costs, which (unless there are restrictions on entry enforced by governments) the process of competition will subsequently begin to erode (Steele, 1992). As Schumpeter (1962) always emphasised, even the most entrenched corporate interests are subject to constant attacks (actual and potential) as the gale of creative destruction sweeps through the economy. The historical record demonstrates that industries that have periodically come to be 'monopolised' by a small group of firms, have subsequently shown a trend towards de-concentration as the lure of higher profits stimulates new market entrants (Brozen, 1982; Steele, 1992).[3] Seen from this perspective, governments are inherently more monopolistic than private markets, because public agencies and political parties are, to a large extent, insulated from new 'market entrants' and the resultant competitive discovery process.

Given the informational advantages of the market system, according to the Virginia school of public choice theory, it follows that the most effective way to allocate environmental resources in accordance with public preferences would be to establish a market in these very resources (Baden and Stroup, 1981; Anderson and Leal 1991). This line of argument draws on the Coasian or property rights tradition, which suggests that defining and enforcing an adequate system of property rights so that people can capture the benefits from 'making a market' in externalities, may obviate the need for government intervention (Coase, 1960; Demsetz, 1967; Alchian and Demsetz, 1973). Coase's followers argue that the presence of externalities and collective/public goods problems indicates the presence of *obstacles* to market exchange and in particular the high cost of establishing property rights in aspects of the environment (Dahlman, 1979). It may, for example, be relatively easy for a landowner to exclude non-payers from the benefits of a park (e.g. by erecting a high fence), but it may be much more difficult for property owners to capture the full benefits from the maintenance of clean air. It is these obstacles or *transaction costs,* which are the principal causes of 'market failure'.

Transaction costs are not, however, the sole preserve of the market system and from the perspective of public choice theory it is to commit the nirvana fallacy to suggest that the alternative to markets is a government immune from similar costs. Just as planners may lack the information to correct for market failures, so too they may operate within an institutional setting where there is insufficient incentive to internalise costs. Public choice theory suggests that the interaction of voters, interest groups, politicians and bureaucrats within the 'political market' of planning, is characterised by a distinctive set of transaction costs and incentive structures, that may result in chronic examples of 'government failure'. When considering the case for planning, therefore, what is needed is a framework that examines the extent to which institutional provisions in the state sector encourage, or inhibit the flow of information and the internalisation of external costs. This book uses public choice theory and the concept of the political market in planning to provide such a framework. In doing so, it argues that the contemporary environmental policy literature may be over-optimistic of the potential for planning to improve on the environmental performance of a competitive market system.

PLANNING AND THE POLITICAL MARKET: PUBLIC CHOICE AND THE POLITICS OF GOVERNMENT FAILURE

Advocates of planning, whether of the technocratic or democratic variety, often assume that the decisions of individuals' operating within the state sector are not driven by the self-interest deemed to characterise private markets. As Tullock (1977, p. 3) puts it,

The conventional wisdom holds that the market is made up of private citizens trying to benefit themselves but that government is concerned with something called the public interest.

The Hayekian analysis of dispersed information exposes the difficulties for planners in knowing what the public interest actually is. Even the most public spirited of planners may not possess the information regarding individual preferences and relative scarcities, which only market pricing can make available to them. According to public choice theory, however, even if these problems could somehow be overcome, this does not necessarily mean that planners will act to achieve the desired goals. From the perspective of public choice theory political actors are not 'economic eunuchs' concerned to maximise 'social welfare', but instead are rational actors pursuing individual self-interest. The ability of planning to correct for market failures, therefore, may be dependent not only on the informational requirements of planning but on the *economic incentives provided by the democratic polity.*

The informational or Hayekian based critique of planning is conceptually distinct from the analysis of political self interest put forward by the Virginia school of public choice, but in practice these arguments are closely linked. From a Virginia school perspective, it is partly as a consequence of the insuperable information problems involved in knowing the content of the 'public interest', that individual agents operating within the political system are likely to act according to interests that they *do actually know*, i.e. their own interests and those of their immediate circle.[4] The starting assumption of public choice theory, therefore, is that political actors follow their own interests and not the public interest. This concept of rational self-interest need not infer the specific motivations of individual actors, whether they are focused on expected pecuniary income, power, status, social approval or the pursuit of an ideological project.[5] It does suggest, however, that individuals respond to changes in perceived net wealth (however conceived) at the margin and do so irrespective of other arguments in their utility functions.

It should be recognised at this point, that the assumption of rational self-interest does not require that individuals are *fully* rational in the sense of the perfectly informed actors that populate the models of orthodox neo-classical economics. Individuals are limited in their capacity to make fully rational calculations of interest due to the cognitive limits of the human mind (Simon, 1957). 'Bounded rationality' does not, however, imply that agents stumble without purpose in a world of complete ignorance and that no meaningful statements can be made about the pattern of their behaviour. Rather, it implies that people act purposefully in pursuit of their interests, but only up to a certain point. In Virginia public choice theory, therefore, all individuals are viewed as rational utility maximisers but are variously limited in information and cognitive abilities in pursuit of this objective.

The Virginia school of public choice theory also maintains a subjective conception of cost – it is not possible for an outside observer to quantify specific aspects of an individuals utility function and to attach precise measurements to individual preferences. What it is possible to do, however, is to observe the *general institutional structure through which these preferences are expressed* (Buchanan, 1969, 1987). Individuals may be motivated by a range of goals, but their ability to achieve these different goals will be dependent, in part at least, on the institutional environment in which they are operating. An individual pursuing her goals in an environment characterised by monopoly may, for example, face a different set of opportunities and constraints than if she pursues the same goals in a more competitive situation.

The policies produced by the operation of the democratic process, therefore, may be analysed in terms of the underlying opportunities and constraints that face the different actors on both the 'demand' and 'supply' sides of the political market (Buchanan, 1969, 1987). To use the term institutional 'failure' (market or government) in this context is to refer to institutions that are *not* held to reflect public preferences for such things as environmental protection. And, by implication to suggest that a *different* set of institutions may make it *easier* for such preferences to be fulfilled (Kasper and Streit, 1998). It is never possible to say categorically that the gains to any one group from a particular policy may outweigh the losses to another group since the relevant costs and benefits are subjective.[6] What the analyst may do, however, is to observe whether there are any *structural biases* within the political market that may prevent the interests of particular groups in society from being considered within the decision making procedure. The normative assumption underlying this approach, therefore, is a liberal one – that political and economic institutions should be judged on their ability to meet individual preferences (Kasper and Streit, 1998).

The Demand Side

According to public choice theory the principal source of 'government failure' on the demand side of the political market stems from the existence of *collective action problems*. A collective action problem exists when an individual's contribution to the achievement of a common interest is unlikely to have a sufficient impact on the advancement of that interest to warrant the costs of political engagement. Following the seminal work of Olson (1965), public choice theory suggests that political activism for public policies, which would benefit large numbers of individuals, is unlikely to be forthcoming. *Ceteris paribus*, the larger the number of people belonging to an interest group, the *less likely* it is that any single individual will be pivotal to the success of the organisation. Because the results of political participation are non-excludable and indivisible (i.e. they are a collective good), each individual may be better off if she 'free rides' on the political participation of others, reaping the benefits without incurring the costs. Larger interest groups, therefore, may suffer from a problem of chronic under-mobilisation in the political market place of planning, *unless* they can supply private inducements or selective incentives to their potential members. In small group situations, by contrast, the collective action problem may be more easily overcome. If the personal benefits from successful political organisation are highly concentrated on relatively few people, then the higher per capita stake may outweigh the costs of participation, and it may be easier to monitor and punish examples of 'free-riding' behaviour.

From a public choice perspective, it is this underlying logic of collective action and inaction that is likely to result in the frequent capture of the political market in planning by special interest groups or rent seekers. A special interest issue is defined as one that generates substantial personal benefits for a limited, identifiable number of constituents, whilst imposing a small individual cost on a large number of unidentified members of the public. Rent seeking interests in the construction industry and local residents associations may, for example, have sufficient incentive to lobby for planning policies (e.g. regulations that restrict competition in the property market) that will concentrate benefits on their relatively few members. Consumers of new buildings on the other hand, although greater in number, may not have their interests (lower prices and developments with higher environmental standards, for example) reflected in the political market. Whilst the gains to the special interests *may* be less than the total losses to the consumers (though these costs can never be objectively measured), the interests of the latter are unlikely to be represented, because losses are thinly dispersed across an unidentified public, none of whom may have sufficient incentive to mobilise (MacAvoy, 1965; Stigler, 1975; Buchanan and Tullock, 1982; Olson, 1982; Poole, 1985; Bartel and Thomas, 1987; Benson, 1990; Robinson, 1993). In turn, the possibility of extracting such special interest privileges may encourage the diversion of resources into re-distributive activities and away from the production of additional wealth.

The problem of special interest capture on the demand side of the political market may be compounded by the insufficient incentive which voters may have to monitor the actions of politicians and public sector bureaucrats. Because the gathering and processing of information is a cost, voters may seek detailed information only to the extent that they can influence the relevant decisions (Aranson, 1990; Buchanan, 1975, 1986; Tullock, 1977, 1989, 1993; Mitchell and Simmons, 1995). Consumers in the private marketplace, even if not 'perfectly' informed, may have an incentive to discover information, because payment is direct and individuals are faced with the immediate consequence of any purchasing errors. In representative politics, however, voters may 'under-invest' in political information because the costs of acquiring accurate data are extremely high, compared to the infinitesimal influence any individual has on the outcome of an election. An individual is unlikely to examine the effects of land use planning, when her vote is unlikely to have any direct influence on the policies concerned and she will have to pay the cost of taxation irrespective of her participation. Voters, therefore, are faced with a situation where it is rational to be ignorant of the policy process a tendency which may account for the failure of many voters to know even the name of their own MP, let alone the small print of planning legislation (Downs, 1957, Tullock, 1989; Mitchell and Simmons, 1995).

In modern democracies this rational ignorance effect may be magnified still further because the state intervenes in so many areas of economic and social life that it is virtually impossible for voters ever to be informed across the whole policy spectrum (Mitchell, 1988; Tullock, 1989). Voters do not vote on individual issues (which environmental designations? which building regulations? which agricultural policies? etc.), but instead are presented with a 'take it or leave it' set of policy bundles. One cannot choose which particular land use policies to support, but instead must elect a representative who will speak on every single issue. Not only is the chance of each voter affecting the result of an election reduced to almost zero, but there is equally little opportunity to influence the content of the political agenda. From the perspective of public choice theory, therefore, the claims for the dialogic capacities of democracy made by the collaborative planning theorists are optimistic in the extreme. Far from providing an arena for informed debate and consensus-building between individual citizens, the quality of public debate is likely to be poor because of chronic rational ignorance. As a consequence the political agenda of planning is likely to be set by politicians, bureaucrats and rent seeking interest groups, who will have a greater capacity to dictate the choice of policy options.

The Supply Side

'Government failures' on the 'demand side' of the political market in planning are, according to public choice theory, mirrored by the structure of incentives facing political actors on the 'supply side'. Foremost amongst these is the tendency for political markets to induce chronic *short-termism* in decision-making. In the 'political market' politicians do not possess property rights in resources and as a consequence may be unable to reap a sufficient return from successful management (Baden and Stroup, 1979). Politicians cannot 'sell shares' in the government of a nation's resources to future political actors. On the contrary, benefits of decisions taken in the present may well accrue when the originating administration is long gone and when a different party may be in power. Decisions about the location of new housing development may, for example, be taken by local politicians concerned about the immediate impact on their own constituents and not according to the future benefits available to the wider community living outside of the constituency concerned. The time horizon of the politician, therefore, may not extend significantly beyond the date of the next election and planning may be based on short-term political gain, rather than long-term sustainable management (Baden and Stroup, 1979; Anderson and Leal, 1991).

This tendency towards government failure on the 'supply' side may be exacerbated by the monopoly characteristics of the political market. In most representative democracies power is concentrated in the hands of a small group of political parties. Unlike private markets, competition (actual or potential) is severely limited, because elections are held over discrete periods of time and once elected, the party/parties in power may use the coercive monopoly of the state to extract resources from the rest of society. The limited scope of competition reduces the level of information generated by the political process and may further allow politicians to disguise the extent to which governments respond to the short-term demands of special interests. The information generated by political markets, therefore, may often be characterised by sloganising, ideological advertising and a chronic reliance on crude party identification strategies (Buchanan, 1986; Tullock, 1989; Mitchell and Simmons, 1995).

A final, but equally important source of government failure may result from the monopoly power of the administrative state bureaucracy (Niskanen, 1971, 1995; Borcherding, 1977). Planning bureaucrats do not hold private property rights in the resources they control and so cannot capture the benefits or bear the costs of their decisions (Baden and Stroup, 1979). Rather, the ability of the bureaucrat to pursue her goals may often be dependent on the size of the agency budget (Niskanen, 1971, 1995; De Alessi, 1974; Borcherding, 1977; Libecap, 1981; Anderson, 1983). Planners, therefore, may have strong incentives to support those policies and interest groups, which will expand the size of the planning agency. Bureaucrats are often monopoly suppliers of services and may use this privileged position to inflate estimates of production costs and to push through policies, which are favourable to their own interests, irrespective of any wider political demand. Politicians, on the other hand, may have relatively little incentive to push for reductions in inappropriate expenditures because any costs savings may be invisibly dispersed across the electorate at large (Niskanen, 1971, 1995; De Alessi, 1974).

THE POLITICS OF PLANNING AND THE CONTRIBUTION OF PUBLIC CHOICE THEORY

The public choice analysis of the political market, sketched above, suggests that the contemporary enthusiasm for planning within the environmental policy literature is misplaced. Not only is it unlikely that planning can 'improve' on the operation of markets due to chronic informational problems exposed by the Austrian/Hayekian school, but there are good reasons to believe that the institutional reality of planning will be characterised by special interest politics and chronic bureaucratisation. This book argues that it is these symptoms of institutional failure, highlighted by public choice theory, which often correspond with the practical experience of land use planning.

In Britain, numerous authors have complained of the frequent capture of the planning system by vested interests and its failure to elicit effective public participation from all sections of the population. Powerful groups representing agriculture and the construction industry have often been the major beneficiaries (Ball, 1983; Lowe et al., 1986; Rydin, 1986). Consumers and taxpayers, on the other hand, have suffered losses by way of the higher prices and increased taxes that have resulted from the regulatory regime (Evans, 1988,

1991; Pennington, 1996). Correspondingly, planning has on many occasions been subject to short-term political manoeuvrings in order to secure electoral advantage. The phenomenon of 'Nimbyism' (Not in My Backyard) by localised homeowner coalitions seeking to maintain property values has, for example, become virtually synonymous with the practice of development control (Hall et al., 1973; Herington, 1984, 1990; Shucksmith, 1990; Evans, 1988, 1991; Simmie, 1993). In the meantime, the suspicion exists that planning is a highly inefficient and cumbersome activity exercised according to the bureaucratic imperatives of professional planners and not according to some neutral judgement of the 'public interest'. In the British case, land use regulation continues to grow, but there is little indication that the increased expenditure on planning has resulted in a proportionate improvement in public satisfaction (Ehrman, 1988; Evans, 1991; Simmie, 1993; Pennington, 1996).

It is largely because of its ability to explain the existence of such institutional failures within the modern state that public choice theory has stimulated an increasing degree of interest within contemporary political science. Public choice is not, however, the only perspective which has sought to move beyond a reliance on the neutral, though technocratic view of planning put forward by welfare economics, or the notion of democracy as a process of consensus building, as emphasised by the collaborative planning theorists. A number of alternative approaches also attempt to examine the dynamics of planning by analysing the exercise of power in the policy process and the significance of political bargaining. Pluralist, structuralist and historical/ institutionalist perspectives have, for example, frequently been used to explain the political economy of planning in Britain and other industrialised countries. It is appropriate, therefore, to examine some of the specific advantages of public choice theory with respect to these alternatives.

One important advantage of adopting a public choice framework, is the potential to develop a fuller understanding of the exercise of power within political economy. Existing analyses of planning often draw on pluralist accounts, which focus on the observable competition between different sets of organised groups within the political system (Truman, 1951; Latham, 1952; Dahl, 1961). Although pluralism recognises the existence of inequalities of power between different groups, these inequalities are usually interpreted as a reflection of the underlying pattern of social preferences as represented by the relative strength of the groups. Pluralism, therefore, tends to see power within western democracies as widely diffused among an array of competing interests, where any group can ensure that its political preferences are adopted if it is sufficiently determined. Within this context, the state is often seen as a neutral arbiter between competing interest groups and to the extent that government employees have interests of their own these will be kept in check by the monitoring activities of politicians eager to ensure re-election. In the specific context of planning, pluralists have often concentrated on the competing demands of construction companies, the farming lobby and environmental organisations, each of which express a different interest in the use of land

(Healey, 1990; Bramley et al., 1995). If politicians introduce planning policies in accordance with the demands of the construction industry for more building land then from a pluralist perspective this is taken to reflect the power of construction interests and the relative lack of public opposition to the policies that they support. Similarly, if the planning bureaucracy introduces a new set of land use regulations, that are in accordance with the demands of the environmental lobby then this should be interpreted as a reflection of the electoral support for environmental interests within society at large.

The continuing problem with such pluralist conceptions of power is the failure to recognise the potential significance of collective action problems and transaction costs within the 'political market'. By focusing on organised groupings, pluralism neglects the chronic mobilisation problems that may cause some groups to be under-organised or to remain completely latent within the political system. As Olson (1965) famously pointed out, that a group may fail to mobilise is *not* necessarily a reflection of apathy or tacit support for the status quo, as pluralism might suggest, but instead may be a product of the *structure of incentives* that faces the group membership concerned. As Chapter 3 will show, the number of consumers who would benefit from a reform of land use planning, may be substantially greater than the 'nimbyist' interests who seek to maintain the status quo. The former may, however, face an insurmountable collective action problem, because of the inherent difficulties of monitoring free-riding behaviour in such a large group. Likewise, according to public choice theory, if the planning bureaucracy introduces policies that accord with the demands of environmentalists this cannot simply be taken as a reflection of electoral support for the policies concerned. On the contrary, as Chapters 4 and 5 will demonstrate, where voters are rationally ignorant and face collective action problems and when politicians have little incentive to monitor bureaucratic actions, policy may reflect the ability of special interests and monopoly bureaucrats to push through measures which advance their own interests and not those of the electorate at large. Public choice theory can, therefore, expose important asymmetries of political power, which are neglected by more pluralistic accounts. More specifically it can help to explain whom the winners and losers in the political market are, according to the structure of incentives that the relevant actors face.

The relative neglect of collective action problems and transactions costs by pluralism has also been reflected in the tendency for authors in the structuralist tradition to commit what Dowding (1991, 1995) has referred to as the *blame fallacy*. This charge involves the attribution of political power to an individual or group because the particular actors benefit from the actions of the state, irrespective of whether the individuals concerned have the incentive or capacity to exert such political influence. Structuralist attempts to explain the politics of planning are often guilty of this blame fallacy. Neo-Marxist and elitist approaches have, for example, suggested that the political operation of land use planning reflects the pay-offs, which are available to powerful class based interests. In neo-Marxist accounts corporate interests in the construction industry are deemed to exercise power because planning may ensure a carefully controlled supply of new development onto the market, reducing the possibility of oversupply and thus boosting profit rates (Harvey, 1973, 1985; Castells, 1977; Ball, 1983; Ambrose, 1986). In elitist accounts (Schattschneider, 1960; Bachratz and Baratz, 1970), meanwhile, farmers, rural homeowners and planning bureaucrats are also considered politically powerful classes; farmers because of the privileges often granted to the agricultural sector – such as exclusion from planning control – (Murdoch and Marsden, 1994); home-owners because of the protection to property values, that planning is often deemed to afford (Shucksmith, 1990); and finally planning professionals because the exercise of land use policies often accords with their own professional values (Reade, 1987). Seen through a structuralist lens, the benefits that flow to these groups reflect the superior economic power of such elites within the political economy and their ability to crush the interests of the individuals and groups that lose as a result.

As Chapters 3 to 6 of this book show, it is undoubtedly the case, that the interests highlighted by structuralist theories have indeed benefited from the operation of land use planning. From the perspective of public choice theory, however, it is inadequate to attribute political power to a group simply because it benefits from a policy, or because it is associated with a particular class or other such elite. Structuralist theories say little about the actual choice processes which transform individual action into the collective outcomes and social structures that we observe and thus provide at best, only a partial account of the way that political power is accumulated and *how* it is actually exercised (Dowding, 1991; Chong, 1995).[7] Neo-Marxist and elitist accounts, for example, do not explain *how* it is that thousands of builders, farmers, homeowners and planning bureaucrats have been able to *organise* in order to manipulate land use planning in their own class interests. Neither is it clear that the accumulation of political power by the beneficiaries of planning is achieved by overtly crushing opposing interests within the political economy. As Chapters 3 and 5 illustrate, consumers are often important 'losers' in the political market of planning, yet these interests are seldom represented by a visible lobby group that could possibly be said to have been crushed. By focus-ing on the significance of collective action problems and transaction costs, therefore, a public choice framework can provide an account of the factors that allow some groups to obtain access to the levers of political power and prevent others from becoming established. It can, in particular, explain how different interest groups are able to exercise political power according to their ability or inability to overcome collective action problems and similar incentive based constraints. In doing so, public choice theory can provide the important *micro-foundations*, which are notably lacking from structuralist accounts of the politics of planning.

An additional advantage of public choice lies in its ability to further specify the *causal* mechanisms, which lie behind the political economy of planning. Alternative perspectives often focus on the contribution of social institutions to the maintenance of society, or of people's attachment to social norms and practices. In structuralist approaches, for example, the political longevity of many planning policies is explained in terms of their ability to bring social legitimacy to capitalist land use decisions by reconciling the allegedly conflicting objectives of securing profits and maintaining environmental amenities (Ball, 1983; Short et al., 1986). Historical/ institutionalist explanations, on the other hand, focus on policy inertia within the structures of the state itself. According to this approach, many governments have long regarded land use planning as a powerful tool for responding to environmental concerns. Hence, amidst growing public pressure for environmental protection, governments have been happy to load additional responsibilities onto their land use planning systems (Healey et al., 1988; Healey, 1992).

Structuralist and institutionalist accounts do offer some important insights and most public choice theorists would certainly accept that the range of rational choices available to individuals i.e. their feasible choice set is, in part at least, affected by pre-given institutional factors (Ward, 1995). As Chapter 6 illustrates, differences between the bureaucratic and political strategies of planners in Britain and the United States may in part be explained by the different institutional arrangements which govern the financing of local government services in these respective countries. Public choice theory does not desire to minimise the significance of such social structures and institutions but rather seeks to illuminate the incentives that are provided by these structures and how individual choices are exercised *within them*. Institutionalist explanations, by contrast, are not always clear in specifying what the causal mechanisms actually are. It is not obvious, for example, *why* planning has been a useful tool in maintaining political stability and *why* it has attracted support from so many different interests. The attraction of public choice theory, therefore, is its ability to expose some, if not all of the causal mechanisms that may be at play. More specifically, what are the possible rewards to politicians (such as improving the chances of re-election) and bureaucrats (such as higher budgets and job security) that are associated with the institutions of planning and how might these differ according to the policies adopted?

It should also be noted that the adoption of a public choice approach to the analysis of political behaviour, does not, as is often suggested (Self, 1989), require the assumption that individual preferences are set in stone, rather than shaped by the institutions and social structures around them. Recent theoretical and empirical work has, for example, stressed the ability of politicians, bureaucrats and interest groups to use the powers provided by the modern state in an attempt to shape or mould the preferences of the electorate at large (Dunleavy and Ward, 1981; Dunleavy, 1991; Kuran, 1995). Although not the specific concern of this book, the possibility of such 'preference-shaping' behaviour may be of particular importance given the tendency towards rational ignorance on behalf of the electorate and the reliance of voters on the information provided by pressure groups, bureaucrats and politicians themselves. It is possible, therefore, to accept that individuals might be actively persuaded to support particular policies, whilst maintaining a basic framework that focuses on the electoral and budgetary strategies of politicians and bureaucrats, the rent seeking of interest groups and the overall structure of incentives that may discriminate against dispersed interests within the political game (Kuran, 1995).

Notwithstanding the above advantages, the empirical claims and methodological underpinnings of public choice theory, have been the subjects of considerable criticism. These objections, crystallised in the recent work of Green and Shapiro (1994) have prompted a vigorous debate within political science and at first sight appear to represent a fundamental challenge to the public choice mode of analysis. The basis of this critique is twofold, focusing on alleged empirical and methodological 'pathologies' of the rational actor model.

The first branch of Green and Shapiro's challenge to public choice theory questions the empirical contribution of the approach. According to this perspective, the self- interest/rational actor model has had relatively little success in explaining many of the empirical realities that characterise political economy. And, where there have been apparent successes, these are largely the product of poorly specified hypotheses, which allow the public choice theorists to claim support for their theories without providing precise statistical measures of observed phenomena that can be attributed directly to the processes of rational action. The response to Olson's theory of interest groups and collective action is illustrative of this critique.

Olson (1965) argues that in the absence of selective, private incentives, self interested individuals are less likely to engage in political activity on behalf of large groups because there is always an overwhelming incentive to 'free-ride'. Green and Shapiro, however, point out that large scale political mobilisations *do* occur on a regular basis and suggest that the only way the public choice theorist may account for such behaviour is to import some aspect of altruistic motivation into individual utility functions. Moreover, to the extent that interest groups do mobilise because of selective incentives, public choice itself offers no hard and fast statistical predictions of what the precise rate of mobilisation will actually be. Writing in a similar vein, Green and Shapiro (1994) also highlight the failure of public choice to account for the paradox of voting. In a real world election it is formally irrational for anyone to vote because each individual may have no more than an infinitesimal chance of affecting the final result (Downs, 1957). The experience of elections in most modern democracies, however, shows that millions of people *do vote* and hence appear to be exhibiting *irrational* behaviour.

Moving on from these alleged empirical deficiencies of public choice, Green and Shapiro (1994) extend their critique to focus specifically on the methodological response of its advocates, when confronted with such disconfirming evidence. According to this line of argument, public choice scholarship is characterised by a tendency towards post hoc theorising, where faced with evidence that contradicts the initial theory, the author simply designs a new model to fit the existing data. The attempt by Downs (1957) to 'save' his account of voting is cited as the classic example in this regard. Faced with the reality that voters do actually go to the polls and therefore appear to act irrationally, Downs responded by suggesting that rational individuals participated in elections because of a 'desire to preserve the democratic system.' But, the critics argue, what exactly is left of a distinctive public choice approach if any conceivable form of motivation may be included in the cost calculus of the individual actors? If public choice theory cannot be confined to such 'hard edged' assumptions as the maximisation of pecuniary gain then it assumes the status of an irrefutable tautology and is devoid of explanatory power.

The critiques advanced by Green and Shapiro appear, at first sight, to constitute an important challenge to public choice theory. On closer reflection, however, it becomes clear that they are based on a serious misunderstanding of what public choice theory attempts to achieve and a decidedly narrow view of successful contributions within the social sciences (Chong, 1995; Fiorina, 1995; Ferejohn and Satz, 1995; Shepsle, 1995).

First, it should be noted that most public choice theorists do not purport to explain *all* human behaviour in terms of individual self interest, but they do contend that this assumption allows the development of generalised theories which may usefully account for observable realities within the political economy. Olson's theory of groups, for example, *does not* suggest that *no* large interest groups will organise to achieve collective goods. Neither, does it suggest that *no* individual would join such a group in the absence of selective incentives. Rather, Olson argues that *ceteris paribus* it will be *more difficult* to mobilise larger than smaller groups, but the actual level of mobilisation will be determined by a host of other factors, which may include altruistic motivations (Fiorina, 1995).

Green and Shapiro (1994) object that the empirical power of public choice theory is minimal, given the inability of scholars to specify with quantitative precision what the rate of mobilisation will be in the absence of selective incentives. In doing so, however, they imply that no social scientific research which does not use 'state of the art' statistical techniques to quantify the effect of specific variables may legitimately be considered a useful empirical contribution. This is a rather odd position given the notorious difficulty within social science of controlling for the multitudinous and often unobservable variables affecting the nature of social outcomes that simply *cannot* be controlled for without the laboratory conditions available in the natural sciences (Caldwell, 1994; Fiorina, 1995; Shepsle, 1995).

The empirical power of public choice, therefore, lies not in the quantitative measure of specific variables, but in its ability to provide explanations for a variety of otherwise *unexplained* phenomena. In this sense, public choice can make useful empirical contributions by following Hayek's (1959) advice on the appropriate method of social science, i.e. that it should focus on 'prediction in principle' rather than attempt to 'predict in detail' the quantitative magnitude of social phenomena. Within this context, the self-interest postulate in Olson's theory does not account for the mobilisation of all interest groups and neither does it have the capacity to predict the precise level of mobilisation in any given situation. What it does do, however, is to provide one of the most compelling explanations for the empirical finding that the full spectrum of economic interests and in particular consumers and taxpayers, are not fully represented by organised groups.

Second, Green and Shapiro are right to criticise 'bolt-on' reformulations of public choice models, but only in so far as these reduce the approach to a set of tautologies, devoid of any problem solving power. This was clearly the case when Downs argued that voters go to the polls to do their share in preserving the democratic system. In doing so, Downs violated the central assumption of public choice analysis – that individuals choose among alternative courses of action according to the relative advantage to *themselves*. As Chong (1995, p. 45) has noted, however, the fact that Downs engaged in post-hoc theorising in a tautological way, does not discredit the enterprise of post hoc theory development *per se*. On the contrary, theory modification in the light of dis-confirming evidence is an essential part of the research process and so long as it avoids tautological explanations, by definition increases the empirical power of theory. Recent developments in collective action theory have, for example, indicated the significance of non-material selective incentives, in the mobilisation of particular types of interest group, to supplement Olson's emphasis on material selective incentives (Opp, 1986; Chong, 1991, 1995). Far from reducing the rational actor model to a tautology, these developments have strengthened collective action theory because they are careful to specify the particular empirical contexts where such incentives are likely to apply. So long as the assumptions are laid out clearly in advance, it remains a matter of empirical enquiry, which particular modifications augment the problem solving power of the public choice approach, from those that diminish it to an un-falsifiable tautology (Chong, 1995; Ward, 1995).

None of the above is to suggest that public choice theory is without its weaknesses and can provide an all encompassing account of the political process. There are a number of areas where the approach is undoubtedly weak, most notably perhaps, in accounting for the shifting ideologies that are an important part of political life. Public choice theory is able to say relatively little about the rise of new value systems, such as environmentalism, for example, though as will be seen in chapter 3 it has much to offer in analysing the way that such movements are politically organised. A fully comprehensive account of political decision-making procedures would seek to explore the complex inter-relationships that exist, between ideologies, and the exercise of rational self-interest (North, 1990). It is not the purpose of this book, however, to develop such an account. In so far as beliefs and ideologies are considered, these are analysed as structural constraints, which provide the context in which self-interested choices are made. The purpose of adopting public choice theory in this book is to identify some *underlying regularities* within the decision-procedures of the British planning system, that may usefully be explained in rational actor terms.

Ultimately, the contribution of any theory or research paradigm must be assessed by its ability to generate insights into social phenomena and it is in doing so that public choice theory has proven its worthiness as a method of analysis. The contribution of the public choice school to the analysis of 'government failures' set out in this chapter, provides a useful account of the social outcomes that we may observe when individuals act within the confines of representative politics when compared with private markets. Within this context, perhaps the greatest attraction of public choice is its potential to develop normative proposals for institutional reform. By focusing on the institutional incentive structures that may result in examples of government failure, public choice can suggest alternative institutional arrangements that can *change* the structure of incentives and thus *improve* the outcomes of the decision-making process. *Improving* outcomes in this sense, referring to the production of outputs that are more in tune with the pattern of public preferences.

It is this normative strand of public choice theory that is central to the current debate on the future role of land use planning. Many authors recognise that the experience of planning in Britain and other western democracies has failed to live up to expectations, but continue to argue that comprehensive regulation is essential if the environmental 'failures' of the market system are to be avoided. Advocates of cost/benefit analysis suggest that 'better evaluation techniques' provide the key to improved performance. Collaborative planning enthusiasts, by contrast, argue that 'more public participation' or 'greater democracy', hold the key to better policy outcomes. If, however, the deficiencies of planning lie in these very notions of 'neutral' planning and 'effective public participation', then it is difficult to see what the contribution of 'better evaluation techniques' or 'greater democracy' could actually be. By neglecting to explore the institutional roots of planning failure contemporary planning theory is in danger of sustaining the status quo.

Public choice theory, on the other hand, suggests an explicit focus on the institutional causes of planning failure. More specifically, a public choice approach can suggest institutional alternatives to the contemporary practice of planning that can help increase the flow of information, overcome collective action problems, reduce transaction costs, break up monopolies and ensure that individuals bear more of the costs and benefits of their actions. If the existence of government failures is attributable to the existing institutions of planning, then it may only be as a result of root and branch reform that the planning failures of the past will be avoided in the future.

THE BRITISH PLANNING SYSTEM AS A CASE STUDY

The following chapters explore the institutional failures of planning from the perspective of public choice theory. Chapter 2 documents the growth of land use planning in Britain and other western democracies and outlines in detail, some of the consequences associated with such policies. These have included higher house prices, greater congestion in cities, longer commuting distances and the continued dependence of rural areas on environmentally damaging farm practices. The purpose of the analysis is to set the scene for an account of the *institutional processes* that have produced these particular outcomes and the extent to which these processes are afflicted by 'government failure'.

Chapter 3 is the first of the chapters to explore the institutional incentive structures within the political market of planning. Focusing on the 'demand side', it shows how special interest coalitions representing agriculture, the construction industry and nimbyist (Not in My Backyard) conservation groupings have been able to manipulate the planning system in order to extract rents from the regulatory regime. The chapter suggests that these groups have been disproportionately represented in the political market because of their greater ability to overcome the collective action problem. The interests of consumers, taxpayers and the mass of the urban population, by contrast, are frequently ignored within the political market because of their structural inability to overcome the logic of collective action.

Chapter 4 turns to the 'supply side' of the political market and suggests that land use planning is a highly bureaucratic activity, exercised according to the budgetary imperatives of planners and not according to the wishes of the community as a whole. In the British case, restrictive land use regulation continues to grow, but there is little indication that the increased expenditure on planning has resulted in a proportionate improvement in bureaucratic perform-ance (Evans, 1991; Simmie, 1993; Pennington 1996, 1997a). Rather, the experience of planning may reflect the monopoly power of planning bureaucrats who have a constant incentive to maximise budgets and regulation.

Much of the recent political popularity of planning in Britain has been stimulated by the growing significance of environmental issues within the electorate at large. As Chapter 5 shows, however, the response of the political market in planning has not necessarily reflected the environmental priorities of the voters. On the contrary, special interests and public sector bureaucrats may have manipulated the rational ignorance of the electorate to obtain an over emphasis on those elements of planning that maximise bureaucratic power and which concentrate benefits on special interest rent seekers.

Chapter 6 turns to the experience of pro-growth planning in Britain. Whereas chapters 3–5 highlight the institutional conditions, which often restrict economic development, the analysis focuses on examples of 'boosterist' or growth promotion planning. The chapter argues that where institutional incentives allow coalitions of special interests and public sector bureaucrats to capture the benefits from growth, then the political market may allow inappropriate forms of development to proceed. Whether planning is characterised by 'anti-growth' or 'pro-growth' policies the political market in planning appears to be institutionally *biased* towards the interest groups and public sector bureaucrats who control the regulatory regime.

Given the widespread existence of 'planning failure' documented throughout the book, the concluding chapter turns to the normative implications to be derived from the public choice analysis. It argues that problems of special interest capture and bureaucratic expansionism may result from incentive structures, which are an endemic feature of the political market in planning. The analysis suggests, therefore, that moves to privatise land development rights, at the individual or neighbourhood/community level and to extend the role of market processes, might prove a more efficient and equitable way of allocating land uses than a continued reliance on the regulatory state.

Much of the material in the following chapters draws on the experience of land use planning in the British institutional context. The primary reason for this focus is the comprehensive nature of land use planning in the United Kingdom. The 1947 Town and Country Planning Act effectively nationalised the right to develop land and introduced one of the most far reaching systems of government control over land use in the industrialised world. In subsequent years, important elements of this system have been imitated in a variety of other countries (Canada and Australia, for example) and the British system continues to be advocated as a model in societies (the United States, for example) often perceived to have less comprehensive planning regimes. An empirical focus on the British experience, therefore, has much to offer, not only in terms of the British planning system but also to the potential experience of planning in other countries as well.

A second reason for focusing on Britain is that the rise of the environmental agenda and its relationship with land use planning has proved to be particularly pronounced within this country. In recent years much has been made of the potential for land use planning to play an important role in helping to achieve the goal of 'sustainable development'. A British focus, therefore, can reveal much about the political processes that have driven the sustainability agenda and provides an opportunity to assess the extent to which the institutional structures of planning are indeed compatible with this goal.

Planning systems do, of course, come in a variety of different forms and there are limits to the general applicability of conclusions derived from an individual case. The analysis presented in this book should, however, be sufficiently general to have resonance with readers whose interests extend beyond the British scenario. Chapter 2, for example, concentrates on the impact of policies that have been implemented to a greater or lesser extent across the industrialised world. In so far as there are differences between British experience and other countries these are likely to be matters of degree and not of fundamental substance. Similarly, the general theoretical framework exploring the relationships between the key actors on the demand and supply sides of the political market in planning are likely to be of relevance in many different countries, at least in terms of the questions asked and in providing a benchmark for future international comparison. The more specific claims concerning the interactions of interest groups, politicians and bureaucrats documented in these chapters may, of course, vary in their applicability outside of Britain, depending on the institutional arrangements concerned.

Finally, the normative analysis presented in Chapter 7 should also be sufficiently general to interest readers unfamiliar with the British planning experience. The claim that market processes and property rights solutions may provide a more effective way of internalising externalities and improving environmental quality than statutory land use planning is a theoretical argument, the scope of which is not limited to the confines of Britain. All readers will not, of course, welcome these conclusions. It is hoped, however, that they will be accepted as a contribution to the environmental policy debate and will challenge dissenters to produce alternative proposals that can tackle the institutional failures of planning outlined in the pages that follow.

2

THE IMPACT OF PLANNING

INTRODUCTION

Chapter 1 outlined the contribution of public choice theory to the analysis of 'government failures'. In this chapter attention turns to the practical experience of land use planning as a possible example of government failure. The first section summarises the institutional practice of planning and outlines the growth of statutory land use regulation in Britain and other western democracies. The chapter then moves on to examine the consequences of planning, focusing on the urban containment policies which have been the principal manifestation of land use controls throughout the industrialised world. By noting the effect of these policies the analysis highlights the importance of avoiding the 'nirvana fallacy' when considering the case for planning intervention in the market for land. In doing so, the chapter sets the scene for the subsequent account of the institutional failings in the political market that have produced some apparent policy contradictions within the British land use planning system.

THE BRITISH LAND USE PLANNING SYSTEM

The history of statutory planning control in the United Kingdom can be traced back to the public health legislation of the late nineteenth and early twentieth centuries. The Public Health Act of 1875 and the Housing and Town Planning Act of 1909, heralded an end to an era of relative laissez faire, bringing as they did the first attempt to regulate the use of land in the interests of 'public welfare' (Cherry, 1996). Significant though this legislation was it did not attempt to alter the overall pattern of development produced by private developers and landowners with decisions over the use of land remaining largely a matter for market forces. It was not until the 1947 planning legislation that the British government sought a more fundamental realignment of the relationship between the state and the private sector.

Enacted in August 1947 and implemented on 1 July 1948, the provisions of the 1947 Town and Country Planning Act brought about by far the most significant expansion of government control over land use in the history of the United Kingdom. The implementation of this legislation under the Labour administration of Clement Attlee, saw a massive transfer of property rights from private individuals to the state. Under the 1947 Act private ownership of land was maintained, but development rights transferred to local authority planning departments and the Ministry of Housing and Local Government (since 1970 the Department of the Environment – DoE and now, the Department of Environment, Transport and the Regions – DETR). Thereafter, with the exception of agricultural land uses, anyone wanting to develop his/her property had to apply to the local authority for planning permission, which would be approved or rejected according to a local development plan. The magnitude of this change has been captured eloquently by two leading planning lawyers:

> It is impossible to exaggerate the importance of July 1st 1948 from the viewpoint of the local planning authority, the landowner, or the building developer, for the 1947 Act conferred some of the most drastic and far reaching provisions ever enacted affecting the ownership of land and the liberty of the owner to develop and use his own land. Indeed, after 1947 ownership of land carries with it nothing more than the right to go on using it for existing purposes. (Grant and Heap, 1991, p. 18)

The initial intent of the post-war planning system was to establish an apparatus of central economic planning, where economic development and environmental regulation would be administered by a 'top down' system in which local planning authorities would be responsible for the implementation of plans developed at the national and regional levels. In subsequent years, however, the emphasis on 'top-down' planning was gradually replaced by moves to increase the role of the private sector and more localised control. The shift towards decentralisation occurred as the inability of central government to exert complete control over all development, was revealed (Deakin, 1985; Marsden et al., 1993; Cherry, 1996).

The framers of the 1947 legislation had assumed that the state itself would become the dominant actor in the development process with local authorities purchasing land for development as required. Under this system, however, landowners were to receive none of the gain resulting from the appreciation in land values, which occurred when local authorities purchased property, or planning permission for private development was granted. Rather, a 100 per cent development charge was to be levied on all such profits. These provisions effectively removed any incentive for landowners to part with their property and combined with the financial constraints on local authority land acquisition, brought about by burgeoning public sector spending deficits, were thought to be stifling the progress of urban re-development required after the war. As a consequence, the incoming Conservative administration of 1953 re-established market value as the basis for land transactions and the development charge was abolished. Whilst subsequent Labour administrations reintroduced a development tax on land (as with the Land Commission Act of 1967 – revoked by the Conservatives in 1971), this was never at the punitive levels introduced under the 1947 legislation. The British land use planning system, therefore, increasingly became a 'mixed economy' mechanism, which sought to guide and regulate private sector development rather than one, which sought to supplant the operation of the land market *per se*.

The development of a mixed economy model of planning has also coincided with increasing demands for more local control and public participation to inject greater accountability into the planning system. The 1968 Town & Country Planning Act replaced the 1947 development plan system with a new framework dividing responsibility between Structure (at the county level) and Local plans (at the district level) and introduced provisions for public consultation. The 1971 Town & Country Planning Act, meanwhile, introduced a system of public participation in the plan making process following the recommendations of the Skeffington Report (1969). The latter Act extended the right of members of the public to make objections to the policies laid out in plans and for the first time to be consulted during the actual process of plan preparation. More recently, the 1991 Planning and Compensation Act has extended the power of local authorities to adopt their own development plans without direct permission from the Secretary of State.

Notwithstanding these moves towards decentralisation, the British planning system remains a comprehensive system of statutory land use regulation with a considerable element of central government control. The fundamental principle that land ownership alone confers no right to develop has remained. Very few developments may proceed without the express permission of the local planning authority, which is obliged by law to prepare a local development plan. Regional level planning in the UK has been particularly weak reflecting the lack of an effective government structure at this level. The strong national policy framework administered by the Department of Environment, Transport and the Regions (DETR) (previously the Department of Environment – DoE) has remained at the hub of the planning system and retains considerable powers to affect the land-use policies adopted by individual local authorities. The DETR issues a wide range of policy circulars and Planning Policy Guidance Notes (PPGs), which form the basis for plan preparation at the local authority scale. Local planning officials do enjoy a considerable degree of discretion over the formulation of plans and the granting of individual planning permissions, but the DETR has powers to ensure that these decisions do not depart fundamentally from national planning policy. The Secretary of State for the Environment, Transport and the Regions retains ultimate responsibility for the planning system and retains the right to overturn the decisions of local planning authorities through the national appeals system or through the power to 'call in' local development plans for revision and amendment should these depart from national guidelines.

The institutional resilience of the post war planning framework was demonstrated most clearly by its' ability to withstand the broader shift towards privatisation developed by the Conservative government of Margaret Thatcher, first elected in May 1979. In line with the goal of reducing state intervention and freeing up market forces, the Conservative governments of the 1980s and 1990s attempted to reduce regulatory red-tape and to create a more flexible regime which would respond more quickly to economic change. In actual fact, however, deregulatory initiatives in the field of land use planning did not extend very far and paled into insignificance when compared with the moves towards full-scale privatisation of previously nationalised industries. Although some commentators have suggested that the Thatcher administration set about dismantling the post war planning system (Ambrose, 1986; Thornley, 1991), as Healey et al. (1988) have suggested, there is an unfortunate tendency for many such authors to confuse the rhetoric of 'Thatcherism' with the reality of policy implementation on the ground (see also, Marsh and Rhodes, 1992).

The Conservatives did reduce the scope of traditional land use planning in inner urban areas with the adoption of Simplified Planning Zones (SPZs) and Urban Development Corporations (UDCs), which transferred planning powers away from elected planning authorities and placed them in the hands of centrally appointed boards. Similarly, changes to the Use Classes Order (which determines whether planning permission is, or is not required for particular types of development) in 1987, removed the necessity to obtain planning permission for a limited number of very minor developments. Elsewhere, however, the fundamentals of the planning system remained untouched and indeed, by the end of the Thatcher decade moves were already afoot to strengthen the regulatory regime in response to the then rapid growth of environmental concerns.

One of the most important reasons underlying the failure of the Thatcher government to change the institutional framework of the land use planning system appears to have stemmed from its lack of clear policy objectives in this particular field (Allmendinger, 1997). Elsewhere, and especially with respect to policies such as the 'right to buy' council houses and the privatisation of nationalised industries, the Conservatives pursued a clear strategy of transferring control of previously state-owned assets into the private sector. This strategy of privatisation was theoretically influenced by elements of the market liberal/ public choice account of bureaucratic decision-making outlined in Chapter 1. Nationalised industries, it was argued, were suffering from chronic inefficiency as a product of their monopolistic position within the public sector. The solution to this problem was to transfer such industries into the private sector, opening them up to market forces in order that increasing competition and an end to government subsidies might bring about a reduction in bureaucratic inadequacies. Whilst it was not always clear that introducing competition was the primary policy goal,[1] programmes such as the right to buy and the sale of nationalised corporations represented a marked shift in policy from anything witnessed in the rest of the post war period. In turn, this allowed the Conservative government to communicate such policies to the general electorate in clear ideological terms and, at least to some extent, allowed it to resist pressures from interest groups in the industries concerned to maintain the status quo.

In other policy areas, by contrast, the approach put forward by the Thatcher administration was notably more tentative. With respect to the National Health Service and education policy, for example, privatisation was never seriously on the agenda and the Conservative approach focused on a rather vague set of commitments to 'increase choice' and to 'reduce red tape' (Marsh and Rhodes, 1992). The greater hesitancy in such fields stemmed in part from the continued ideological support within the electorate for the state provision of such services and the perceived electoral disadvantages of radical reform. In addition, however, the lack of clear policy commitments was also a product of ideological tensions within the Conservative Party itself. The British Conservative Party is not and never has been, committed to classical liberalism or libertarianism which argues for a minimal state, confined to the enforcement of private contracts (Nozick, 1974). The fundamentally illiberal stance of many 'Thatcherites' on matters such as immigration, family policy, attitudes to homosexuality and other aspects of personal behaviour reveals a deeply traditionalist approach and support for a *strong* rather than a minimal state (Gamble, 1988). Even with regard to economic affairs, a substantial element within the Conservative Party and especially the so-called 'One Nation' tradition, has always envisioned an extensive role for the state in the provision of welfare services, the protection of 'cultural heritage' and in asserting a strongly traditionalist 'moral tone' (Norton and Aughey, 1981).

It would appear to have been a combination of such Burkean traditionalism and also a perception that planning still retained a degree of ideological backing from the electorate at large, that accounted for the lack of a clear oppositional stance to land use planning from the Thatcher administration. The new policy developments that were introduced, such as Urban Development Corporations and Simplified Planning Zones could not properly be described as privatisation, or even de-regulation, but rather were representative of a *different type* of planning style, focused on using public sector monies to 'lever' in private capital through corporatist decision-making procedures (Brownhill, 1990; Imrie and Thomas, 1993). Whilst the government maintained a rhetoric of 'reducing regulation' and 'streamlining' decision-making, no attempt was made to privatise the planning system and the lack of clear policy objectives left considerable decision-making autonomy to local authority planners (Brindley et al., 1989; Allemendinger, 1997). In turn, it was arguably this lack of clearly expressed policy objectives and a sufficiently coherent ideological stance to challenge the planning system that allowed considerable leeway for interest groups and planners to seize the policy initiative in response to the emerging environmental agenda. Lacking a clear intellectual framework with which to respond to this agenda the Thatcher government and the subsequent Major administration was not in a position to resist the growing pressure to expand the regulatory regime.

Pressure to strengthen the powers of the land use planning system in recent years has undoubtedly been a product of the growing influence of environmental concerns. The Report of the United Nations World Commission on Environment and Development (1987), *Our Common Future*, popularised the notion of 'sustainable development', which has subsequently become a watchword within the planning profession. Correspondingly, domestic political pressure from a more environmentally conscious electorate, prompted by concerns over issues such as 'global warming' and ozone depletion has ensured that 'the environment' has staked a new claim to the political agenda. In terms of planning, this was reflected with the passage of the 1991 Planning and Compensation Act widely hailed as, 'one of the most important pieces of environmental legislation in the last twenty years,' (Burton, 1991, p. 70).

The Planning and Compensation Act did not fundamentally alter the structures of the land use planning system, but nonetheless strengthened the role of the plan and environmental criteria within the decision-making process. Section 54 a, in particular, introduced a requirement that all development control decisions should be made in accordance with the local plan. This replaced the previous 'presumption in favour of development', where the plan was but one of a number of 'material considerations' (such as changing market conditions) to be taken into account when considering the merits of a particular planning application. As a consequence, the ability of developers to use the national appeals procedure (now performed by the Planning Inspectorate), to push through proposals which are a response to market conditions but are not in accord with the strictures of the local plan, has been reduced. It is this policy framework which formed the inheritance of the new Labour administration elected in May 1997. The new government has yet to indicate an intention to substantial reform in the field of land use planning, confining itself instead to the creation of the new DETR (an amalgam of the former Department of Environment and Department of Transport) and a continued commitment to expand the scope of public participation within environmental decision-making (DETR, 1998).

If the institutional structures of land use planning in the UK have remained largely immune from reform so too has the policy focus of the planning system. In 1973, Hall et al. completed the first comprehensive analysis of British land use planning, the title of which – *The Containment of Urban England*, reveals the very essence of post-war land use regulation. First proposed in the Barlow Report (1940), the key priority of planning controls in the post-war era has been an attempt to restrict the outward growth of urban areas. The principal mechanism for the achievement of this objective has been the designation of special areas in which planning permissions involving new urban developments are unlikely to be allowed. Probably the most famous of these is the Green Belt, originally recommended to local planning authorities by Duncan Sandys in the Ministry of Housing and Local Government Circular 42/1955.

Throughout the post-war period the emphasis on containment has been justified, at least in part, in terms of the 'market failure' arguments discussed in Chapter 1 (Klosterman, 1985; Thornley, 1991). Initial arguments for land use planning as advanced in the Barlow Report and its subsidiary Scott (1942) on Rural Land Use, suggested that restrictive land use controls were an essential mechanism to avoid the loss of open landscapes and fertile agricultural land and to prevent problems of congestion and pollution within the cities themselves. Several trends were cited in justification of a policy focus on urban containment.

These included; a massive suburban housing boom in the inter-war period, which saw the construction of 2.7 million new homes between 1930 and 1940; the rapid loss of agricultural land, running at approximately 30 000 ha per year in the 1930s; growing problems of urban congestion, especially in South East England; and increasing economic disparities between an expanding Midlands and South East and declining areas of the old industrial North (Hall, 1975). Such problems were seen as the inevitable result of 'haphazard' market processes and, imbued with the ideas of rationalist planning, post-war politicians pursued the goal of urban containment to bring about a 'less wasteful' and 'more efficient' use of land. Containment was to reduce pressure on the countryside and in particular agricultural land. It was to encourage redevelopment in the depressed areas of the north by restricting development opportunities in the more prosperous south. And, it was to improve living conditions in the congested cities by enabling a controlled and contained dispersal of the population out of the older urban areas and into self contained 'New Towns' (Hall, 1975; Cherry, 1996).

Throughout the post-war period, the policy commitment to urban containment has been maintained, irrespective of the political party in power. The Thatcher government did attempt briefly to introduce a modest amount of liberalisation with proposals to draw back the boundaries of Green Belts issued in 1983. Similarly, in 1987 the so-called ALURE (Alternative Land Use and the Rural Economy) proposals suggested that farming uses should cease to have first claim on the countryside. These proposals, however, were quickly dropped following substantial opposition from interest groups, such as the Council for the Protection of Rural England (CPRE) and the National Farmers Union (NFU) and from within the ranks of the Conservative Party itself. The traditionalist or Burkean element within the party, strongly represented in the rural shire counties was vociferous in expressing its desire to use the powers provided by the land use planning system to preserve the countryside and a traditional image of rural life. Partly as a consequence of this, the Thatcher decade as a whole saw the biggest *expansion* in the Green Belt system since the implementation of the 1947 Act. Between 1979 and 1991 the area of designated Green Belt increased from 1.7 to 4.2 million acres (+147 per cent) to account for 14 per cent of the land area of England and Wales (Cullingworth and Nadin, 1994).

The abandonment of Conservative attempts to liberalise the planning system in the 1980s was to herald the arrival of the still more stringent commitment to urban containment, which characterises the practice of planning in Britain today. Speeded by the growth of environmental concerns, both within and outside the United Kingdom, the passage of legislation in the early 1990s marked an expansion of the regulatory regime and a pronounced tightening of existing restrictions. The Planning and Compensation Act (1991), for example, makes an explicit commitment to countryside protection and to the prevention of 'urban sprawl'. In addition to the existing argument for containment on the grounds of countryside protection, the new legislation and a raft of policy guidance's (now known as Planning Policy Guidance Notes – PPGs) issued by the DETR, suggest a need to integrate land use policies with a wider environmental strategy aimed at the achievement of 'sustainable development'. In response to the international environmental agenda set by the 'Earth Summit' in Rio de Janeiro (1992), a new argument has been advanced which suggests that the land use planning system should be utilised as a strategic device to minimise the use of non-renewable resources that would otherwise be overexploited in the context of a market economy (DoE PPG12). The planning system should, through a strategy of urban containment, discourage the use of 'non-renewable' green field sites and concentrate new developments on 'recycled' brown-field sites in existing urban centres. In so doing, it is argued that land use planning can contribute to a reorientation of the urban system, moving it away from an emphasis on low density suburban developments, heavily reliant on road transport and in particular the private car, towards a more high density, compacted form of development serviced by public transport. By reducing transport distances, it is suggested that planning can help to reduce the emmittance of pollutants and 'green house' gases such as Carbon Dioxide (DoE PPG2, PPG6, PPG12 and PPG13).

At present approximately 1.64 million hectares (ha) of England & Wales or 11 per cent of the total land area is devoted to urban land uses. (Cullingworth and Nadin, 1994). The major impact of post war planning regulations, therefore, has been a reduction in the rate at which land transfers from rural to urban uses. The 1980s, in particular, saw the lowest rate of rural land development since the implementation of the 1947 Act. Between 1980 and 1990, 5,000 ha (or 0.03 per cent) of the land area) transferred out of agricultural production and into urban uses, a third of the figure in the 1950s and 1960s and a mere fifth of the rate witnessed in the inter-war period (Cullingworth and Nadin, 1994). Some of this reduction was attributable to the effects of population stabilisation and economic slowdown, but the planning system would appear to have had a very significant impact, given that the demand for housing in rural and suburban locations has risen continually in recent years (Evans, 1988, 1991; Bramley et al., 1995).

The clearest manifestation of the commitment to continue this restrictive policy stance can be seen in the response to the latest projections on the demand for housing land. In 1996, the then Secretary of State for the Environment, John Gummer MP, set a target that 60 per cent of new dwellings should be built on land within the boundaries of existing towns and cities, rather than on green-field sites (DoE, 1996). More recently, the New Labour administration has committed itself to an eventual target of 75 per cent brown-field development in order to achieve the policy goal of more compact towns and cities (DETR, 1998). Together with the already substantial catalogue of restrictive designations, documented in Table 2.1, Table 2.2 and Figure 2.1, the British land use planning system would now appear to be present a bigger obstacle to urban developments in the countryside than at any point since 1947.

Table 2.1 Land Use Designations in the United Kingdom

AGLQ	Area of Great Landscape Quality
AGLV	Area of Great Landscape Value
AONB	Area of Outstanding Natural Beauty
ASI	Area of Scientific Interest
ASSI	Area of Special Scientific Interest
ESA	Environmentally Sensitive Area
CPZ	Coastal Protection Zone
GB	Green Belt
HC	Heritage Coast
LCA	Local Conservation Area
LNR	Local Nature Reserve
NNR	National Nature Reserve
NP	National Park
NSA	National Scenic Area
RS	Ramsar Site
SSSI	Site of Special Scientific Interest
SCA	Special Conservation Area
SPA	Special Protection Area

Table 2.2 Major Designations in England and Wales as a Percentage of Land Area

Designation	Area/millions ha.	% of Land Area
Green Belt	2.18	14.5
AONB	2.25	15.0
National Park	1.35	9.0
SSSI	1.05	7.0
Total	6.83	45.5
England and Wales	**15.03**	**100.0**

Source: Computed from Cullingworth and Nadin (1994, Chs 5 and 8).

PLANNING SYSTEMS IN OTHER WESTERN DEMOCRACIES

As was noted previously, planning in the United Kingdom remains a relatively centralised system with a considerable element of national government control over matters such as urban containment policy. Outside of the UK, planning systems in the former British colonies of Canada and Australia have developed in a similar way. Elsewhere, in the western democracies, however, land use planning takes on a number of somewhat different institutional forms.

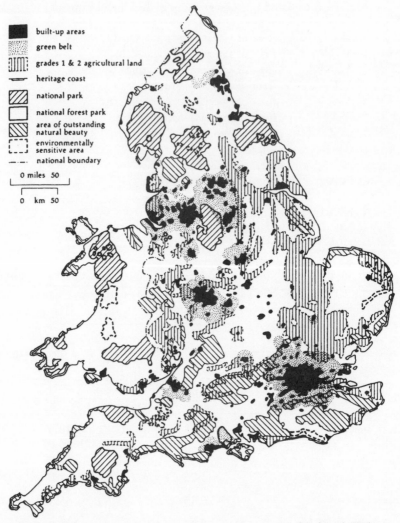

Figure 2.1   Statutory Land Use Designations in England and Wales

If the British planning system is marked by a tendency towards centralisation and policy standardisation, the experience of planning in the United States is one of fragmentation and decentralisation. This reflects, to a large extent, the significance of the federal governmental structure and the importance given to the states within the American constitution. The Ninth and Tenth Amendments to the US constitution restrict the rights of the Federal government in Washington DC, to infringe on the rights of states and citizens. As a result, planning and land use regulations have tended to be exercised primarily by local authorities and the states. No American State, however, has created a set of procedures equivalent to the British system where planning permission from the local authority is required for almost all forms of development. The American model has instead been based on the use of local zoning ordinances, which specify where and what classes of development are to be permitted within particular zones (industrial, residential, agricultural etc.). So long as the development in question conforms to the overall class specified in a particular zone, then the development may proceed as a matter of private right and *not* as a matter of public permission. Within this context, public participation in planning occurs in two different ways. As in Britain, citizens have the right to attend and make public comment on plans and planning decisions in the hope of influencing these decisions through the political process. In contrast to Britain, however, certain broader based decisions such as re-zonings or the extension of zoning ordinance powers at the state level are also subject to public participation by way of a referendum.

Unlike the UK, much of the United States consists of a vast undeveloped landmass, which allows for a wider degree of choice and mobility for individuals and businesses. Some individuals choose to move to localities which are highly regulated whilst others prefer to move to rural areas which are often less rigid in the application of land use controls. Within this context, the limited role of central government involvement in land use control has permitted the development of a more diverse pattern of planning practice than the centralised procedures found in Britain. Some local planning systems are so extensive that the areas concerned are referred to as 'planned communities' (Staley, 1994). These communities are now increasingly common, especially in the more populous states such as California and Florida. In other parts of the country, however, communities are entirely or almost entirely unplanned. Many rural areas in the largely undeveloped interior of the country allow virtually any piece of land to be developed in the way that the owner sees fit. This is not the case, however, in the so called 'public lands' of the Rocky Mountains and the far West, where over two thirds of the land area is held in direct public ownership by government agencies such as the Forest Service, the Bureau of Reclamation, the Army Core of Engineers and the National Parks Service.

In contrast to the model of planning in the United States, planning systems throughout Western Europe have been characterised by a more activist role for central government. European planning practice is, however, far from homogenous, with Newman and Thornley (1996) able to identify three institutional types of planning, in addition to the British system.

Planning systems of the 'Napoleonic' type including countries such as France, Spain, Italy and the Benelux, are characterised by an approach which involves the interaction of different layers of government at the central, regional and local scales. There is a tendency under such systems to prepare a national code of planning regulations and to create a hierarchy of plans based upon a zoning approach, which correspond with the different tiers of government. In France, for example, there are four layers of government with an interest in planning – the central state, region, departement and commune. The state produces national rules and guidelines and determines major decisions over large-scale infrastructure projects. The regions can produce development plans on the basis of the national framework, which lay out in general terms a regional based strategy. Departements have no specific land use planning function but have a wide range of functions, which impact on land use issues and planning decisions. Communes, meanwhile, represent the lowest level of the French planning hierarchy and it is at this level where there is the greatest opportunity for public participation in the process of plan preparation, usually by way of public hearings. All communes with a population of over 50,000 have a plan, the production of which is not obligatory but brings with it the power to determine applications to develop and for some communes the right to buy key development sites. French planning, therefore, provides considerable powers for communes, including the right to compulsory purchase, which has allowed many authorities to build up substantial tracts of public sector land.

In the 'Germanic' tradition of planning (Germany, Austria, Switzerland), the regulation of land use is based on a strong legal framework and a relatively decentralised decision-making structure. These aspects are reflected by the strong legal backing given to plans and permissions and considerable variation in planning practice across the different states or Lander (Cantons in Switzerland), which produce their own planning laws. In Germany the role of the federal government is confined to the setting out of a general framework of regulations to ensure a modicum of consistency in the planning legislation of each state. All sixteen Lander are obliged to set up state-wide plans, which contain broad statements of intent concerning matters such as settlement patterns and environmental protection policies. The responsibility for the implementation of land use and development control, meanwhile, is devolved down to local authorities (gemeinden). These authorities prepare both broad based zoning statements and a legally binding local plan, which determines the accepted uses. Approval of local plans has to be obtained from the relevant Lander, but this can only be withheld on legal grounds and not on matters of planning substance. The process of granting or refusing planning permission then becomes an administrative task of checking conformity with the plan which is not without similarity to the current 'plan–led' development control system operating in the UK.

Outside of the United Kingdom, the model of planning that has developed in the Scandinavian countries and especially in Sweden represents the most comprehensive system of government land use control, with most developments requiring some sort of planning permission or equivalent. Unlike the UK system, however, the Swedish model allows considerably more autonomy for local authority decision-makers. National level planning in Sweden has been reduced to a minimum and regional planning is only very weakly developed. The locus of decision-making, therefore, rests firmly with the local authorities or municipalities. These jurisdictions prepare both a broad general plan which takes into account national planning guidelines on matters such as ecologically sensitive areas, national recreational areas and water supply, and a detailed local plan which is the legally binding instrument brought into play when a change in land use is proposed. Within this context, the Swedish system has gone further than any other in granting considerable powers to the public sector to be actively involved in the development process itself and in the business of land acquisition. In this sense, the Swedish system of land development is something akin to the original British planning model where land was to be purchased and developed by the state and most of the development gains to landowners were to be taxed away through a development charge. Land assembly in Sweden is often carried out by local authorities, which can use powers of compulsory purchase to obtain land at prices only marginally above existing use value. This land is then contracted out to private firms for development purposes with the completed housing units sold at prices set by the state and under the full gamut of local planning controls.

Notwithstanding these differences in institutional practice, a common feature of planning throughout the western democracies has been the tendency to adopt growth management or urban containment regulations, though nowhere has the focus of policy been so centred on this approach as in the UK. In the former British colonies of Canada and Australia the concept of developing green belts appears to have been 'transported', albeit in a less thoroughgoing form, with cities such as Ottawa and Brisbane adopting urban containment as a key policy goal. In Europe, meanwhile, France, the Netherlands and Germany have long established policies for the management of urban growth. Planning in these countries has, however, tended to be based on the designation of green wedges or green corridors as opposed to the continuous green belts found around the entire outer boundary of many British cities. The intention here has been to *break up* the contiguous nature of urban development rather than to stop the outward growth of urban areas *per se*. In countries such as Sweden, meanwhile, the high degree of public sector involvement in both the ownership and development of land has enabled the Swedish Local State to exercise a profound impact on the evolving pattern of urban growth. Public sector ownership has enabled planners to keep certain areas free from new development for conservation purposes, though the high importance given to the autonomy of local municipalities has prevented any overall strategy of urban containment from being implemented across the country as a whole. The much lower population to land ratio found in much of Scandinavia (Sweden has approximately one eighth of the population of Britain in almost twice the land area) has meant that urban containment has been somewhat less of a priority than in countries such as Britain.

Of all western countries, the United States has often been considered to have the least developed of planning systems and the weakest commitment to urban containment policies. Indeed, the use of the pejorative term 'urban sprawl' has often been synonymous with the depiction of American urban development. In actual fact, however, a mere 3.2 per cent of the land area of the 48 contiguous states is devoted to urban land uses with the vast majority of the country devoted to either cropland, forests or wilderness areas (Fischel, 1985, p. 20). As Simmie (1993) observes, such figures make it difficult to argue for a policy of urban containment on the grounds of land shortage. Nonetheless, from the early 1970s and accelerating through the 1980s and 1990s, there have been progressively more attempts by local authorities to introduce various growth management policies. In 1972 there were only a dozen local authorities nation-wide with growth controls, but by 1974 this figure had risen to 200. By the mid-1980s in states such as California and Florida over 80 per cent of communities had adopted growth control policies. More recently, state-wide growth control initiatives have emerged in states such as Oregon, California, Florida and New Jersey. In cities such as Portland in Oregon, for example, state level mandates on growth controls have enabled the introduction of 'urban-growth boundaries' which come close to the kind of urban containment policies currently found in the UK (Staley, 1994).

THE CONSEQUENCES OF PLANNING

The foregoing analysis has revealed some of the institutional practices of land use planning in Britain and other western democracies and the extent to which urban containment or growth management policies have formed the core of government attempts to regulate the market in land. In Britain, the containment of urban development has been the clearest manifestation of land use regulation in the 50 years since the 1947 Act. It is quite remarkable that the Thatcher government, supposedly committed to a policy of 'deregulation', actually presided over the biggest increase in the area of statutory environmental designations in the history of the planning system (Ehrman, 1990; Cullingworth and Nadin, 1994).

With the rise of the environmental agenda, government support for urban containment policies throughout the western democracies appears to have strengthened still further. As was noted above and in Chapter 1, this support is often based on the need to correct for environmental 'market failures' and specifically the prevalence of externalities. Restrictive planning controls, how-ever, and in particular urban containment policies produce various 'negative externalities' of their own. Focusing on the British experience, it is to the sources of these externalities that attention now turns. Although some criticisms of arguments in favour of policies such as urban containment will be made, the aim of the analysis is *not* to indict these policies *per se*, but to highlight some of the effects of planning and the possible conflicts of interest that exist within the planning system. In the final analysis it is not possible to prove that the costs of such policies are greater than the benefits, because these costs are subjective. It is, however, possible to consider the ability of the decision-making procedures to ensure adequate consideration of all the different interests affected by land use planning. This is the fundamental issue that will be considered at length in the remaining chapters of the book. For the time being, however, the analysis concentrates on the *effects* of land use planning rather than on the decision making processes within the planning system.

PLANNING & HOUSE PRICES

Perhaps the clearest and most well debated feature of planning or growth controls is their effect on the price of housing. Economic theory teaches that given a constant demand, restrictions in the supply of a commodity will increase the price of that commodity. Rising prices will in turn act to choke off demand to ensure that the quantity demanded equals the quantity supplied. Environmental designations such as green belts effectively remove substantial areas of the countryside from the urban land market and so one would expect to witness an upward effect on the price of land for housing and other urban developments as a result of such controls.

Empirical evidence in support of the view that containment policies have increased prices in the UK has been provided by Evans (1988, 1991) who examines data from the Department of the Environment's index of housing land prices between 1965 and 1985. According to this analysis, housing land prices increased by over 1000 per cent during this period, compared to only a 400 per cent increase in general prices (Evans, 1988, p. 17–22). This data confirms the earlier work of Hall et al. (1973), which suggested that the proportion of land costs in the price of new housing units increased from between 4 per cent and 8 per cent in 1960 to between 18 per cent and 38 per cent a decade later (Hall et al., 1973, pp. 399–400) – by the late 1980s the figure was well over 40 per cent (Ehrman, 1988, p. 17). In short, it appears that the market for land in Britain has responded to the increasing relative scarcity brought about by containment policies in precisely the way the economist would predict. As a consequence, the principal beneficiaries of land use planning have been existing owners of property who have seen a continual appreciation of their assets at the expense of decreased housing opportunities in rural and suburban areas. Wealth has, therefore, been redistributed in favour of a relatively richer group of property owners at the expense of a relatively poorer set of consumers (Simmie 1993).

As Veljanowski (1988) observes, one would expect at the very least that planning restrictions would lead to relative shortages of land and as a result higher prices – but this position has not been exempt from theoretical challenge. On the contrary, it is often argued that since the supply of undeveloped land is fixed, its value is determined by the demand for land, which in turn is derived from the economic value of its uses – and not the availability of land itself (Neuberger and Nichol, 1975; Ball, 1983; Grigson, 1986). This line of reasoning derives from the application of Ricardian rent theory which states, 'Corn is not high because a rent is paid, but a rent is paid because corn is high'. In the specific case of housing land, therefore, prices are determined by the supply and price of the existing housing stock, and not the availability of land itself.

As Evans (1988) proceeds, however, the theoretical challenge to the contention that planning controls increase prices is based on a serious misapplication of the Ricardian analysis. Land use planning restricts the supply of *all developed land* and it is this restriction which *must* contribute to increased house prices, at least in the long run. In the short run, the supply of housing is likely to be relatively inelastic because it takes time for house-builders to assemble land and to increase production in response to a price rise; and as Goodchild and Munton (1985) note, the extent to which landowners bring forward development land may be constrained by a range of non-pecuniary personal motivations, including attachments to a particular plot. In the long run, however, the supply of land for development is elastic, because land can be transferred from less valued uses such as agriculture to more valued uses such as housing. It is this process that urban containment policies restrict and thus contribute to increased prices. As Evans (1988) argues, accepting the Ricardian analysis that the price of housing land is determined by the supply and price of housing does not alter the fact that the existing supply of housing is affected by the supply of housing land. 'Both land prices and house prices are determined simultaneously by demand and by supply. Restricting the supply of land, i.e. through planning controls, will raise the price of both.' (Evans, 1987, p. 3).

Empirical support for the Evans thesis is provided by comparing the difference between the price of land for housing and the price of land for the next most valued use – usually agriculture i.e. the opportunity cost of housing land. Table 2.3 displays the results of the most recent research, which compares land prices for agriculture and housing in four British case studies. The effect appears to be most marked in South East England where restrictions are often most severe, but even in the North of England planning controls have constrained

Table 2.3 Housing Land and Agricultural Land Prices in Four British Case Studies

	Housing £ per ha	Agriculture £ per ha	Agricultural as a % of Housing
Reigate			
1975	75 000	1 620	2.2
1990	972 000	4 940	0.5
Wokingham			
1975	67 000	1 980	3.0
1990	1 070 000	6 790	0.6
Beverley			
1975	19 000	1 750	9.2
1990	480 000	4 940	1.0
Barnsley			
1975	27 000	1 450	5.4
1990	210 000	6 180	2.9

Source: Gerald Eve and Cambridge Department of Land Economy (1992, p. 26).

supply to such an extent that the price of land for housing far exceeds its agricultural value. The difference in the two prices is maintained by restricting the transfer of land from one market to the other, which is precisely the intention of urban containment policies.

Low income groups, have been especially disadvantaged by this process, because the planning system has reduced the total housing stock available and has thus thwarted the operation of the so-called 'filtering effect'. The more new houses that are built (even if many of these are at the 'top end' of the market), the more used housing becomes available and the more the relative price of housing will fall. Urban containment policies have reduced the level of new building and have thus slowed down the filtering process by which affluent homes reach the lower income groups. This position may also have been made worsened by other government interventions in the housing market, such as rent control and security of tenure legislation that have discouraged the process where previously owner-occupied homes are split up into smaller flats and let out to lower income people (Minford et al., 1987).

It should be noted at this point that critics of 'filtering theory' have argued that it represents little more than a theoretical apology for policies that often assist the better off (Short, 1982, pp. 198–210). Suggesting that building homes, irrespective of the income bracket of the buyers is an effective way of increasing access to all income groups is, it is argued, to divert attention away from more re-distributive policies which could increase housing access for the poor. As Fischel (1985) points out, however, to pursue this line of criticism is to completely confuse a *deliberate policy* of subsidising the construction of homes for the affluent – as has been the case in the UK and USA through policies such as mortgage tax relief – with the entirely beneficial *process* of filtering itself. If planning controls act to discourage new development, whether at the 'top' or the 'bottom' end of the market, then they will reduce the increase in the total housing stock and result in higher prices for both low and higher income groups alike. One may still wish to introduce other ways of improving access to the housing market for low income groups (by increasing welfare benefits, for example), but this would not be to deny the continued importance of the filtering process in ensuring that an adequate supply of housing space is available for those on low incomes.

Outside of Britain, evidence that restrictive planning controls have driven up the cost of housing and reduced access for those on lower incomes is widespread. Working in Canada, Derkowski (1975) and Martin (1975) show how urban containment policies introduced around cities such as Toronto, Ottawa, Edmonton and Vancouver have increased prices. Staley's (1994) analysis suggests that similar processes may be underway following the introduction of environmental designations in Hong Kong. In the United States, meanwhile, numerous analyses have concluded that the introduction of growth management policies has brought about price rises (Frech and Lafferty, 1976, 1984; Frieden, 1979; Rosen and Katz, 1981; Schwartz et al., 1981, 1984; Mercer and Morgan, 1982; Dowall, 1984). Typically, these studies compare the trend of house prices before and after the introduction of growth management/urban containment policies, such as the California Coastal Zone Commission. All of these studies confirm that the introduction of planning restrictions does indeed contribute to higher housing costs. Whilst the statistical reliability of the precise magnitude of the price rises attributed to planning must be questioned (Kneisel, 1979, for example, suggests that Californian planning restrictions may have been responsible for as much as a 21 per cent increase in the cost of housing), that restrictions have been responsible for price inflation is in little doubt.

Further evidence for this position has been marshalled by Simmie (1993) in a comparative analysis of land use regulation in California (USA) and the United Kingdom. Taking the experience of California and using secondary sources, Simmie examines the impact of containment policies by first looking at the pattern of house prices before growth management policies were introduced; second comparing these with the pattern of prices after regulation increased; and finally comparing this experience with the still more stringent containment regime operating in the United Kingdom. The studies summarised by Simmie conclude that housing land prices in California increased substantially after the introduction of land use controls, but that in turn these increases were not of the order often experienced in the UK and especially in South East England.

It is not only via the designation of environmental sites that land use planning may have contributed to increases in the price of housing. Additional research suggests that the British planning system barely responds to increases in market demand by increasing the number of planning permissions approved (Bramley et al., 1995). The length of time taken to evaluate planning applications and the complex procedures involved in the drafting of local development plans all impose substantial cost and time delays on developers, which reduce their ability to respond to increases in demand. In recent times these delays have become particularly severe following the 1991 Planning and Compensation Act, which as Cullingworth and Nadin (1994, p. 59) note, increased the length of the public inquiry procedure, where it is not uncommon for developers to pay out over £500,000 in consultancy and legal fees, from about 7 weeks in 1988 to 22 weeks in 1992. Research suggests that it can take as long as four years for developers to proceed from the plan consultation stage to the commencement of new building (Gerald Eve, 1992; Simmie, 1993). As the supply side response of developers to market demand is constrained by land use regulation, so the relative scarcity of housing stock increases and prices rise.

Despite the wealth of evidence confirming the contribution of urban containment policies to rising property prices, a number of authors have suggested that the rise in the cost of housing land can be attributed to the process of property speculation and monopolistic behaviour in the land market rather than to the effect of planning restrictions (Ball, 1983; Barlow and Duncan, 1992). Speculation involves holding land off the market for a while in the hope of attaining a higher price at a later point in time. According to critics of land speculation, therefore, the market price obtained is not 'deserved', for the landowner has rarely expended capital and labour to improve the land commensurate with the price at which it is subsequently sold. Rather, the vendor is extracting a 'development gain', in effect, a 'tax' levied on the house-builder's profits and ultimately on the consumer, purely to affect a change in land ownership (Barlow and Duncan, 1992, p. 137). This 'tax' is likely to be especially high where ownership is concentrated in private hands and where property owners can reap additional rewards from the exercise of monopoly power. Seen through this lens, the problem is not that planning controls in countries such as Britain are too restrictive but that the British planning system lacks the powers to tackle the existence of speculative behaviour. Thus, Barlow and Duncan (1992) argue that the French and in particular the Swedish system of land use planning and housing finance have fared far better than their British equivalent in keeping land and house prices under control.

The above arguments continue to attract attention in the debate over land and house prices in a number of different countries but are, at root, fallacious. To start, critics of land speculation ignore the crucial role that *all* speculative activity plays in the production and discovery of information within the market system. The implicit assumption behind the critics' argument is that a 'socially efficient' pattern of land uses is *objectively identifiable* and that it is the process of land speculation, which prevents this pattern of resource allocation from being achieved. As we saw in Chapter 1 (pp. 7–9), however, it is precisely because knowledge concerning the demand and supply of land in different uses is *not pre-given* that entrepreneurial action within the market system is required. A successful speculator is one who predicts the future market trend accurately, buying when the price is relatively low and selling when the price is relatively high. The profits obtained through land speculation, therefore, are not 'undeserved' but are the reward for bearing risks and searching out land which is relatively under-priced in a particular use in order to sell in markets where it is relatively over-priced. The price of land is determined by the demand for it and the price which people bid serves to allocate land to its most productive uses. High land prices, therefore, are caused by high demand and limited supply, not by speculators profits.

Under the conditions of uncertainty, which characterise *all* entrepreneurial action, the forecasts on which speculators base their decisions may, of course, be imperfect, but competitive decision-making and the discovery process which comes into operation as decisions are made generates new knowledge as resources flow to the most successful market participants. The necessity to forecast the demand for land cannot be avoided and, if not performed by specialised private speculators, must be performed by government officials. The fundamental difference between private and government forecasting, however, is that private speculators who guess wrong, lose money and over time may be driven out of business, whereas government officials are not subject to a similar competitive procedure which can weed out those who make consistently bad decisions. The potential for the resultant planning failure was demonstrated most clearly in Britain during the 1970s when urban local authorities purchased substantial urban land banks for the purposes of public sector redevelopment schemes. The failure of local authorities to anticipate the subsequent decline in demand for many of these sites and their refusal to sell at lower prices in a declining market was the primary cause of the huge levels of local government debt that built up in the late 1970s and early 1980s and the maintenance of vast tracts of vacant public sector land which came to characterise many British cities during this period of time (Chisholm and Kivell, 1987; Loveless; 1987; Denman and Goodchild, 1989).

The theoretical flaws in the critiques of speculation have also been reflected in the interpretation of the evidence on housing land prices. Barlow and Duncan (1992), for example, quote the Swedish case approvingly, noting that under the system of local authority land banking and compulsory purchase the price of new housing land has been kept low. It is, however, hardly surprising that a policy which confiscates property in land, combined with a policy of selling the developed land at government controlled prices, keeps down the price of new housing. What the Swedish land banking policy does is to take away the potential gains of increased values from the original owners of land and gives these gains to builders or first time buyers who subsequently sell the property on. Why this is considered socially desirable is far from clear. Moreover, Barlow and Duncan's analysis says nothing about the *allocative* effect of the Swedish system because it completely ignores the opportunity costs involved. To sell land to housing developers at little more than the existing use value (usually agriculture), plus servicing costs is to *subsidise* the purchase of land for housing. Under these conditions, the allocative role of market prices is suppressed and land which may be better suited for other purposes, (retail or industrial use, for example) may instead be developed for housing. It may well be that it is the propensity for Swedish planners to allocate *too much* land to the pursuit of subsidised housing and other 'welfarist' policies that has been a contributory factor in the declining fortunes of Sweden's economy over the last twenty years (Fry, 1979; Stein, 1982; Rojas, 1998). In addition, because the incentive to economise on housing land has been reduced this development may occur at too low a density. Whereas land prices and as a result dwelling densities (see pp. 48–50 below) in Britain, may be kept *artificially high*, because of planning controls, in Sweden the dominance of local municipalities in the land market may keep the price of housing land *artificially low*.

Authors such as Barlow and Duncan (1992) are on safer ground when they suggest that problems of monopoly power in the speculative market are partly responsible for the rise in house prices experienced under the British system. Monopoly in the land market, however, is largely a function of planning restrictions and is not an intrinsic characteristic of this particular market. Of course, individual plots of land may attract a price premium due to the uniqueness of each location, but there are nearly always sufficient substitute sites to avoid this becoming a serious issue (Evans, 1985; Goodchild and Munton,

1985; ASI [Adam Smith Institute], 1988; Gerald Eve, 1992). Planning restrictions, on the other hand, can and do contribute to problems of monopoly by limiting the number of sites on which new development may take place. Under competitive market conditions, speculators and developers have limited potential to exert an upward effect on prices in the long term, because each wants to sell when prices are high and will fear that should she wait too long, other landholders will enter the fray, reaping the reward of selling at the top of the market and hence bringing prices down. Planning restrictions, however, reduce the number of sites where development can take place. A speculator or developer holding a site with planning permission has little incentive to sell the site or develop it herself, safe in the knowledge that prices are likely to go on rising because of the artificial scarcity brought about by planning restrictions. Under these conditions, land is kept off the market for an inordinate length of time, contributing still further to shortages. Analysis in Britain and the United States has repeatedly shown that the introduction of urban containment policies fundamentally alters the structure of land and property markets towards a monopolistic situation (Dowall, 1984; Landis, 1986; Evans, 1988, 1991; Simmie, 1993; Pennington, 1997a). Examining the planning process in the city of Chester, for example, Pennington (1997a, p. 201) found that the granting of a *single* planning permission in 1990 accounted for 11 per cent of the new homes permitted to be built in the town over a five year period.

Overall, the evidence on prices supports the view that the restrictions imposed on urban development by planning are responsible for higher housing costs. What does remain a matter of contention, however, is the magnitude of the price increases which can be attributed to containment oriented policies. For the UK, Cheshire and Sheppard (1989) used econometric techniques to compare the relatively more relaxed planning regime in Darlington, Durham with the more restrictive policies in Reading, Berkshire to examine the impact of restrictive controls. The results of their analysis suggested that housing costs in central Reading would be 12 per cent lower in the town centre and 4 per cent lower in the suburbs if the more relaxed policies were adopted (pp. 469–85 – see also Cheshire and Sheppard, 1997). In a further study, however, Bramley et al. (1995) suggest in their econometric model that a relaxation of Green Belt designations would result in only a 2 per cent reduction in housing costs across South East England (Bramley et al., 1995, Ch. 7). According to this analysis, if planning controls were relaxed substantially, the fall in housing costs would not be that significant because consumers would respond to lower prices by consuming more land which would in turn force up the cost of housing units. Cheshire and Sheppard (1989) and Evans (1988, 1991) accept that 'density effects' may be in operation and that the effect of containment policies in Britain may be not so much on the numbers of housing units and the price per unit (though these may be significant, depending on which econometric analysis one is to believe), but more on the type, size and density of the units which are developed. It is this 'density effect' which appears to represent the second major externality associated with planning controls in Britain.

Planning and Dwelling Densities

If there remains debate concerning the extent to which land use restrictions in Britain have forced up the price of housing, there is little doubt that containment policies have had a substantial effect on the densities at which people live. Economists, such as Evans (1988, 1991) argue that when planning restricts the supply of land for housing, it inevitably tends to raise densities as developers cram more units onto ever smaller plots and that this obliges households to consume less space than they would otherwise prefer – the 'Rabbit Hutches on Postage Stamps' syndrome (Evans, 1991). As opportunities for new building on green-field sites are restricted, developers respond to the shortage by seeking out any remaining open land within existing urban areas. The resultant 'in-filling' of urban open space and the loss of garden space in suburban estates, increases the density of urban development above the level, which accords with consumer preferences and adds to urban congestion (Simmie, 1993).

There is now a substantial body of evidence, which highlights the rise in dwelling densities experienced in Britain as a result of planning. Research by Gerald Eve and Cambridge Department of Land Economy (1992), for example, compares the density of new detached housing in four British case studies over the 40 year period from 1950 to 1990. The empirical results, presented in Table 2.4 indicate a significant increase in densities over the period of study. A second manifestation of this effect has been examined by Cheshire and Sheppard (1989), Evans (1988, 1991) and Bramley et al. (1995), all of whom note the increasing trend towards low space consuming developments such as flats and maisonettes and away from more spacious dwellings such as detached houses and bungalows. According to Evans (1988) between 1969 and 1985 the proportion of newly constructed buildings mortgaged with building societies which were bungalows, fell from 25 per cent of the total to only 11 per cent, whereas the proportion which were flats, maisonettes or terraced houses increased from less than 10 per cent to over 25 per cent (pp. 20–22). This shift

Table 2.4 Density of Detached Housing in Four British Case Studies

	Density per hectare				
	1950s	1960s	1970s	Early 1980s	Late 1980s
Reigate	20.14	9.75	18.16	23.86	29.92
Wokingham	16.72	15.65	25.55	23.11	21.77
Beverley	na	14.38	22.09	na	27.38
Barnsley	na	39.44	27.11	40.94	na

Source: Gerald Eve and Cambridge Department of Land Economy (1992, p. 31).

has occurred because of the increase in the relative price of housing land and not because the size of households is becoming smaller and hence requiring smaller units of housing. If the latter had been the dominant reason for the shift in dwelling types, one would have expected the price of the smaller units to have increased faster than the larger units, when in fact the evidence points to the opposite effect.

Bramley et al. (1995) concur with this analysis by observing the different proportions of dwelling types in different regions of the country. In South East England, where land prices are highest and containment controls tend to be the toughest, the proportion of flats and maisonettes is substantially higher than in areas of lesser demand and relatively more liberal policies, especially in parts of the West Midlands. Thus, flats formed nearly a third of new output in Berkshire, compared to only 3 per cent in Staffordshire. In further work Bramley et al. (1995) offer additional support for this thesis with an eco-nometric analysis of planning restraints and dwelling densities from which they conclude that there is a positive relationship between the degree of planning restraint and the density of new development – the more restrictive is the planning policy, the higher is the density of new housing construction (Bramley et al., 1995, Ch. 8).

Evans (1988) adds and interesting twist to the density thesis by suggesting that falling architectural and environmental standards, can also be attributed to the effect of restrictive planning controls. According to this view, given the restricted supply of land the profitability of obtaining planning permission for a developer is far higher than the profits to be made from the design of attractive buildings. Or, as Veljanowski (1988) puts it, given the absolute shortage of development land due to planning the value of a house, or any building *per se* is exceptionally high, but the marginal profitability of that house or building being well designed is low. Since property has been made an artificially scarce commodity more or less any kind of building can be put up and sold.

The policy of urban in-filling is now an explicit component of the British government's commitment to improve environmental quality and to implement the goal of sustainable development. It is, however, far from clear that any such 'improvements' will occur. Increasing dwelling densities in the cities still further, may save some environmental amenities by stopping green-field development on the urban fringe, but environmental conditions in the cities themselves may decline as urban congestion and air pollution may worsen. Indeed, a case could be made that in order to improve environmental quality in the towns, brown-field sites could be converted into green open spaces such as urban nature reserves, rather than developed as housing. Seen in this context, it may be the lack of such environmental amenities that is encouraging people to escape the cities and to move towards the suburbs and the countryside (Gordan and Richardson, 1997). In truth, it is difficult to assess just what the desirable level of urban dwelling densities actually is especially in terms of what accords with consumer preferences. Land use policy in the UK has historically been focused in favour of urban containment and higher density development, so there has been little chance for people to experiment in order to experience the different costs and benefits associated with a wider variety of urban forms.

One of the major effects of British urban containment policies has been to increase the density of residential development, but this is not always and everywhere the effect of restrictive planning controls. On the contrary, in some countries the effect of planning restrictions has been to *decrease* dwelling densities below what might have occurred in an unfettered market and to create a scattered pattern of development. The most striking example of this phenomenon can be seen through the effect of planning controls on dwelling densities in the United States. Whereas British attempts to restrict urban development in the countryside have taken the form of refusing planning permissions in Green Belts, with high density development crammed onto the remaining sites, the US zoning system has sought to restrict the total number of houses built through a process of 'large lot zoning'. This system operates by specifying a minimum lot size for each house constructed. Early growth management policies in states such as New Jersey required minimum lots of 5 acres per home (Frieden, 1982). In recent years, however, with the rise of the environmental agenda, this process has intensified. In California, for example, some planning authorities have created zoning districts that require minimum lot sizes of 20, 40 and even as much as 60 acres per single family home. This kind of regulation presents a formidable barrier to new house-building in suburban and semi-rural areas and has quite obvious distributive effects, with only the wealthiest of households able to afford the cost of such large sites. Moreover, as Fischel (1985) suggests, growth management policies of this sort have contributed to the very sort of low-density urban sprawl which their proponents' claim they are supposed to prevent. The emphasis on large lot zoning has created a highly dispersed 'leap frog' pattern of development, which has continually forced suburban development further and further out beyond the major towns and cities.

Planning and Transport Patterns

In addition to the price and density effects, it is now increasingly apparent that planning has been responsible, at least in part, for a shift in the nature of transport and commuting patterns. Although much of the growth in demand for long distance commuting may be attributed to the effects of a subsidised road system and in particular the absence of road pricing mechanisms (ASI, 1988; Hibbs, 1992), analysis has confirmed that Green Belts and equivalent controls may exacerbate these trends (Hall et al., 1973; Herington, 1984, 1990; Downs 1992; DoE; 1993a).

In the case of the UK, the major effect of planning controls has been the *physical* containment of urban areas, but these controls have only partially succeeded in preventing the *functional* decentralisation of cities and of the population itself (Simmie, 1993). Throughout the entire post-war period there has been an important shift in the pattern of residential location, away from the major conurbations towards the smaller 'commuter' towns, outside of the traditional metropolitan areas. In turn, as people have left the older cities they have been accommodated in high-density suburban estates or in rural villages. This outward flow of resident populations has not, however, been matched by a concurrent shift in the pattern of employment. Employment levels in the inner cities have fallen, but not to the same extent as population levels. The result has been an increase in the proportion of employment opportunities taken by commuters, often living a substantial distance away from their place of work. These distances have been increased by green belts and other designations that restrict development on the rural/urban fringe and hence shift development pressure further away from the urban core. This, in turn may increase the demand for long distance commuting and hence more roads (Herington, 1984, 1990; DoE, 1993a; Simmie, 1993).

As Simmie (1993) observes, the trend towards increased commuting has been particularly marked around the free-standing cities beyond the green belts. In these areas, population has remained fairly stable, but there has been a significant increase in the level of employment opportunities. The new jobs have been taken by individuals living outside the areas concerned, usually in neighbouring towns or rural villages. Environmental designations have thus contributed to an increase in commuting distances, because they prevent families from living in homes within close proximity of their chosen place of work. Instead, people must commute between towns or between towns and rural villages and as a consequence there has been an increase in the demand for road links between these areas (Simmie, 1993; DoE, 1993a).

Outside of Britain and especially in the United States planning controls may also have contributed to the phenomenon of long distance commuting. In both Britain and the United States, the absence of urban containment or growth management policies, would probably have resulted in new development for housing and other purposes taking place on greenfield sites at the edge of existing conurbations that would in turn have resulted in a gradual outward expansion of the contiguous urban area. In the British case, designations such as Green Belts have prevented this pattern and have instead acted to push the new development that has been allowed beyond the boundaries of the Green Belt, thus lengthening the commuting distance for those who live in the suburbs but work in the cities. Zoning policies in the United States have also operated to encourage such leap frog patterns, but with one important difference. Whereas leap frog development in Britain has tended to occur in the form of nucleated settlements, large lot zoning policies in the US have encouraged highly dispersed leap frog development which has heightened the demand for new road links and lengthened commuting distances to an even greater extent (Fischel, 1985; Simmie, 1993).

Setting aside the significance of the 'leap frog' effect on commuting distances, contemporary advocates of urban containment policies argue that more compact forms of development have an important role to play in reducing the need for automobile use and combined with public transport subsidies can make a significant contribution to reducing car use and hence vehicular emissions (Urban Task Force, 1999). Authors such as Newman and Kenworthy (1989) have produced empirical data, which appears to suggest that the lower the density of urban development the greater is the consumption of the gasoline/petrol, which in turn leads to higher levels of air pollution. According to this perspective, higher density developments reduce the need for longer distance trips, as people are able to access a wider range of services within a smaller surface area (see also Banister, 1997). This would appear to be the argument that has informed the British government's restrictive stance on out of town shopping developments and in favour of town centre re-development. High-density development accompanied by town centre shopping serviced by public transport is thought to reduce the need for the use of the private car.

The transport related rationale for urban containment is now widely cited by politicians and environmental campaigners alike, yet it is far from established that 'compact city' policies are indeed capable of producing the desired reduction in transport-related emissions that their advocates suggest. Whilst subsidised road transport has undoubtedly been an important factor in contributing to increased car based travel and hence pollution, public transport has also been in receipt of substantial government subsidies throughout most of the post war period. Indeed, in the United States public transit subsidies have by far and away *exceeded* those granted to road building and the private car, yet the use of public transit has continued to decline (Cervero, 1993, 1994; Altshuler and Gomez Ibanez, 1993; Gordan and Richardson, 1997). Whether the *financial* subsidies given to public transport have surpassed those flowing to the private automobile to an extent which sufficiently reflects the *non-financial* environmental benefits of the former is open to debate. The point remains, however, that public transit *has* been in receipt of substantial government subsidies.[2]

A number of authors have also challenged the alleged relationship between urban density and transport energy consumption. Using data from 32 cities around the world Newman and Kenworthy (1989) suggest that for every decrease in urban density there is correspondingly a rise in the level of automobile use. Recent research by Breheny et al. (1998), however, calls into question the validity of these findings. According to these authors, the Newman and Kenworthy data are heavily skewed by results from ultra high density cities such as Hong Kong and ultra low density areas such as Pheonix (USA). Whilst it does seem to be the case that extremely low density development results in more automobile use than extremely high density equivalents, for those cities that fall in between these polar cases, there is little if any evidence to suggest that those with lower density development experience significantly more in the way of car-based energy consumption. In addition, Hall (1999), has suggested that much of any observable difference between high and low density areas is not so much a product of their direct effect on car use, but stems from the fact that higher density areas often have higher proportions of low income people who *do not own cars*.

A number of authors (Crane, 1996) have also put forward the view that compact city policies may in certain circumstances actually *increase* rather than reduce automobile use, because shorter origin-destination trips reduces the average cost per trip. Cheaper trips may mean more vehicle trips and it is conceivable, therefore, that total vehicle miles travelled may increase in higher density developments (see also, Cervero, 1993, 1994; Altshuler and Gomez Ibanez, 1993; Gordan and Richardson, 1997). Seen through this lens, much maligned out of town shopping developments, may actually represent a more environmentally sensitive option than town centre equivalents. Although people tend to travel longer distances to the former, the frequency of these visits tends to be much less, so it is not at all clear that discriminating against such developments in the planning system will do anything to reduce auto-based pollution.

In practice, there would seem to be considerable uncertainty concerning the effect of different urban forms on transit patterns and pollution levels (positive or negative). It is somewhat surprising, therefore, that given the extent of these uncertainties politicians and planners in Britain and increasingly in other countries appear to be pursuing such an unswerving emphasis on urban containment, rather than adopt a more experimental or piecemeal approach.

Planning and the Decline of the Cities

A further argument put forward in support of urban containment or 'compact city' policies is that by preventing development in the countryside and on the urban fringe, planning controls can help to re-direct economic activity back to the older urban areas and thus help to improve economic fortunes and the quality of life in the inner city. Notwithstanding the existence of urban containment policies, evidence from both Britain and the United States suggests that the major areas that continue to experience economic growth are the suburbs and semi-rural areas. It is difficult, therefore, to see how a policy of urban containment can prevent such processes, which are, in part at least, a reflection of the fundamental economic shift away from city based manufacturing, towards highly mobile forms of service sector employment. More often than not, imposing extra restrictions on rural and suburban development does not redirect economic activity back to the cities, but actually stops this development from taking place anywhere at all (Evans, 1988; Simmie, 1993). Even in the continental European countries which have traditionally witnessed a more compact form of development, decentralisation appears to be underway, albeit with something of a time lag when compared to the experience of the United States and to a lesser extent Britain (Gordan and Richardson, 1997). A case can be made, however, that planning policies have actually contributed to the speeding up of the decentralising trend.

In addition to the problems of congestion highlighted earlier, one of the major reasons for the flight from the cities may have been the failure of business interests and urban local authorities to deliver the residential and shopping environments and other services, (schools, crime prevention etc.) that their residents prefer (Gordan and Richardson, 1997). In Britain, for example, town centre shopping developments are often seen as dirty and inconvenient when compared to 'out of town' shopping malls (Burke and Shackleton, 1996). Adopting a still more stringent emphasis on containment under these conditions may be equivalent to granting failing town centre businesses a monopoly market and urban local authorities monopolistic control over the local tax base. In these circumstances, without competition from potential 'out of town' or 'edge of town' development, urban businesses and local authorities may have little incentive to improve the quality of services that they provide and of finding more innovative ways of making urban environments attractive places in which to live.

It may even be argued that it is the relative lack of competition brought about by *existing* planning/containment policies that has perpetuated the lack of economic dynamism in the cities themselves. Inner city areas that are already protected from competition by containment policies, are prone to higher taxes, poor services, regulations that thwart the development of small businesses by low-income people, rent controls that remove the incentives for property owners to improve the quality of the housing stock and a high percentage of public sector land ownership (Loveless, 1983, 1987; Denman and Goodchild, 1989; Simmie, 1993). As wealthier sections of the population who can afford inflated prices in the suburbs leave, the cities have increasingly become the reserve of those excluded from the rest of society – the poor and the unemployed.

Within this context, successive governments in Britain and in the United States have sought to 'regenerate' urban areas through policies of direct intervention in the urban land market. Rather than pursue a de-regulatory agenda, business interests and local authorities in both Britain and the United States have sought large scale injections of public sector monies in order to fund highly visible re-development schemes (Frieden and Sagalyn, 1989; Mills, 1991; Salins, 1994; Gordan and Richardson, 1997). In the 1960s and 1970s these were based on the large scale building of public sector housing and slum clearance programmes. More recently, policies such as Enterprise Zones and Urban Development Corporations introduced in the 1980s and 1990s have been highlighted as examples of a 'property-led' form of urban planning typified by prestige projects such as the Canary Wharf redevelopment and the Millennium Dome. In this model, substantial public subsidies have been injected into declining urban areas in the hope of 'levering in' still greater amounts of private investment capital to stimulate regeneration of the urban property market. Notwithstanding the substantial amounts of public funding that have been invested in urban renewal programmes of this sort, there is little to suggest that they have been successful in reversing the long-term economic decline of many inner urban areas. On the one hand such schemes have been criticised for their minimal impact on employment levels and on the other for exacerbating social inequalities within the areas concerned (Brownhill, 1990; Imrie and Thomas, 1993; Gordan and Richardson, 1997).

Planning: Environmental or Agricultural Protection?

A fifth external effect, which may be attributed to the operation of land use planning, concerns the impact on the countryside of the land uses that have been favoured under the planning system and especially the privileges granted to the agricultural sector.

It is often thought that planning controls and site designations such as Green Belts are primarily an act of environmental policy. In practice, however, the environmental focus of land use planning in Britain has been confined purely to the preoccupation with urban containment to the neglect of what actually happens in the countryside itself (Evans, 1991, 1996; Pennington, 1996). Existing uses of land in rural areas and agriculture, in particular, have been exempted from the controls governing alternative forms of development. Thus, planning permissions for farm buildings, fences and hedgerow grubbing are often not required. In reality, therefore, the town planning legislation has been inextricably linked to the regime of subsidised farming also introduced in 1947 (via the Agriculture Act) and since 1973, the Common Agricultural Policy (CAP) of the European Union. The designation of green belts, and other controls on rural land development has prevented housing developments in the countryside. The countryside, however, has not been conserved for environmental purposes, but rather for the expansion of subsidised farming which has had a devastating impact on the rural landscape throughout Western Europe.

The environmental impact of agricultural support policy in Britain is now well documented (Bowers and Cheshire, 1983; Munton, 1983; Lowe et al., 1986). With farm subsidies positively related to the level of production, land prices have risen as the possession of agricultural land has become in effect a license to receive subsidies. In turn, higher land prices have raised the real cost of land above that of labour and heavily subsidised capital inputs, thus encouraging farmers to intensify the use of land, which has usually meant the removal of hedgerows, the adoption of 'prairie farming' techniques and the widespread use of chemical fertilisers and pesticides. Consequently, agricultural production has increasingly extended onto marginal lands, otherwise unsuitable for farming with a concurrent loss of habitats, including an 80 per cent reduction in chalk downland, a 60 per cent reduction in heath-land, and a 50 per cent reduction in meadowland (Lowe et al., 1986 pp. 65–8).

It is often suggested that the environmental problems associated with agricultural over-production are not the direct result of planning but rather stem from the absence of planning controls. The solution to the externalities produced by the farming industry, therefore, is to impose the full gamut of urban planning regulations on the agricultural sector (Lowe et al., 1986). There are two problems with this particular line of argument. First, the introduction of a still further set of regulatory controls seems a highly inefficient way of dealing with a problem that might not exist on anything like the present scale, were it not for the existing level of state intervention in the countryside. The most likely outcome of such a policy is a 'cycle of interventionism' typified at present by the so-called agri-environment schemes that pay farmers additional subsidies for not destroying habitats, which they might not be destroying in the first place, were it not for the level of state support. Rather than introduce still more regulation, an alternative route would be to remove the existing government subsidies that are the proximate cause of the problem (Ridley, 1996; Pennington, 1996). Second, there is an implicit assumption that the developments which might replace some agricultural land uses should subsidies be removed, are inherently 'bad' for the environment. Rural housing and leisure developments interspersed with woodland, are, however, perfectly compatible with maintaining habitat and species diversity, yet such developments are ruled out of court under the contemporary British planning system. By designating sites which effectively forbid such developments the planning system has reinforced the position of subsidised farming and it can be argued, has prevented the transfer of land to more highly valued and in many cases less environmentally damaging uses (Evans 1996; Pennington 1996).

In the immediate post-war period, policy-makers justified the introduction of agricultural subsidies on the grounds of avoiding food shortages. In the intervening years, however, transfer payments have been expanded to such an extent, in particular under the CAP, that there is now massive over-production and a surplus of agricultural land, which could be as high as 12 million acres (Shucksmith, 1990). By restricting the development of non-farm businesses in the countryside, the planning system has added substantially to the burden of taxation by maintaining the dependence of farmers on subsidies and the continual expansion of the CAP budget – now approaching £4 billion. On the one hand, farmers are subsidised to produce food for a market which does not exist or to restore habitats which may not have been destroyed in the first place where it not for the CAP, whilst on the other, the relative shortage of building land drives up house prices and may contribute still further to urban congestion.

CONCLUSION: PLANNING AS GOVERNMENT FAILURE?

This chapter has sought to summarise the principal consequences of land use planning and has highlighted the major external effects generated within the British planning system. Within the British context the emphasis on more stringent urban planning controls now forms a key plank of government commitments to the policy goal of sustainable development. As the foregoing analysis has shown, however, there is evidence to suggest that the historic policy focus of the British planning system may actually conflict with a number of other policy objectives with respect to housing, the environment and agriculture.

First, all major political parties, continue to profess a desire to increase the affordability of housing, yet the commitment to urban containment implies an increase in the relative cost of land and hence higher prices for housing developments. Second, politicians and planners claim to seek an improvement in the quality of urban environments, when it is far from clear that the desire to provide the majority of new housing in existing urban areas is compatible with this objective. Third, policy suggests that planning should encourage a more compact form of development to reduce commuting distances, when there is evidence to suggest that green belts and equivalent controls may actually increase the tendency toward long distance commuting. Fourth, current policy is based on the notion that planning should seek to redirect investment to inner urban areas when past experience suggests that such policies may, in part at least, have been a contributing factor in the decline of these very areas. Finally, politicians claim to support a reduction in the burden of agricultural support yet the stringent commitment to containment restricts alternative business development and thus seems more likely to increase the burden of taxation.

The presence of the externalities and potential policy contradictions generated by the planning system *does not*, by any means, prove that these costs outweigh the potential benefits of planning. In the British case these have centred predominantly on the maintenance of open countryside around the major towns and cities. Whilst some authors are clearly of the opinion that the environmental and social benefits of urban containment are insufficient (see, for example Simmie, 1993), others contend that the advantages of protecting Green Belts and other such zones are more than adequate to warrant the relevant costs (Urban Task Force, 1999). No attempt, it should be noted, has been made in this chapter to *measure* the costs and benefits associated with planning as might be required by an adherent of social cost/benefit analysis. On the contrary, from the perspective of Virginia public choice theory, the values that individuals attach to environmental goods are known only to the individuals themselves and it is only through the actual exchange of goods in a market where property rights are assigned that the relative value of these goods can be made known.[3] It is *not* possible, therefore, for an outside observer to attach precise costs and benefits to the operation of the planning system. Indeed, the disagreements that exist between the supporters and opponents of policies such as urban containment merely serve to illustrate the subjective nature of these supposedly 'neutral' techniques.

If it is *not possible to measure* the effects of planning what it *is* possible to do, is to *examine the institutional process that has produced the relevant policy outcomes*. In order to evaluate the practice of planning, therefore, attention should focus on the *process* of planning and the *structure of incentives* provided by the institutions through which planning policies are formulated and enacted. What the existence of potential external effects associated with land use planning suggests, is the need to avoid the 'nirvana fallacy' when considering the merits of planning intervention in the market for land. Market failures exist when the institutions of private property and voluntary contract fail to take account the costs that may be imposed on individuals who are not party to such contracts. Government failures, on the other hand, exist where democratic processes are structured so that, individuals within the political system are not held to account for the consequences of their actions and the political market does not represent the underlying structure of public preferences.

To an extent, of course, the externalisation of costs is an inherent feature of democratic decision-making – unless there is unanimity across the electorate with respect to a particular policy issue, it is inevitable that sections of the population will have to bear the costs of policies that they themselves do not support. Identifying government failures in terms of departures from unanimity is, therefore, too broad a definition, since virtually any democratic decision may be said to have failed when judged by such standards. A more appropriate position for the purposes of policy analysis is to identify government failure when the democratic process is biased in favour of certain groups, *which systematically gain at the expense of others*. Thus, if land use planning policies reflect the ability of special interest groups, public sector bureaucrats and elected representatives to *capture* the political market, then it may be possible to indict such policies as an example of 'government failure'. This book examines the decision-procedures of the British land use planning system for signs of such structural bias and institutional failure. The following chapters use the public choice framework set out in Chapter 1 to examine both the demand and supply sides of the political market in this regard. Three general themes shape the focus of these chapters:

1. The experience of planning reflects the existence of collective action problems on the 'demand' side of the political market. Interest groups which are able to overcome the logic of collective action are the principal beneficiaries of the planning system, whereas as those unable to do so are the principal bearers of the costs.
2. The experience of planning reflects the economic interests of bureaucratic actors on the 'supply side' of the political market and in particular the monopoly power of the administrative state bureaucracy to support policies which expand the size of the planning budget.
3. The experience of planning reflects the incentive for politicians on the 'supply side' of the political market to respond to the combined demands of special interest groups and public sector bureaucrats in order to secure electoral and patronage benefits from the passage of planning legislation.

If the experience of land use regulation can be attributed to such government failures, then the theoretical case for planning in its present institutional form must be open to serious question.

3

INTEREST GROUPS, COLLECTIVE ACTION AND PLANNING

INTRODUCTION

This chapter uses public choice theory to explore the role of interest groups on the demand side of the political market in planning. The emphasis on interest groups and collective action problems is important given the current significance attributed to the role of public participation within the environmental policy literature, and collaborative planning theory in particular. In recent years there has been a renewed advocacy of public participation as a means of improving the accountability of the planning system to the community at large. Public choice theory, by contrast, is highly sceptical of the merits of public participation arguing that special interest capture and rent seeking are an *endemic* feature of political markets. Seen from this perspective, public participation in planning and the policies that result are likely to be *structurally biased* towards those interest groups that are advantaged by their greater ability to overcome the *logic of collective action*.

It is the contention of this chapter that the policy focus of land use planning system in Britain, outlined in Chapter 2 has indeed reflected the processes of special interest capture highlighted by public choice theory. The analysis suggests that decision-making biases evident in the British planning system are not a reflection of insufficient opportunities for public involvement but are rather the product of underlying collective action problems, which may continue to result in chronic examples of 'government failure'. The chapter provides an exposition of the key theoretical concepts in the public choice theory of interest groups and collective action, which are then used as a refractive lens through which to view the behaviour of the major winners and losers in the political market of town and country planning.

INTEREST GROUPS, COLLECTIVE ACTION AND GOVERNMENT FAILURE

Within the literature of environmental policy and planning expanding the role of public participation in decision-making is considered to be at the heart of attempts to improve the democratic accountability of decision-making. Collaborative planning theory, in particular, suggests that the active involvement of interest groups or 'stakeholders' within the political process is essential if the full spectrum of public preferences is to be properly reflected and a process of democratic consensus building is to occur (Jacobs, 1992; Dryzek, 1996; Healey, 1997). Advocates of collaborative planning do, of course, recognise that the reality of public participation does not always conform to this pluralist ideal. Those influenced by Marxist arguments suggest that within the prevailing capitalist economy, the interests of business are always likely to be dominant (Ambrose, 1986). Elite theorists, meanwhile, suggest that bureaucratic structures may obstruct public participation and there may be biases and prejudices displayed towards certain groups (Marsden et al., 1993). The assumption is made, however, that if the political process could somehow be 'opened up' and the relevant stakeholders treated with equal respect then the democratic process would necessarily be open to all who are sufficiently determined to register their preferences. It has been one of the principal contributions of public choice theory to question this assumption.

From the perspective of public choice theory access to the political marketplace of democracy is *endemically asymmetric*. Seen through this lens, power can never be diffused through democratic processes in the way that the collaborative planning theorists suggest. Inequalities of access to the political process are not, as Marxists and elite theorists suggest, a reflection of money power (though this may be a contributory factor), which may simply be solved through a redistribution of wealth. Rather, they are a product of underlying *incentive structures* that are an inherent feature of the political marketplace itself. More specifically, unequal access to the political process reflects the differential ability of groups to overcome what Olson (1965) has termed the 'logic of collective action' – the ability of groups to mobilise.

The Logic of Collective Action

The mobilisation of an interest group is a key factor, which affects its ability to participate effectively in the political market place. Where large numbers of individuals remain unorganised, their ability to attract support from politicians and bureaucrats is seriously undermined and their preferences may be neglected. Within this context, it was the insight of Mancur Olson (1965) to note that political activism for public policies that benefit large numbers of individuals is unlikely to be forthcoming. According to Olson, a single individual's participation will not have a sufficient impact on the political process to make up for the costs of engagement. Because the results of interest group lobbying are non-excludable and indivisible (i.e. they are a collective good) it is rational for individuals to 'free ride' on the membership of others, reaping the benefits without incurring the costs. And, since most individuals will reason in this way, collective action is unlikely to occur.

When recast in the language of game theory, the decision to join an interest group resembles an n-person prisoners' dilemma (PD) game (Hardin, 1982; Chong, 1991). In the prisoners' dilemma each individual is engaged in a game against all the other actors and has a choice of co-operating or not co-operating in a collective venture the benefits of which cannot be obtained by a single individual acting alone. In the 'one-shot' prisoners' dilemma, all players would be better off if they co-operated in the provision of the collective good, but each individual player prefers defection, irrespective of whether the other players *do* or *do not* co-operate. If an individual co-operates whilst the others defect, then she incurs the costs of engagement without deriving sufficient benefits. If, on the other hand, she defects whilst the others co-operate, she can obtain the benefits of collective action without paying her share of the costs. In such a situation, the course of action, which is optimal from the point of view of the individual proves, therefore, to be sub-optimal with regard to the interests of the group.

The public choice approach suggests that collective action problems such as the prisoners' dilemma strike differentially across the political market place depending on the character of the interest group concerned. For large groups the benefits of membership to an individual are so discounted by the irrelevance of an individual contribution to supply that it is seldom worthwhile to join such a group. Smaller groups, by contrast, may have sufficiently few potential members that each may be aware of the others free-riding behaviour. In these situations potential group members may engage in a process of strategic bargaining which transforms the 'one shot' prisoners' dilemma game into an *iterated* scenario. When prisoners' dilemmas are played an indeterminate number of times, players may develop co-operative strategies where each player co-operates on the first play and thereafter mimics the other players preceding move. 'Tit for Tat' strategies can lead to co-operative solutions to the collective action problem, but this is less likely to occur in large number situations where it is not possible to monitor the other players' behaviour (Axelrod, 1984; Taylor, 1987; Chong, 1991).

Small groups, therefore, are structurally advantaged in the political marketplace by their greater ability to overcome the collective action problem. A small group of firms in a concentrated industry, for example, are more likely to know the names of the other firms in the industry concerned and may as a result be able to engage in strategic behaviour (Hardin, 1982). Producer interests in an industry with a more diffuse market structure, meanwhile, may fall into the category of intermediate or medium sized groups. Labour unions may also be intermediate groups, especially where the industry in which the potential members work is in a fixed locality and potential free-riders may be known to one another. Intermediate producer groups may be less likely to engage in collective action than producers in a more concentrated industry, because the potential membership is greater and it is more difficult to monitor free-riding. They are, however, far more likely to mobilise than consumer groups where the size of the potential membership is such that it is virtually impossible to monitor and penalise defection (Olson, 1965; Hardin, 1982).

Another category of groups, which may find it easier to overcome the collective action problem are what Olson (1965) terms privileged groups. A *privileged group* exists where the gains to at least one member from acting alone to achieve the collective good exceed the costs of doing so. Any industry, which would benefit from trade protection, for example, is privileged if the gains to at least one firm are higher than that firm's share of lobbying costs. Privileged groups do not, however, escape the collective action problem completely; they are subject to a different version of this problem.

In the prisoners dilemma game no individual can provide sufficient quantities of the collective good to warrant the costs of engagement and the worst case scenario for the individual actor is that she co-operates to organising the political lobby, whilst the other actors defect. In a privileged group, however, there is at least one actor who could derive sufficient benefits from acting to provide the lobbying effort *alone*. The worst case scenario for this actor is that nobody co-operates and none of the political good is provided. Whilst it may be possible for this individual to provide a sufficient quantity of the collective good on her own, she will *still prefer that the other group members contribute to the collective action whilst she herself defects*. In this situation a pattern of strategic behaviour emerges which is known as a Chicken Game (CG). If there is more than one actor who would pay the full cost of the lobby should she have to (the privileged members of the privileged group), each of these actors has an incentive to pre-commit to a strategy of defection in an attempt to force the other(s) into payment. If there is only one such actor, she also has an incentive to pre-commit, in order to force the smaller actors to pay their share. Some of the actors in the Chicken Game may, however, recognise the danger of pre-commitment to defection and, unless they are habitual risk takers willing to take the chance that none of the good will be provided, at least some collective action may occur (Taylor and Ward, 1982). This action may tend, however, to be rather unstable because of the ongoing incentive to pre-commit to a strategy of non-co-operation.

Given the prevalence of such collective action problems, public choice theory suggests that for larger groups to attain a satisfactory degree of mobilisation they must provide benefits on an individual or private basis – benefits that may only be obtained by joining the group. The provision of private benefits or *selective incentives* may take on a number of different forms. *Material* selective incentives include the provision of services such as specialised insurance or health care benefits, which are made available as a by-product of membership. Alternatively, where a group has attained a degree of political power and established access to the state, group leaders may 'colonise' particular agencies and render group membership a prerequisite for access to state benefits. In addition, penalties might be applied to recalcitrant individuals, as when trade union dues are extracted through closed shop or union shop arrangements (Dunleavy, 1991; Tullock, 1993).

Non-material selective incentives may also be developed to encourage participation in the groups' affairs (Salisbury, 1969; Moe, 1981; Hirschman, 1982; Opp, 1986; Ostrom, 1990; Chong, 1991). Although not involving any direct material gain to the individuals concerned these incentives are nonetheless a key factor, which may alter the perceived costs and benefits associated with political participation. In these circumstances the act of participation may itself become a benefit rather than a cost (Hirschman, 1982). Within this context, two broad types of non-material benefits can be identified: *solidary* benefits, which include such things as the opportunity to socialise with like-minded people or the desire to avoid the possibility of social stigma/ ostracism resulting from a failure to participate in the collective endeavour (Moe, 1981; Opp, 1986; Ostrom, 1990; Chong, 1991); *and expressive* benefits, which may include the desire to achieve public approval from *being seen* to contribute to a fashionable cause, or the entertainment value of taking part in events which are perceived to be of major public significance (Opp, 1986; Chong, 1991).

A further strategy that may stimulate collective action is to rely on a political entrepreneur to enhance the view that individual participation is significant, so that the discounting of benefits is reduced. According to Dunleavy (1991), people recognise that their individual contribution to group effectiveness is lower in larger groups, but they may also perceive a larger group to be more politically viable, thus lowering the perceived costs of membership. In response to this phenomenon, Dunleavy suggests that political entrepreneurs may send out 'mixed messages' to their potential members and in particular may adopt 'size manipulation strategies'. Because people may be more likely to support an apparently large and powerful interest group, political entrepreneurs may stress the scale of wider public support for the group aims in order to increase the perceived viability of the group. At the same time, however, in order to counteract the disincentive effects of increased group size, leaders may create local branches or sections focused on smaller, more localised issues, where an individual may perceive her personal contribution to the supply of group benefits to be that much greater.

Notwithstanding these different strategies to stimulate mobilisation, according to public choice theory, the logic of collective action remains a troublesome problem especially for larger and more diffuse groups. Whilst certain large groups may periodically manage to overcome collective problems, in general there remains a structural bias within the political market which is likely to favour, smaller, more concentrated lobbies with a higher per capita stake. In turn, it is this structural bias which allows special interest rent seekers to capture the political market, systematically transferring wealth and other benefits to themselves, at the expense of the community at large.

INTEREST GROUPS, COLLECTIVE ACTION AND THE POLITICAL MARKET IN PLANNING

Having outlined the key factors which may affect character of public participation in the political market the remainder of this chapter sets out to examine the characteristics of interest group participation in the British land use planning system. The purpose of the analysis is to link the policy focus of the British planning system and in particular the emphasis on urban containment, to the underlying incentive structures that face the major actors within the political marketplace. Each of the key winners and losers is analysed in terms of the character of benefits they derive from the existing policy framework and their ability to overcome the collective action problem.

The Building Lobby

As one would expect from public choice theory producer interests have been important beneficiaries of decision-making with the British planning system. Perhaps the most successful of these groups have been construction interests and in particular, the house building lobby. This interest is represented in the political market by groups such as the House Builders Federation (HBF), the Volume Builders Study Group (VBSG) and the Building Employers Confederation (BEC).

For house building interests the benefits (rents) extracted through the political process are dependent on the rate of land release for residential purposes via the planning system. Developers favour a greater level of land release than either the conservation or the farming lobbies (see, pp. 68–81 below), but it would be a mistake to view the building lobby as supporting levels of development which might be feasible in a land market free from statutory controls. On the contrary, the ability of the house builders and in particular the larger developers to extract rents is dependent on a regulated land use system and it is *control over the regulatory process* which forms the focus of their lobbying activity (Rydin, 1986; Evans, 1991).

House building firms require sites available for development as construction on existing sites nears completion, so that the firms resources can be transferred easily from one site to another (Goodchild and Munton, 1985). Consequently, it is necessary for many firms to hold 'land-banks' of sites with planning permission. Obtaining planning permission requires time and money to participate in the plan-making process where potential sites are identified for release and later on individual planning applications. The granting of planning permission for a parcel of land confers a *monopoly right* on the owner as other potential sites are *excluded* from the land market. Developers who are able to secure planning permissions for their land banks are thus able to secure higher prices and profits than in a fully competitive market. In accordance with Stigler's (1975) economic theory of regulation, the corporate builders favour a controlled system which provides permission to develop their own land, *whilst restricting access to land for potential competitors*. As Evans (1988, 1991) points out, the bulk of profits derived from UK house building are often not the product of building homes, but rather the monopoly gains derived from the sale of land-banks with planning permission. A similar pattern of rent seeking appears also to have developed in the retail sector and in particular with respect to the activities of the large supermarket chains. Having already built a substantial number of 'edge of town' and 'out of town' shopping centres throughout the 1980s the British corporate retailers have put up little opposition to new government restrictions designed to bring a halt to such developments. Indeed, as the opportunities that this regulation provides to restrict entry into the food retail market and in particular to keep out foreign owned concerns have become apparent, British firms have increasingly begun to support such restrictive planning measures (Burke and Shackleton, 1996).

Given the importance of land-banks to the economic fortunes of the house builders, it is periods of economic growth and property market boom which bring forth the most vigorous lobbying by groups such as the HBF. As land prices soar due to restricted supply developers lobby for greater control over the regulatory process in order to reap monopoly profits from the *controlled release of the land which they own*. In the 1980s this was exemplified in the setting up of a 'New Homes Marketing Board' by the HBF/BEC to advertise the case for greater land release (Pennington, 1997a, p. 96). Similarly, the HBF and VBSG played an important role in the formulation of DoE circulars 9/80, 16/84 and 14/85, all of which increased the involvement of developers in the identification of new housing sites during the 1980s (Rydin, 1986).

A second source of rent seeking gain for the large house builders is derived through the increasing exclusion of small firms from the housing market and hence a further reduction in competition. The acquisition of planning permissions requires the use of rent seeking expenditures in the form of planning consultancies, legal fees and the costs of application and appeal. Smaller firms are at a disadvantage because resource constraints limit the number of applications they can make, which increases the risk of not obtaining any planning permissions. Larger, corporate firms are able to afford a greater number of planning applications to spread the associated risks. This pattern is reinforced because the costs of application and appeal in the British planning system do not increase proportionately with the size of a development. The cost of a planning permission for a development of 500 homes is lower per house than the cost of permission to build five homes (Cullingworth and Nadin, 1994; Evans 1988, 1991). Small firms are often driven out of business due to the resultant land shortages and between 1972 and 1974 almost 2,000 firms were lost (net), largely due to corporate take-overs. As Table 3.1 indicates, the trend towards concentration in the building industry appears to have continued into the 1990s. According to the National Housing and Building Council, in 1992 the top 32 companies supplied almost half of total production, with each building 500 units or more. At the other end of the market there were more than 6,000 companies building fewer than ten houses per year (Bramley et al., 1995). Undoubtedly, some of this concentration may be accounted for by genuine efficiencies due to economies of scale and the ability of large firms to spread the risks of production in what is often a highly volatile market. As Evans (1988, 1991) contends, however, the peculiar incentives in the planning system which favour land release on very large sites must be a critical factor, given the relatively low start-up costs for house building firms.

From the perspective of public choice theory, the undoubted success of the house-building lobby in the political marketplace of planning is a reflection of its structural ability to overcome the collective action problem. In 1994 the

Table 3.1   Structure of the UK House Building Industry – Starts by Size of Output (%)

Units	1977	1982	1987	1992
0	0	0	0	0
1–10	16	14	13	12
11–30	13	10	11	9
31–100	14	12	13	13
101–500	22	18	18	21
501–2000	35	17	16	18
2000+	Incl. Above	25	25	26

Source: Bramley et al. (1995, p. 89).

HBF had 3,500 members and an income of £5 million derived from large regionally based firms or corporate multinationals, whose combined output accounted for almost 80 per cent of new housing construction in the UK. The VBSG, on the other hand, consists of eight mega-corporate concerns including firms such as Christian Salvesen and Barratts. The BEC, meanwhile, has some 12,000 members, including all HBF members (HBF is a subgroup) and a range of other construction interests including representatives of the road-building lobby (Pennington, 1997a, p. 95).

As a producer interest in a relatively concentrated industry, the large building firms in particular, are a relatively small group who are likely to find themselves in a situation which resembles the iterated prisoners' dilemma. With only 30 or so large national producers supplying half of the new homes market it would be relatively easy to identify free-riding behaviour should member firms attempt to gain the benefits of lobbying without paying their share of the costs. These firms could develop tit for tat strategies, which could help to ensure the continuing support of the member firms to the lobby. This is an even more likely scenario for the very largest firms represented by the VBSG. The eight corporate giants in this group are in a position where strategic behaviour to discourage free riding is a clear possibility.

There is also evidence to suggest that building interests in the HBF have been able to benefit from the 'size manipulation strategies' discussed by Dunleavy (1991), in order to encourage membership from the somewhat more numerous regionally based producers. The HBF has created nine regional branches throughout the country, which are the focus of the groups' lobbying activity at the regional and county level when regional planning guidance and structure plans are being prepared. Within the national context, these regional based producers might have incentives to free ride on the HBF's national political campaigns because their individual contribution to the national policy process is likely to be negligible. At the regional level, however, the likelihood of each individual firm being decisive to the success of collective action is considerably higher and the incentive to join the building lobby is correspondingly greater. Within a regional housing market, the number of large firms is far fewer, than the total number of such firms operating within the national market. In these circumstances, large regional producers are much more likely to know the names of the other potential member firms within their region and the possibility of monitoring free-riding behaviour in a more strategic context is increased.

In addition to the above strategies the building lobby is also able to offer selective incentives to its potential members. The HBF, for example, offers a magazine service and is a member of the National Housing and Building Council, which issues various design awards and charter marks and hence provides a valuable marketing ploy to the member firms. Equally, the federation's technical knowledge and expertise in the planning arena are often indispensable for firms attempting to secure a place for their individual developments in the local plan process. In certain circumstances, it might also be the case that at the local level, in particular, the building lobby constitutes a privileged group. In this situation, individual developers may be prepared to bear a disproportionate share of lobbying costs. This scenario is especially relevant at the structure and the local plan making stage, where it is common for developers to pay out hundreds of thousands of pounds on consulting and legal fees during local plan inquiries, because the monopoly gains from land banks with planning permission are potentially huge. In a study of the local plan process in Chester, for example, Pennington (1997a, p. 202) found that a consortium of four large producers paid approximately £240,000 in lobbying costs at the local plan inquiry. If the big developers are to get their own sites allocated for development to the exclusion of smaller competitors and potential market entrants, then it is imperative that they engage in political lobbying at the plan making stage. In such a situation, the large builders' lobby is protected from the problem of Chicken pre-commitment strategies, which can undermine collective action in privileged groups. In this case, any potential member who threatened the other member firms with a pre-commitment to defect would simply not have her land banks identified for development within the planning process and would thus receive none of the potential gains.

If the larger corporate developers have been important beneficiaries from the British planning system, the same cannot be said for the small firms sector. Small firms have lost out significantly because of their inability to access land with planning permission in a tightly regulated system. The Federation of Master Builders (FMB) which has some 9,000 members, consisting mostly of small and medium sized firms is the principal lobby group representing this sector (Pennington, 1997a, p. 95). The FMB has lobbied repeatedly for a liberalisation of planning controls but appears to have had a negligible impact on the planning process when compared with groups such as the HBF (Rydin, 1986; Pennington, 1997a). In terms of public choice theory, this is not at all surprising given that the FMB is a far less mobilised and well-organised lobby than groups representing the corporate developers. Where the HBF have full time political lobbyists and a specialist team of planning experts, the FMB simply does not have the resources to employ staff for these purposes (Rydin, 1986; Pennington, 1997a, p. 97). This lack of resources is partly a reflection of the smaller size and economic power of the member firms, but also a product of the more substantial collective action problem that these firms may face. With at least 20,000 small building firms in the country, the sector has a much larger potential membership than the corporate interests represented by the HBF. Even at the local scale, the number of potential member firms is sufficiently great that it is more difficult to monitor any free-riding behaviour or to develop a process of strategic bargaining. In order to get its members the FMB has to rely disproportionately on selective incentives and in particular an attempt to license entry into the sector by developing a code of practice to 'guarantee' against 'black market' firms operating outside the realm of statutory building regulations (Pennington, 1997a, p. 97).

The Agricultural Lobby

A second set of producer interests that are important beneficiaries of the British planning system is the agricultural lobby. This interest is represented by the National Farmers Union (NFU) and the Country Landowners Association (CLA), the former the traditional representative of the tenant farming community and the latter, the interests of land owning farmers. The rent seeking activities of farmers are central to the release of land for development and their lobbying behaviour within the town and country planning system. The principal form of rent extraction has occurred through the continuation of farm subsidies following the Agriculture Act (1947) – more recently (since 1973) the Common Agricultural Policy (CAP) of the European Community/ European Union (EC/EU) and the continued ability of the farm lobby to remain exempt from key aspects of statutory planning control.

Within the context of agricultural support the NFU has always advocated restrictive planning controls and hence a reduced level of urban development, because planning permissions for non-agricultural uses often result in a notice to quit for its' tenant members. The NFU were thus strong supporters of the 1947 planning legislation which redistributed development rights away from landowners in favour of tenants and combined with agricultural support guaranteed the incomes of farmers (Newby, 1985). Land owning farmers, meanwhile, have been prepared to tolerate the loss of development rights so long as farm subsidies provide an income which can compensate for the lost ability to diversify out of agricultural production (Evans, 1991; Marsden et al., 1993). At the same time, however, both the agricultural lobby groups have been vociferous in their campaign to maintain the exemption of *agricultural land uses* from statutory planning controls. Environmental campaigners have complained of the continuing damages wrought by agricultural production to the countryside and have repeatedly argued for the introduction of statutory regulation over agricultural uses. The farmers, however, appear to have been remarkably successful is dissuading the government of the merits of this case (Lowe et al., 1986; Winter, 1996; Pennington, 1996, 1999).

When farm subsidies are growing, both the NFU and CLA are supportive of a strict system of planning control and urban containment. If, however, subsidy levels and hence, farm incomes start to decline, the pattern of rent seeking assumes a somewhat different character as the groups' search for alternative sources of revenue. The NFU has tended towards the development of an alternative rationale for farm subsidies and in particular has sought support from the environmental lobby to support subsidies for landscape conservation, the first example of which was the introduction of conservation subsidies in the 1986 Agriculture Act. CLA members, on the other hand, whilst supporting conservation subsidies, have tended to shift their emphasis to a selective liberalisation of planning controls to enable diversification out of agricultural uses, which includes the release of land for residential development. In more recent times and as the proportion of owner occupier farmers within its ranks has risen, the NFU position has moved towards that of the CLA in supporting a selective liberalisation. As with the CLA, however, the NFU do not support a total liberalisation because the monopoly gains derived from the scarcity value of land are dependent on the maintenance of regulation and the avoidance of a free market (Marsden et al., 1993).

The shifting pattern of rent seeking is depicted in Table 3.2, which shows the trends in Ministy of Agriculture, Fisheries and Food (MAFF) farm subsidies, conservation subsidies and farm incomes over the period 1982–95 and the major changes in governmental policy which have formed the focus of lobbying activity. Of particular interest is the shift in farmers' lobbying, first from a defence of agricultural support and opposition to deregulation of planning, second to an emphasis on selective liberalisation and third, a shift back towards farm support, but reoriented towards a 'conservation' agenda.

In 1980/1981 the principal focus of NFU/CLA lobbying was the Wildlife and Countryside Act, which brought farmers into direct conflict with environmentalists in groups such as The Royal Society for the Protection of Birds (RSPB) and Friends of the Earth (FoE). Subsidies at this time were at an all time high and the farmers sought to defend the basis of support from an assault by the environmentalists who highlighted the destructive impact of subsidised agriculture on habitats such as hedgerows and wetlands. The environmental lobby failed in its attempt to enact statutory planning controls over agriculture and the eventual outcome was a net increase in farm subsidies as payments were offered for conservation activities *on top* of existing farm support (Lowe et al., 1986; Winter, 1996; Pennington, 1996).

By 1983, the agriculturalists and especially the NFU were joining forces with the conservationists as the focus of lobbying shifted to the defence of Green Belt policy from the prospect of liberalisation. Tenant farmers saw a threat to their tenured/subsidised position if the rural land market was liberalised and having joined in a national campaign with the Council for the Protection of Rural

Table 3.2　Subsidies, Farm Incomes and Lobbying

Year	Agri. Subsidies	Conserv. Subsidies	Farm Incomes	Policy
1981	2.20	0.012	140	W&C
1982	2.00	0.015	130	
1983	1.97	0.015	124	GB
1984	2.22	0.018	165	GB
1985	1.95	0.030	96	
1986	2.17	0.040	111	Agri. Act
1987	2.72	0.042	115	ALURE
1988	2.64	0.046	93	ALURE
1989	1.67	0.076	107	
1990	1.81	0.080	100	
1991	1.77	0.129	95	
1992	1.86	0.133	113	MacSharry
1993	3.00	0.097	154	
1994	3.00	0.141	160	
1995	na.	0.150	180	

Notes: Subsidies in £ billions (1993 prices). Incomes in Index form: 1990 =100
Source: Computed from MAFF/Countryside Commission and English Nature Annual Reports and Farm Income Survey.

England, secured the signatures of well over one hundred, mostly Conservative MPs who saw to it that the proposals were thrown out (Elson, 1986).

The attitude of the farmers was somewhat different in the period 1987/88 when the so-called ALURE proposals (Alternative Land Use and the Rural Economy) were introduced. The growing burden of the CAP on the European Community budget made the issue of agricultural subsidies more visible than at any time since the war and subsidy levels were reduced for the first time in 1984. Faced with declining incomes, farmers sought alternative sources of revenue, including the potential for housing and leisure developments in the countryside, which were suggested in the ALURE proposals (Marsden et al., 1993; Pennington, 1996).

With the conservation lobby campaigning successfully against the deregulation of the rural land market (see below, pp. 72–77), the focus of agricultural lobbying shifted again during the 1990s. The NFU/CLA joined forces with the conservation lobby to defend farm subsidies, but instead reoriented towards landscape conservation. Indeed, with its new 'Countryside Membership Scheme' the NFU has recently sought to attract small landholders as new members in order to obtain conservation payments (NFU Annual Report, 1993, p. 20). The farmers have thus gained an important new ally in the pursuit of their rent seeking activities. This push to demand an extension of agricultural subsidies on conservationist grounds has been heightened still further, following the recent collapse in farm incomes brought about by the crisis over BSE/mad cow disease.

Just as the building lobby has been able to exert political influence by overcoming the logic of collective action, so too the agricultural lobby has been enable to articulate its demands within the political market through its ability to manage the collective action problem. The farming interest is highly mobilised with the vast majority of farmers subscribing to one or both of the major lobby groups. The NFU has a total membership of 114,000 representing approximately 80 per cent of all farmers in the United Kingdom and the CLA has a further 50,000 members ranging from small owner-occupier farmers to the large commercial estates. High levels of mobilisation are reflected in terms of financial strength with NFU coffers totalling £21.4 million in the year 1992/93, sufficient to employ 800 staff nation-wide, including a full time team of political lobbyists. The CLA, meanwhile, had a total income of £4.2 million in 1992/93 and employed 50 full time staff, including ten professional advisors, a political lobbyist and a specialist media consultant (Pennington, 1997a, pp. 78–9).

The NFU and CLA appear to have adopted a number of strategies in their attempt to overcome the collective action problem. As with the building lobby, both the NFU and CLA administer much of their membership affairs through their local and county branches where the contribution of each potential member is more significant and it is easier to monitor free-riding behaviour. The free rider problem, however, remains potentially more significant for the agricultural lobby, even at the local level, because of the nature of the farming industry itself. There are considerably more farmers than house building firms and many of the relevant farms are highly scattered, especially in the more remote rural areas so it is much more difficult for the NFU and CLA to monitor examples of free riding behaviour. A more likely explanation for their ability to overcome the collective action problem, therefore, would point to the array of selective incentives, which are administered through the local branches.

Both the NFU and the CLA employ material selective incentives, administered by the local and county branches to encourage member participation. The NFU, for example, offers low cost insurance policies tailored to the special needs of farmers and legal services to members only. In addition, both groups offer a wide range of advice services designed to help farmers in the running of their businesses. This advice covers the vast machinery of government surrounding the farmer, which ranges through the implementation of health and safety regulations, employment regulations, landlord/ tenant dispute resolutions and planning legislation, to name but a few (Howarth, 1990, p. 108). The national headquarters of both organisations have, in the meantime, benefited enormously from the complicated system of agricultural support, which they have helped to create. The technical nature of the regulatory controls which emanate from the Ministry of Agriculture, Fisheries and Food (MAFF), requires a team of policy experts to broker advice to individual farmers usually through the local branches in order to gain access to agricultural grants. Consequently, as Howarth (1990,

p. 108) points out, there is virtually no problem a farmer can have for which the County Secretary cannot provide assistance. The average farmer, therefore, simply cannot afford not be a member of at least one of the major lobbying groups.

In addition to these material selective incentives a range of non-material solidary benefits are also potentially important. As was noted earlier, farming is often an extremely isolated activity especially in the more remote rural areas. In these circumstances there are important participation benefits to be gleaned from the membership of a group such as the NFU. Meetings at the local branches may, for example, provide significant opportunities to develop social networks and share news with other member farmers. In many cases, the local NFU branches, host social events and groupings, such as the Young Farmers, which are often an important source of entertainment for those living an otherwise isolated lifestyle. Combined with the powerful material selective incentives discussed above, the agricultural lobby is thus able to offer a highly attractive package of benefits, which may help to explain its considerable success in dealing with the collective action problem.

The Local Amenity/Nimby Lobby

The third and perhaps the most important set of lobby groups within the decision procedures of the land use planning system, is the environmental lobby. The British environmental movement represents an extremely diverse set of organisations including groups such as the Council for the Protection of Rural England (CPRE), The Royal Society for Nature Conservation (RSNC), The Royal Society for the Protection of Birds (RSPB) and Friends of the Earth(FoE). These groups have a range of different aims and objectives, but it is appropriate to distinguish between two broad types of environmental organisation and the character of the benefits that they seek to obtain from the planning system.

On the one hand, there are those groups that are concerned predominantly with aspects of environmental conservation at the *local scale* and in particular the preservation of amenity values. The benefits sought by these groups are often 'site specific' and pertain to aspects of the local environment such as the desire to maintain particular open spaces. Correspondingly, they may also encompass benefits such as the preservation of local property values, which are often connected to environmental assets such as the existence of an attractive view. It is for this reason that such groups are often labelled as NIMBYist (Not In My Backyard). The principal representative of this type of organisation in the British planning system is the CPRE. Founded in 1926, the CPRE is a national organisation which campaigns on a wide range of environmental issues such as species diversity and wildlife conservation, so it would be inappropriate to caricature this group as a purely nimbyist lobby. There is, however, little doubt that is from the local amenity interest that the bulk of its members are derived (Herington, 1984; Short et al., 1986; Shucksmith, 1990). Other environmental organisations, by contrast, draw on a more diverse membership and are focused on broader aspects of environmental protection. Some of these groups have an explicitly ideological commitment to reducing both the impact and the overall level of economic development in order to preserve environmental assets for the public at large (McCormick, 1991; Rawcliffe, 1998). Each of the different groups, however, tends to have a particular target area for its lobbying activity. FoE, for example has had a recent focus on transport issues and in particular attempts to reduce the environmental effects of car use. The RSPB, on the other hand, as its name suggests, focuses on countryside issues that affect the protection of wild birds (Rawcliffe, 1998).

The environmental lobby as a whole campaigns for the extension and enforcement of statutory planning controls such as Green Belts, Areas of Outstanding Natural Beauty (AONBs) and Sites of Special Scientific Interest (SSSIs), to prevent the transfer of land from rural uses such as agriculture, to urban uses such as housing. Within this context, however, it is the CPRE that appears to have exerted by far the most significant impact on the land use planning system and the policy of urban containment in particular. This influence has been pronounced at both the national and local scales.

At the national level, the CPRE ran three extremely effective political campaigns during the 1980s. In 1983/84, its lobbying activity was instrumental in gaining the support of over 100 Conservative MPs, which led to the abandonment of proposals put forward by the then Secretary of State for the Environment, Patrick Jenkin, to liberalise Green Belt policy (Elson, 1986). A similarly successful campaign was conducted against the so-called ALURE (Alternative Land Use and the Rural Economy) proposals in 1987. Again, having mobilised a considerable level of support from back bench Conservative MPs the government effectively abandoned a scheme which was designed to allow greater scope for non-agricultural land uses in the countryside (Marsden et al., 1993: Pennington, 1996). It was, however, with the implementation of the 1991 Planning and Compensation Act, that the CPRE achieved perhaps its greatest victory in recent years. In this case, it was an amendment sponsored by the CPRE and inserted during the final parliamentary stages of the Planning and Compensation Bill (1991), which resulted in the new plan-led development control system (Burton, 1991; Marsden et al., 1993). The subsequent requirement for all planning applications to be judged in accordance with the local development plan has reduced the ability of the building lobby to use the Department of Environment, Transport and the Regions (DETR) appeals procedure and placed a new emphasis on the local plan making process. It is at this level that the CPRE have further demonstrated their considerable ability to ensure that politicians and planners maintain a strict focus on urban containment policy.

At the local level, numerous authors have demonstrated the capacity of nimbyist groups to exert political leverage through the procedures of public participation (as at local plan inquiries) and through both formal and informal (behind the scenes) lobbying on individual planning applications. Out of a sample of 4,850 representations at local planning inquiries, for example, Adams

(1995) found that 63 per cent of changes made as a result of lobbying involved a reduction in the amount of new development as against only 13 per cent where development targets were increased. All major empirical studies of planning throughout the non-metropolitan areas – Connell (1972) in Surrey, Lowe (1977) and Buller and Lowe (1982) in East Anglia, Short et al. (1986) in Berkshire, Shucksmith (1990) in the Lake District and Murdoch and Marsden (1995) in Buckinghamshire, have demonstrated the political successes of nimbyism in thwarting the supply of new housing developments in the countryside.

In terms of public choice theory, the political successes of the environmental lobby are often considered somewhat surprising. All the major environmental organisations have witnessed a substantial growth in their memberships over recent years especially during the late 1980s with some estimates suggesting that as many as 1 in 10 people are now affiliated to one environmental group or another (Jordan and Maloney, 1997; Rawcliffe, 1998). The logic of collective action, however, suggests that these groups should face chronic mobilisation problems especially when contrasted with producer interests. Environmental groups in this sense are analogous to consumer interests – unlike producer groups they could in theory have a potential membership which includes any individual in the population making it almost impossible to monitor and penalise free-riding behaviour. How then can the apparent ability of the environmental lobby to overcome the collective action problem be explained?

Any analysis of environmental groups must first recognise the different characteristics of the collective benefits that different sections of the environmental lobby are seeking to obtain. Within this context, it is especially important to distinguish between the local amenity/nimbyist element represented by the CPRE and the rest of the environmental movement.

The CPRE has a national membership of 46,000 individuals with a budget of some £3.1 million and a national headquarters based in London. These national figures, however, mask the underlying scale and character of the membership. In addition to the 46,000 members affiliated to the national group there are approximately 2,600 local amenity and residents associations (average membership 200) that are affiliated to the CPRE through its 45 county branches and a further 200 or so local district branches. The total affiliated membership of the group, therefore, is well over half a million.[1] The CPRE is thus a highly decentralised lobby with much of its campaigning on planning matters occurring at the local authority level through public participation in the plan-making process and on individual planning applications. It is this federated, decentralised structure that would appear crucial to the CPRE's success in overcoming the logic of collective action.

Local CPRE groups campaign for collective goods, the benefits of which are often *site specific* and to a significant extent *confined to individuals in the locality concerned*. Although passers-by may benefit occasionally from designations such as Green Belts, most of the benefits associated with such controls; local open spaces, scenic views, a 'rural character', opportunities for recreation and higher property values, are available only to those who live within the immediate vicinity. As such, 'nimbyist' groups campaigning against development in a part of the Green Belt may have an advantage in trying to overcome the collective action problem. On the one hand, the number of individuals within the locality is likely to be relatively small, so the per capita benefit for individuals to engage in collective action to protect their own 'back yard' is likely to be fairly high. This may be a particularly important factor where homeowner coalitions seeking to protect property values are concerned. In these instances, the equity investment in homeownership may represent a substantial fraction of their personal wealth, thus increasing the relative stake of joining an organisation, which can protect such investments (Fischel, 1985). On the other hand, the relatively small and identifiable group of potential members may allow group organisers to solicit members by targeting the relevant houses in the area concerned and to simply badger people into membership by knocking on the relevant doors. Within this context, there is a strong possibility that potential members may be residential neighbours or known to one another in some other local community capacity. Previous research suggests the importance of local churches, parish councils and residents associations as important networking points for local amenity interests (Murdoch and Marsden, 1995). In this case a local branch of the CPRE may fall into the category of an intermediate group, where there is scope for repeated community interaction and the development of co-operative strategies within the context of the iterated prisoners' dilemma. This may especially be the case in the more rural communities where there may be the possibility of developing sanctions against free riders through strategies of social ostracism (Ellickson, 1991).

The latter point may help to explain why, in comparison with rural amenity groups, urban nimbyist organisations campaigning against development within the cities are relatively less well organised than their rural equivalents. Larkham's (1993) data suggest that the rate of mobilisation for amenity/nimbyist groups within the larger urban areas is considerably lower than in rural villages and small towns. In urban areas the potential membership of such groups is more heterogenous than in rural equivalents – a higher proportion of the population may live and work in the same area and thus have an interest in more development (Danielson, 1976; Komesar, 1978). Moreover, because urban population densities tend to be higher, the potential membership of anti-development groups may be that much larger, thus reducing the significance of an individual contribution to supply. Urban populations tend also to be highly mobile/transient and under these circumstances it may be relatively more difficult for anti-development groups to identify free-riders and to penalise their behaviour through the application of social pressure. A further reason why urban nimbyism is less well supported than its rural equivalent may be the higher proportion of low income people that tend to be concentrated in the cities. From a public choice perspective, low income groups are especially prone to the logic of collective action because of the higher opportunity cost of time that they exhibit. In this case the disincentive to collective action may be especially strong because poorer people have relatively little time to devote to organised politics given their immediate requirement to secure the basic essentials of life.

In addition to the possibility for strategic bargaining and social pressure the CPRE is also able to rely on its ability to provide other non-material selective incentives and, in particular, the existence of solidary benefits associated with participation. Empirical research suggests that the membership of the group is drawn predominantly from older sections of the population and especially the retired (Lowe and Goyder, 1983). In an analysis of local amenity societies in Chester, for example, Pennington (1997a, p. 200) found that all group leaders were over 55 years of age and retired (see also Pennington and Rydin, 2000). It would appear that these groups depend on individuals who are motivated by a strong ideological belief in environmental conservation and exhibit a relatively low opportunity cost of time. Being involved in the running of a group and participating in the planning process provides a source of personal enjoyment, opportunities for socialising and developing friendships. It is not surprising, therefore, that older people tend to dominate the profile of the CPRE. The costs of lobbying local planning authorities are predominantly time related, requiring as they do a substantial amount of preparation in terms of submitting documents to planning committees, attending public inquiries, organising public meetings and repeated lobbying of local politicians and planning bureaucrats. If younger people were to be involved in such activities they would have to take a substantial amount of time off work or at the very least sacrifice a significant proportion of their relatively limited leisure time. Older people, by contrast have relatively more spare time to conduct campaigns and organise group activities and unlike their younger counterparts are more likely to consider such activities as a benefit rather than a cost. Pro-active involvement in the running of a local amenity group, therefore, often provides older people with new opportunities for socialising and personal fulfilment following their retirement (Pennington and Rydin, 2000).

The CPRE is also given active support by a number of other groups with a vested interest in the regulation of the rural land market. The NFU and CLA are associate members as both derive rents from the artificial maintenance of agricultural land and corporate groups including British Petroleum, Shell UK, Enterprise Oil, Esso and Unilever, provided donations totalling £400,000 in 1993 (Pennington, 1997a, p. 92). The oil companies, in particular, have a direct stake in the preservation of subsidised agricultural land, with a significant farming market in the form of fuels, drugs and fertilisers (Body, 1984). Bureaucratic agencies such as the Countryside Commission (now the Countryside Agency) and English Nature, which are responsible for site designation are also major supporters and in 1991 the Countryside Commission grant of £68,000 was the largest single donation received by the group (Pennington, 1997a, p. 92).[2]

Notwithstanding these other sources of support, it is the ability of the CPRE to mobilise a package of benefits at the local scale which is the key to its overcoming the collective action problem. This is not to say that the *rate of mobilisation* achieved is as high as for producer interests in the building and agricultural lobbies, but it does suggest that the local amenity lobby is able to organise a concentrated block of opposition to development at the local level, which experience suggests has been highly successful throughout the British planning system. In turn, it is the historic success of the CPRE locally that has enabled the group to develop a powerful presence at the national scale. Many of the county and district branches of the organisation actually predated the development of a national headquarters. In this particular case it would appear that the size manipulation strategies discussed by Dunleavy (1991) have been turned on their head. Rather than have a national group create local branches in an attempt to attract additional members, it has been the ability of the CPRE to mobilise collective action around nimbyist issues at the local level which has facilitated the development of what is arguably the most influential of the national British environmental lobbies.

Other Environmental Lobbies

If the CPRE has been able to overcome the collective action problem primarily through local means, a rather different pattern emerges when considering the strategies of some of the other major environmental organisations. Although the campaigns of the local amenity lobby may benefit individuals in society at large who wish to prevent development in the countryside, it would appear to be the site specific nature of the benefits that prompts a high degree of this membership. For other environmental groups, by contrast, the potential membership is not so immediately identifiable. Problems such as air pollution although manifested locally, are often derived from trans-boundary sources, which affect much larger numbers of individuals. In the case of urban air pollution, for example, problems associated with vehicular emissions are mobile in source, tend to occur city-wide and there is little prospect of political lobbying in any one locality having any effect on the level of pollution experienced in that particular locality. Similarly, issues such as the loss of farmland birds due to agricultural intensification may occur out of the public eye in parts of the country where few people actually live. In this case, the potential membership of a group seeking to protect the countryside could include almost anyone in the population. Such cases would appear to approximate a pure prisoners' dilemma scenario, with little possibility to develop co-operative strategies through the development of more iterative social relations. In order to mobilise large numbers of individuals, therefore, such groups may have to rely to a disproportionate extent on selective incentives.

The mobilisation of broad base environmental groups may, to an extent, rely on the provision of material benefits, which may only be obtained through membership of the group concerned. Groups such as the RSPB, for example, are often more akin to commercial trading organisations than might be considered a political lobby group. There is evidence to suggest that a proportion of the RSPB's 800,000 membership is tied in with the purchase of private goods such as wildlife magazines and free entry into the 300 bird reserves, which the society owns (Jordan and Maloney, 1997; Rawcliffe, 1998). A similar pattern is evident with the Royal Society for Nature Conservation and its Local Wildlife Trusts with each of its 260,000 members offered free or reduced entry into the 2,000 nature reserves, owned and managed by the individual Trusts. Friends of the Earth (FoE) meanwhile, provides a magazine service that is available to members only.

Whilst material benefits may be one factor influencing membership it seems unlikely that is the possibility of gaining access to what are often relatively small benefits (especially so for FoE) is the dominant factor at play (Jordan and Maloney, 1997; Rawcliffe, 1998). A more complete explanation of collective action by broad-based environmental groups, therefore, would point to their ability to mobilise a range of non-material selective incentives. One important category of non-material incentives provided by the environmental lobby is the participation benefits and in particular the solidary benefits that can be associated with membership. In these circumstances, membership can provide opportunities for socialising and the enjoyment of participating in collective activity with individuals who share a common interest. This form of incentive may be particularly important for the membership of the RSPB and the Wildlife Trusts. These groups provide a number of opportunities for socialising and the development of friendships with 'fellow travellers'. The youth branch of the RSPB, for example, (the Young Ornithologists Club – YOC), often organises bird watching trips for young people through its local branches. The Wildlife Trusts, meanwhile, organise a range of voluntary events, which also perform an important social function for those involved. The Wildlife Trusts, in particular have a membership which is skewed heavily towards both the youngest and oldest sections of the population. These are the groups with a relatively low opportunity cost of time, some of which can be filled by the *entertainment value* of such events. The absence of working age groups from the membership of such organisations is also consistent with such an explanation. These groups have a much higher opportunity cost of time and their limited leisure hours are likely to present them with less of an opportunity to be involved in this type of group activity.

In addition to the solidary benefits discussed above, another source of non-material selective incentives is the expressive benefits that group membership may provide. These may include such things as the social acceptance and status that may be associated with support for a particular cause or the desire to be seen to have taken part in major public events. This type of expressive incentive may be especially important to groups such as FoE. There is evidence to suggest that it was the rise in public awareness of environmental issues and indeed the fact that environmental protection became a 'fashionable' issue during the late 1980s that explains much of the recent growth in membership of FoE and similar groups such as Greenpeace (Jordan and Maloney, 1997).

The rise of environmentalism up the agenda of British politics is usually dated from the period 1985–89. Throughout this period and especially in 1988 a series of high profile environmental threats, including a pollution induced epidemic amongst seals in the North Sea, concerns over housing development on green field sites and the publication of scientific findings on matters such as acid rain, ozone depletion and global warming, prompted a 'green wave' of media and public interest in environmental issues. 'The environment' appeared to have become a fashionable political issue with the trend towards 'green consumerism' – the purchasing of products claiming to minimise environmental damage – becoming firmly established in this period. By the end of the 1980s it appeared that the purchasing of 'green products' was an important way to demonstrate a commitment to an increasingly 'politically correct' cause and thus to obtain social approval, especially amongst the young (Bennie and Rudig, 1993).

As Jordan and Maloney (1997) have argued, groups such as FoE were quick to pick up on such trends and indeed further enhanced these very processes through their own marketing strategies and dealings with the media. These included highly emotive campaign messages usually dispensed through mail-shots and the provision of all manner of paraphernalia – campaign badges, car stickers, posters etc., with which to demonstrate one's environmental consciousness. Young people, in particular, appear to have been attracted by such marketing with FoE recording over 60 per cent of its new members as being under 32 years of age (Jordan and Maloney, 1997, p. 115). Other environmental groups such as the CPRE, RSPB and RSNC also witnessed substantial growth in membership during the late 1980s, due in large part to the 'fashion' for environmentalism. FoE and Greenpeace, however, appear to rely much more extensively on such expressive incentives and far less so on the solidary benefits of participation provided by these other groups. Unlike the CPRE, RSPB and RSNC, which already had substantial memberships prior to the late 1980s, FoE and Greenpeace membership was in fact very small – in 1980 numbering no more than 12,000 and 10,000 members respectively. By 1990, however, following the fashionable 'green wave' FoE membership had risen to over 120,000 and Greenpeace to a phenomenal 320,000.

Within this context, it appears that much of this additional membership is of a *token* or at the very least *passive* nature. The joining of such groups does not by any means suggest that the individuals concerned will become *actively involved* in the policy making process by way of direct lobbying. As Jordan and Maloney (1997) have noted, joining a group such as FoE and Greenpeace is quite a *low cost* activity, a fact repeatedly emphasised by the groups themselves, which requires no more than paying the relatively small membership fee. Members may, as a result, achieve the expressive benefits of participation without taking any more pro-active or costly measures. The general situation has been summarised effectively by Bennie and Rudig (1993, p. 19 – quoted in Jordan and Maloney, 1997, p. 115).

in the United Kingdom, there is evidence that many young people took up 'the environment' as a fashionable issue of the late 1980s but that their commitment to environmental practices and policies remains rather shallow. Buying 'green' products was clearly 'chic' and was practised by a large majority of British youth; a commitment to less glamorous activities such as making less noise and using less energy, however, is comparatively lacking.

This lack of commitment to *active* participation and the reliance of groups such as FoE on expressive benefits have important implications for their role in the planning process. There is evidence to suggest that when it comes to *higher cost* activities such as writing letters to politicians and lobbying bureaucrats, FoE and even groups such as the RSPB, fair badly when compared to the CPRE in overcoming the collective action problem. In contrast to the CPRE, which can also rely on the 'nimby effect' in order to stimulate *active* involvement in the planning process at the local level, groups campaigning for broader environmental protection goals have few ways of stimulating the required collective action. It would appear to be in recognition of this fact that, in an echo of Dunleavy's (1991) 'size manipulation strategies', FoE are increasingly attempting to put the 'think global, act local' slogan into practice by developing local branches to campaign more actively within the planning process (Pennington, 1997a; Rawcliffe, 1998). As the CPRE example, shows, it is at the local level that an individual contribution is likely to have greater significance and where it may be easier to mobilise incentives against free riding behaviour. Even at the local level, however, broader based groups such as FoE lobbying on non-nimbyist issues are likely to face more severe collective action problems. It may, for example, be much more difficult to organise people against air pollution where the effects tend to widely spread and are often derived from mobile sources than to organise against a new housing estate in the Green Belt, where the source of environmental impact is in a fixed locale and the potential costs are concentrated on a more identifiable set of affected parties (Weale, 1992; Pennington, 1996; Rydin, 1998a; Webster, 1998).

Empirical work conducted at the local planning authority level confirms this pattern of participatory bias. In a study of the local plan process in Chester, for example, Pennington (1997a) found that the combined membership of nimbyist organisations explicitly formed to prevent development on specific sites numbered over 1,000, whereas the local FoE group could manage a mere 30 members. A similar pattern of public participation in environmental interest groups is indicated by Pennington and Rydin (2,000) whose comparative analysis of local collective action on open space protection, beach pollution and air pollution confirms a clear bias towards nimbyist issues within the policy process. It would seem that nimbyist groups are much more able to generate *active* participation in the policy process in terms of the lobbying of politicians and bureaucrats, writing letters, organised protest meetings etc. because of the greater incentive for collective action on such issues. In turn, politicians at the national level may be aware that participation in organisations such as FoE, is of a more tokenist nature with a relatively low level commitment to a rather diffuse set of 'environmental concerns' (Pennington, 2000 [forthcoming]). From a public choice perspective it is the bias in environmental collective action that may explain the apparent success of environmental interest groups such as CPRE in the area of urban containment policy and their relative failure to obtain regulatory controls over the subsidised procedures of agricultural production. Whereas the former concentrates benefits on nimbyist lobbies, which are organised and extremely vocal, the latter diffuses costs across a largely unidentified public less well equipped to overcome the free-rider problem.

The Professional Lobby

A fourth set of interests in the political market of planning is the professional lobby, consisting of the Royal Town Planning Institute (RTPI), the Royal Institution of Chartered Surveyors (RICS), the District, County and Metropolitan Planning Officers Societies (D/C/M/POS) and the Town and Country Planning Association (TCPA).

The professional planning lobbies have rent seeking interests on both the demand and supply sides of the political market. On the supply side, planning professionals are public sector bureaucrats responsible for the enforcement of statutory land use regulations. On the demand side, meanwhile, they have a direct stake in the operation of the property market through the process of land assembly, private consultancy and a quasi-legal role in planning applications and appeals. The subsequent chapter considers the role of planners on the supply side, so for the purposes of this analysis attention centres on the process of rent seeking on the demand side.

Demand side rent seeking occurs through the manipulation of the regulatory process in order to maximise the income stream of planning professionals by inflating the demand for private consultancies, marketing and quasi-legal advice from those engaged in the construction of property. In order to achieve planning permission for their proposed developments, private house builders and other developers must submit applications and appeals to the relevant planning authorities and may be required to present evidence at a public inquiry procedure. The professional planning bodies are a major source of representation for private developers, with approximately 55 per cent of all representations presented by chartered town planners or chartered surveyors and the remaining 45 per cent by barristers or solicitors (Adams, 1995, p. 203). Within this context, the professions are able to extract rents from private developers and hence add to the total cost of land use planning in two, key ways. First, because all applications and appeals are judged by professional planners it pays to employ qualified planners as representatives who are then able to extract monopoly charges from this captive market (Adams, 1995). Second, because developers require expert knowledge of the legislative process in order to achieve planning permissions, the professions can extract rents by seeking to lengthen the planning process and to instigate more complicated legal procedures which they themselves are then required to interpret.

The rent seeking fortunes of planning professionals are tied closely to the fortunes of the development process and in particular the state of the property market. In periods of boom the demand for planning consultants and legal advisors is buoyant as private developers submit more planning applications and appeals in order to secure the release of their holdings. In the property boom of the mid 1980s, for example, Coombs (1991, quoted in Adams, 1995) notes that the number of chartered town planners employed by private developers more than doubled between 1984 and 1988. In periods of recession, however, many private planners and consultants may suffer a dramatic decline in their incomes as the demand for consultancies begins to run dry. If incomes are to be maintained, then the professions must look to stimulate the demand for their services by lobbying for changes to the legislative apparatus, which will heighten the demand for private consultancy.

Given these incentives it should come as no great surprise that the centrepiece of professional lobbying during recent years was the major changes in national planning legislation introduced by the 1990 Town and Country Planning Act and the subsequent 1991 Planning and Compensation Act (Pennington, 1997a). The RTPI, RICS, D/C/MPOS and the TCPA all joined with the CPRE in lobbying for the creation of the 'plan-led' development control system, the implications of which appear to be very favourable for professional incomes. As noted earlier the enhanced status of the local plan has increased the significance of the plan making process and reduced the ability of developers to use the appeals procedure. It has thus become essential for developers to make their representations during the plan making stage if they are to stand any chance of receiving a subsequent planning permission. As the plan-making stage has increased in importance so has the length of the entire planning procedure and with it the demand for planning consultants and legal advisors. It is not uncommon for developers to pay out as much as £500,000 for consultancy and legal costs at a planning inquiry the average length of which increased from seven weeks in 1989 to 22 weeks in 1992, i.e. following the Planning and Compensation Act (Cullingworth and Nadin 1994; Adams, 1995).

According to public choice theory, the ability of the professional lobbies to extract rents through the political market of planning stems in large part from the immunity of such professional organisations to the logic of collective action. Typically, these groups exist to provide services to individual members and may effectively license entry into a particular profession or trade. Individuals who have organised themselves for reasons unrelated to lobbying enjoy a comparative advantage in rent seeking because organisation costs once borne, do not add to the marginal cost of lobbying and the free rider problem does not occur (Rowley, 1992, p. 111). The RTPI, for example, is the state registered body for professional planners and under the Royal Charter devises the skills and examination standards necessary to attain corporate membership as a town planner.

The 'Forgotten' Groups: Those Who Suffer In Silence[3]

The interest groups that gain the most from British land use planning all favour a tightly regulated land use system; the construction lobby because of the barriers to competition that are raised within the building industry; the agricultural lobby, because of the protection granted to the subsidised farm sector; the nimby lobby because of the exclusionary protection of amenity and property values; and the professional lobby, because of the rents derived from complicated administrative procedures. Within this context, it is difficult to decipher which of these interests is the most powerful at any particular point in time, though the successes of the CPRE/nimby lobby in recent years appear to suggest that it is this particular section of the environmental interest that is now in the ascendancy. What then of those groups that bear the costs of the regulatory regime? No analysis of collective action and British planning would be complete without considering the major losers from this system.

The most significant of the social groups who may be harmed by the operation of the land use planning system are the consumer interests and in particular the consumers of residential development. As Chapter 2 showed, a primary consequence of planning in the United Kingdom has been a rise in the price of housing, which has been brought about through a combination of restricted land supply and the reduction in competition in the house building industry that has resulted. As prices have risen and as competition within the house building industry has been reduced, consumers have been forced to pay increasingly inflated prices for less housing space and for a poorer quality product. In addition, many housing consumers have had little option than to purchase housing in locations that they would otherwise not prefer. The post war trend towards sub-urbanisation and counter-urbanisation suggests that consumer preferences may favour a more decentralised form of living, yet the British planning system has explicitly sought to thwart the realisation of these preferences.

Virtually all consumers of housing lose out as a result of these processes, but there are those for whom such losses may be more significant. For most individuals the cost of land use planning involves paying a higher price for housing and thus a reduction in disposable income. To those at the margins of the market, however, the effect of the current planning system may be such that they are priced out of the housing market altogether and must rely to an increasing extent on welfare payments such as housing benefit, in order to attain any sort of access to living space. Correspondingly, those individuals unable to obtain jobs in the older urban areas may be prevented by the planning system from moving into the very areas – the suburbs, the market towns and semi-rural areas where the growth in employment opportunities is now occurring. In this sense not only may contemporary planning policies be increasing the cost of housing, but they may also be contributing to the social exclusion of the inner urban poor (Simmie, 1993; Rydin, 1995).

A second set of interests that may have suffered as a consequence of British planning policy, are those of the urban population at large. The majority of people live in towns and cities yet the interests of these groups do not appear to rank highly in the priorities of the planning regime. As development opportunities on green belts and in the broader countryside have been restricted, so the density of new urban development has risen, as increasing amounts of housing have been crammed into the towns. The principal losers from such processes have been the general urban population that has been subjected to higher density and increasingly congested living environments, with chronic problems of air pollution. The amenities of those living in designated areas within the planning system are protected, but there is no compensation for the rest of the population who must continue to endure the increasing congestion and pollution in the towns. Urban interests do, of course, have a stake in preserving the countryside for the purposes of environmental protection and recreation. The planning system, however, has not protected open spaces for the sake of public recreation, but for the subsidised and environmentally damaging practices of modern agri-business.

Added to the housing consumers, the unemployed and the urbanites are a fourth set of interests that lose from the contemporary planning regime. These are the individuals who, but for the policy of urban containment would live in closer proximity to their place of work were it not for a planning system that has encouraged a 'leap-frog' pattern of development. As a consequence of designations such as green belts, those individuals who have moved to the suburbs but continue to work in the towns and cities have been forced to travel a longer distance to their place of employment. It is not surprising, therefore, that Pahl (1975) has described this section of the population as the 'reluctant commuters'.

The final group of individuals who bear the costs of land use planning are the mass of the taxpaying population who are forced to pay the price of the system in a variety of different ways. First there are the direct costs to taxpayers of funding the planning bureaucracy itself. The operating costs of land use planning are currently well over £1.5 billion per annum and have been increasing at well above the rate of inflation and the level of economic growth for a period of over thirty years. (Pennington, 1997a – see also Chapter 4 of this volume). Second there are the substantial indirect costs associated with ever-higher levels of welfare spending. As house prices and labour immobility are increased due to planning restrictions so higher levels of welfare spending are required to support those who are excluded from the housing and employment markets (Minford et al., 1987; Evans, 1988). And third, there are the costs of continuing to fund the inefficiencies of a massively subsidised farming industry. The planning system operates to discourage the transfer of land out of agricultural uses and thus externalises costs onto the taxpayers who continue to pay for the protection of the farming sector (Evans, 1991; Simmie, 1993; Pennington, 1996).

From the perspective of public choice theory the failure of the interests discussed above to have an effective political voice in the British planning system stems from their chronic inability to overcome the collective action problem. Although these groups are potentially far more numerous than the special interests who gain in a concentrated way from planning their interests appear to often be forgotten by politicians and planners alike. These are the individuals too numerous, too weak in terms of identity and with too small a stake to act collectively, in order to challenge the status quo. This problem is particularly severe for the consumers, the unemployed, the taxpayers and the commuters who are so dispersed throughout the population that there is virtually no possibility for co-operative behaviour through strategic interaction. Neither is there the possibility of mobilising a package of selective incentives or participation benefits to stimulate collective action from such individuals. The difficulty here is that the transfers of wealth and other benefits that occur under the guise of the planning system are mostly intangible. Unlike the environmental lobby, which can rely on high profile examples of environmental disaster to attract media attention to form the basis for a package of expressive incentives, the losses that flow from planning are virtually invisible to most individuals and are not easily traced back to the effect of the regulatory regime. Indeed, it is likely that these groups may not even be aware of the scale of the costs that stem from the operation of planning. Transfers of wealth that occur through the mechanism of regulation are often extremely difficult to detect and may be subject to a high degree of rational voter ignorance (Tullock, 1993). Tracing the effects of planning controls would require a substantial amount of research on behalf of individual voters, an effort which may not be worthwhile given the minuscule chance that any single voter may have on the result of an election.

The urban population also appears to be underrepresented in the political market because of the difficulty of overcoming the collective action problem. The increasing density of development that has been brought about by restrictive regulation in the countryside, has affected the majority of urban dwellers, but because the numbers concerned are so great and the process of increasing densities proceeds in an indirect, almost imperceptible way there is little incentive for groups to mobilise on the basis of improving the quality of urban life. Urban interests are, to a limited extent, reflected in the mobilisation of nimbyist groups seeking to prevent the *direct* loss of amenities within the towns themselves – such as urban parks, though as was discussed earlier there are reasons to believe that these organisations are less well mobilised than their rural equivalents. Moreover, in so far as these groups are successful they simply exacerbate the negative effects borne by the other losing groups within the planning regime. On the one hand new development is simply 'shoe-horned' into those urban areas which represent the least point of resistance, thus shifting the problems of congestion and air pollution elsewhere. And, on the other hand, to the extent that new development is stopped altogether, the price of housing and its knock on effects escalates still further.

As Table 3.3 shows, the political market in planning shows clear indications of structural bias in favour of the smaller more concentrated groups and/or

Table 3.3 Interest Groups and the Political Market in Planning

Economic Interest	Formal Group	Total Members	Group Type		Mobilisation Strategies		
			Local Level	National Level	Strategic Interaction	Selective Incentives (a)	Selective Incentives (b)
Winners							
Large Builder	HBF/BEC	12,000	Small	Small			✓
Landed Farmers	CLA	50,000	Intermediate	Large		✓	✓
Tenant Farmers	NFU	114,000	Intermediate	Large		✓	✓
Nimby	CPRE	560,000	Intermediate	Large	✓	✓	✓
Planners	RTPI/RICS	100,000	Professional	Professional			
Losers							
Small Builder	FMB	10,000	Intermediate	Large			✓
Other Environmental	FoE/RSPB	1,200,000	Large	Large		✓	✓
Housing Consumer	None		Latent	Large			
Urban Dweller	None		Latent	Large			
Commuter	None		Latent	Large			
Taxpayer	None		Latent	Large			
Unemployed	None		Latent	Large			

Notes: Selective Incentives a) = material selective incentives. b) = non-material selective incentives.

those which are able to offer a package of selective incentives. The Federation of Master Builders is the one losing group, which falls into the category of an intermediate interest, its lack of success reflecting the numerical superiority of the winning coalition. The non-nimbyist environmental lobby, on the other hand, is the one group that falls into the large/diffuse category at both the local and national levels, which has nonetheless attained a substantial membership. Much of this participation is, however, of a *token* nature and is not matched by *active* lobbying in the actual process of plan preparation at the local level. The saving grace for the broader environmental lobby is that at least *some* of its interests, i.e. preventing development in the countryside, *are* represented by nimbyist groups. The same cannot be said for the consumers, the commuters, the taxpayers and the unemployed, all of which appear to have *no* effective political representation within the planning system and continue to suffer in silence.

CONCLUSION

This chapter has examined the participation of interest groups in the British planning system and in particular the incentives for collective action and inaction that may enable or prevent their mobilisation. In doing so it has suggested that the current policy focus of British land use planning is reflective of the differential effect of collective action problems on the demand side of the political market. More specifically, the emphasis on urban containment policy may be the product of a structural bias that concentrates benefits on rent seeking interests to the detriment of a much wider population that is absent from the realm of organised politics. It is not, of course, possible to demonstrate conclusively that the total costs imposed on the (latent) losers from land use planning are greater than the benefits obtained by the (organised) winners and that the British planning system is therefore 'inefficient' in some objectively identifiable sense.[4] In the final analysis the costs and benefits concerned are subjective and cannot be estimated by an outside observer with the necessary precision. There are, however, strong theoretical and empirical grounds, as outlined in this chapter to suggest the existence of a structural bias within the political market that is likely to *discriminate against* those who lose from the regulatory regime. *If* the total losses experienced by latent groups are indeed in excess of the benefits obtained by the winners there are strong reasons to believe that this will *not* be reflected in the structure of expressed political demand because of the severity of the collective action problems facing the individuals concerned.

If the analysis presented here is accurate then some important questions appear to be raised for the way interest group participation in planning should properly be conceived. The dominant theoretical development in planning in recent years has been the rise of participatory or collaborative planning approaches, which suggest that planning has the potential to empower individuals and groups through a process of democratic dialogue. According to this view, individuals will set aside rational self-interest in order to engage in a shared process of public consensus building with all the relevant 'stakeholders' within the community at large. From the perspective set out in this chapter, however, it requires a truly heroic assumption to suggest that individuals will engage in such activities unless they can gain sufficiently from doing so. Neither does one have to assume that people are particularly egotistical and driven purely by the prospect of material gain in order to reach such a conclusion. People may be driven by non-material or even other-regarding concerns, but in the absence of selective benefits, which can yield a demonstrable return on their individual participation are unlikely to engage in a decision-making process where the effect of their personal contribution is negligible.

The significance of such collective action problems is of particular importance given the substantial evidence of nimbyist participation in the planning system highlighted in this chapter. Collaborative planning theorists tend to advocate participatory planning at the 'local community' scale, yet it is clear that locally 'empowered' groups that block new development have the capacity to impose costs on groups within the rest of society who are less well placed to overcome the logic of collective action. Advocates of collaborative planning are clearly aware of such problems but fail to provide an adequate account of how they are to be overcome. Healey (1997, pp. 307–8), for example, argues that for 'strategic' environmental protection issues, higher level decision-making by bodies such as the European Union, may be required to over-rule such biases. It is far from clear in this account, however, what the basis is for deciding *where* the appropriate boundaries of participation should lie. Moreover, as the British experience suggests, to the extent that higher tiers of decision-making (such as the DETR) are actually favoured, it is not apparent that they can be relied upon to counteract the effects of mobilisation bias within the wider political market. How precisely are groups such as consumers, taxpayers, the urban population at large and others lacking formal political representation to have their interests represented, *whatever the tier of decision-making*? It is difficult to believe that politicians and planners will ignore the forces of special interest politics and will advocate policies that benefit such latent groups, simply because decision-making is moved to a different level.

Public choice theory, therefore, challenges the contemporary enthusiasm for 'collaborative planning', because it suggests that the collective *inaction* of those who lose from the practice of planning is not so easily resolved. Far from providing an arena for 'inclusive' democratic consensus-building, the political market of planning is always likely to be a mechanism which concentrates benefits on organised lobbies that can gain in an identifiable and significant way, to the neglect of those with insufficient incentive to overcome the collective action problem. The consumers of housing, the unemployed, the urbanites, the reluctant commuters and the taxpayers are as much stakeholders in the practice of planning as any other group, yet collaborative planning has still to explain how such interests are to achieve effective representation through the mechanisms of public participation. If the current policy focus of the British planning system is a product of consensus building it seems more likely to be a consensus built on special interest rent seeking than on public deliberation by the community as a whole.

BUDGETS, BUREAUCRATS
AND PLANNING[1]

INTRODUCTION

A defining characteristic of the British land use planning system in the 50 years since its inception has been a consistent tendency towards the growth of regulation. Throughout the post war period, irrespective of the political party in power, there appears to have been an inexorable increase in the scope of the regulations administered by land use planners. This growth of regulation has occurred through the ongoing designation of protected environmental sites such as Green Belts and the increasing complexity of the regulatory process itself, a complexity that has been manifested in the notoriously low productivity rate of the development control procedure.

An indication of the scale of regulatory growth is provided by Peacock (1984), who notes that the number of statutory regulatory instruments available to land use planners increased from 98 to 386 between 1958 and 1979 – an increase of 290 per cent. The 1980s, meanwhile, supposedly a period of deregulation, were also characterised by an overall expansion of the regulatory regime. Early attempts to liberalise controls such as Green Belts were quickly abandoned and by the end of the 1980s comparatively minor moves towards deregulation, such as the extension of the General Development Order, had been overtaken by a new raft of environmental controls. The area of land designated as Green Belt by local planning authorities actually increased from 1.7 to 4.2 million acres between 1979 and 1994 (+147). Other designations also increased apace with the number of designated Sites of Special Scientific Interest (SSSIs) rising from 2,600 in 1982 to 3,800 in 1994. Such was the growth of environmental site designations that by the early 1990s almost 50 per cent of the land area of England and Wales was covered by one or other statutory control.

Following the 1991 Planning and Compensation Act, the 1990s have seen a further continuation of the trend towards regulatory growth. The introduction of the 'plan-led' development control system appears to have increased the complexity of the regulatory process through a lengthening of the plan preparation stage. Between 1988 and 1992, the length of the public enquiry procedure increased from an average of 7 weeks to 22 weeks (Cullingworth and Nadin, 1994, p. 59) and it is now not uncommon for the preparation of local plans and structure plans to take as long as four years (Simmie, 1993).

Correspondingly, the DETR has substantially increased the number of Planning Policy Guidance Notes it produces, with new documents on transport (PPG 13), 'out-of town' retail development (PPG 6) and nature conservation (PPG 8) all adding to the complexity of the planning regime. In addition, the planning system continues to be plagued by a remarkably low level of productivity in the processing of development applications. According to Ehrman (1988) the productivity rate in the late 1980s was a mere one development processed, per month, per worker. Despite central government attempts to speed up the planning process, by the early 1990s fewer applications were being processed within the government target of 8 weeks than at the beginning of the previous decade (Simmie, 1993).

One way of explaining this tendency towards regulatory growth is to adopt a demand side perspective focusing on the role of interest groups within the political market. As Chapter 3 showed, interest groups have always been a key factor in the British planning system and the nimbyist lobby in particular, appears to have been an important element in the recent drive towards the adoption of still more restrictive planning controls. The ability of interest groups to overcome the collective action problem, however, may be worthless unless there are actors on the supply side of the political market with sufficient incentives to cater to their demands. The planning bureaucrats charged with the day to day administration of the land use system are an important group of players on the supply side of the planning process, yet the role of such actors remains relatively unexplored within the environmental policy literature.

This chapter develops an approach to bureaucratic behaviour based on public choice theory in order to explain the part of the planning bureaucracy in the process of regulatory expansion. Through a review of the theoretical literature and the presentation of empirical evidence, the aim is to apply a new analytical framework to understand the operation of the supply side of the British planning system. The chapter opens with some recent theoretical refinements to the public choice theory of bureaucracy and drawing on Dunleavy's (1991) work, outlines a classification of bureaucratic agency types and incentive structures. The subsequent sections present budgetary data on the primary agencies of the land use planning system within the context of the analytical framework. The chapter suggests that land use planning, is dominated by agency types where bureaucrats can best advance their interests by seeking to expand their budgets. Finally, the analysis relates these bureaucratic strategies to the current policy focus of the planning system and in particular the continuing emphasis on urban containment.

BUDGETS, BUREAUCRATS AND GOVERNMENT FAILURE

According to public choice theory, bureaucratic actors are self -interested agents in much the same way as are the entrepreneurs, workers and consumers that populate the private sector. Within this context, public choice argues that the incentive structures facing public sector decision-makers may constitute an important source of 'government failure' on the supply side of the political market. Niskanen (1971), in particular, argues that bureaucratic actors follow their self-interest through the pursuit of budget appropriations. For a firm operating in the private market, the income of the entrepreneur tends to be performance related, because remuneration is dependent on the account of profit and loss. Bureaucracies, by contrast, are public sector organisations where a significant proportion of revenue is derived from budgetary grants. According to Niskanen, therefore, the rational self-interested bureaucrat will seek to maximise her agency budget. A growing agency will tend to employ more staff, add to job security and the perquisites of office and increase the status of the employees.

Government bureaucrats are monopoly suppliers of goods and services within the public sector and from the perspective of public choice theory, this position affords them considerable organisational and informational advantages over the electorate and its political representatives, which may in turn facilitate budget maximisation. Unlike other pressure groups and the mass of the electorate, bureaucrats may not face such substantial collective action problems. With the organisational apparatus of the state already in place the free rider problems discussed in Chapter 3 are minimised and the ease of access to elected officials, characteristic of bureaucratic employment, increases the likelihood of discretionary influence. In addition, as monopoly suppliers, government bureaux are often the only source of output /cost data with respect to their services and may easily inflate cost estimates in order to obtain budget increments. Finally, politicians supplying budgetary grants may have few incentives to examine in detail the resource claims of specific bureaux, because any cost savings are thinly dispersed across the voting population, minimising the per capita gains and hence the potential for electoral award. According to Niskanen, therefore, this combination of incentives result in a radical oversupply of state provided services and regulation and this has contributed significantly to the growth of the modern state.

Figure 4.1 provides a graphical analysis of the oversupply thesis. A private firm operating in a competitive market would expand its output to point E, where the marginal value of production is equal to the marginal cost. Production at this point would provide a consumer surplus (welfare gain) represented by the triangle GEH. Budget maximisation in the public sector, however, may expand output to point F, creating an area of unnecessary production, (EFR), which wipes out all the consumer gains in a process of bureaucratic exploitation.

In his more recent work Niskanen (1995) shifts from the oversupply thesis, towards an emphasis on bureaucratic inefficiency in the production of given outputs. The concept of waste in his original thesis refers specifically to 'allocative inefficiency' as distinct from organisational or 'X-inefficiency'. In the former case, resources are devoted away from their most valued use, which does not necessarily mean that they are produced 'inefficiently' – by using too many staff,

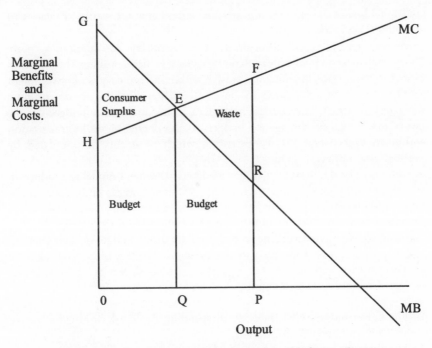

Figure 4.1   Bureaucratic Exploitation by a Niskanen Bureau

for example. In his latest contribution, however, Niskanen suggests that bureaucrats may focus less on the maximisation of output per se and more on the maximisation of their 'discretionary budget'. This represents the difference between the minimum cost of producing a given output and the maximum level of resources that can be extracted from the political authorities for its production. The emphasis of the account, therefore, shifts from oversupply – which may still occur – to the organisational inefficiency of supply, as bureaucrats maximise the level of inputs per unit of output (see also Peacock 1983).

Niskanen's approach remains the most influential account in the public choice literature, but the empirical evidence in favour of his straightforward budget maximisation model has been rather limited. Given that staffing, job security and status are assumed to be a positive monotonic function of budgets, one would expect to find a significant correlation between expenditure and staff increases. This relationship is, however, far from clear with regard to *aggregate* public sector trends in both the US and UK. Peters' (1989) study of Federal bureaux in the USA, for example, revealed hardly any correlation between expenditures and staff increases in both growing ($r = 0.08$) and declining ($r = 0.19$) agencies (Dunleavy, 1991, p. 214). Similarly, Dunsire (1991) reports that during the general decade of cutback management in the UK (1974–85), staffing as a whole was cut much more than expenditures. The only available evidence in support of Niskanen's thesis was a general tendency for bureaux to cut capital before current expenditures, the latter being the source of salary and administration costs.

In response to these difficulties, it is necessary to develop a more disaggregated account of bureaucratic behaviour, which considers the variation of incentives towards bureaucratic growth within different types of government agency. Three factors appear to be particularly influential in determining the extent to which bureaucrats might seek to maximise their budgets; i) the institutional form of the agency budget, ii) the degree of professionalisation within an agency and iii) the extent to which an agency is populated by ideologically motivated staff.

Dunleavy (1991), in particular, has modified Niskanen's model to produce an account, which considers the variation of incentives towards budget maximisation within agencies of differing institutional forms. His basic model distinguishes between three institutional types of budget and then categorises five different agency types according to the character of the budget in their charge.[2]

The proportion of a bureau's total expenditure that falls into each of these categories varies according to the type of bureau, as shown in Table 4.1. The budget classification is as follows:

1. The Core Budget (CB) includes all spending deployed within the bureau itself on staff and administration.
2. The Bureau *element* represents all monies paid out to the private sector as contracts or transfer payments. The CB plus the bureau element is referred to as the Bureau Budget (BB)
3. The Program *element* encompasses all monies which the agency receives but then passes on to other public sector bureaux. The overall budget flowing through the agency is termed the Program Budget. (PB).

Keeping the assumption that bureaucrats desire a mix of job security, perquisites of office and increased status, Dunleavy (1991) suggests that these are primarily associated with the Core Budget (CB) and in certain circumstances to the Bureau Budget (BB). Accordingly, he argues that incentives for budget maximisation are strongest in those agencies where the CB represents a high

Table 4.1 Bureaucratic Agency Types and Budget Form

Agency Type	Budget Form
Delivery	CB most of BB and PB
Regulatory	CB most of BB and PB
Transfer	CB small part of BB, which is most of PB
Contract	CB small part of BB, which is most of PB
Control	CB small part of BB, which is small part of PB

Source: Adapted from Dowding (1995, p. 90).

proportion of the total budget; in Delivery agencies such as the Police Force or the Army, which produce output directly for the consumption of individuals or enterprises; and in Regulatory agencies, such as Health and Safety Directorates, which act to control the behaviour of individuals and firms through the administration of licensing systems or regulatory laws.

In Transfer agencies, such as the Ministry of Agriculture and Contract agencies, such as the defence procurement divisions within the Ministry of Defence, bureaucrats might also pursue a budget maximising strategy. In these cases, subsidy payments or government contracts are destined for the members of highly organised interest groups, (farmers and defence contractors, for example) that are often able to provide a flow back of benefits such as post-retirement deals and other such benefits in exchange for greater subsidies. In all other Transfer and Contract bureaux, however, dealing with a fragmented clientele of consumers there may be relatively fewer incentives to push for budgetary growth. As Dunleavy (1991, p. 194) puts it,

> Why should policy level staff at a welfare agency seek to push up payments to the unemployed – none of whom can provide any reciprocal benefits to bureaucrats?

Similarly, in Control agencies, such as the Department for Education, where budget increments are simply passed on to lower level bureaucracies (individual schools and local authorities), there may also be fewer incentives to budget maximise.[3]

A second factor that may influence the tendency toward bureau expansion, is the degree of professionalisation within different agencies. As Breton and Wintrobe (1975) argue, highly professionalised bureaux often have personnel whose expertise is relatively restricted with possibilities for career advancement residing mainly within the agency. The specialised skills and knowledge acquired by such professions are not easily transferred to other career paths, a tendency that may fuel the pressure to push for bureau growth and the resultant job security. In less professionalised agencies, by contrast, there may be fewer incentives to push for expansion. First, because top bureaucrats may have greater opportunities for advancement outside the agency concerned. And second, because to the extent that senior professionals do budget maximise these incentives may be confined to the relatively small proportion of the overall budget devoted to professional staff. There may be fewer incentives in terms of job security or status for high-grade officials to expand budgets and job opportunities on low skilled workers performing routine tasks. Differences in the degree of professionalisation and the rank structure of departments, therefore, may result in different incentives for growth in agencies of the same institutional form.

In further work, Dunleavy combines his 'bureau shaping' analysis with an account of professional behaviour to explain acquiescence to the growth of contracting out and competitive tendering in local government service delivery

(Dunleavy, 1991; Dunleavy and Biggs, 1995). Niskanenesque accounts predict that contracting out exposes bureaucrats to greater competition and should therefore provoke strong opposition. In practice, however, some policy level bureaucrats have accepted contracting out with comparatively little in the way of resistance (Ascher, 1987). Dunleavy explains this trend by arguing that so long as the impact of contracting out (i.e. potential job losses) falls on low grade staff, senior bureaucrats in local delivery bureaux are unlikely to witness a decline in their opportunities for promotion and prestige, should routine tasks carried out by low skilled workers be 'hived-off' to private contractors. Why should senior bureaucrats care how many workers perform the refuse collection service or fill the potholes in the road? The greater the grade distinctions between policy level staff and implementation staff, therefore, the less likely it is that self-interested managers will pursue outright budget maximisation and oppose contracting out. By contrast, highly professionalised bureaux with relatively few low-grade functions are more likely to pursue open-ended bureaucratic growth and to resist any transfer of functions to private contractors.

A third and final variable, which may affect incentives towards bureaucratic growth is the importance of ideological motivation and the existence of expressive benefits. Bureaucrats may not be driven by purely material incentives, but by a range of non-material elements or moral motivations within their utility functions. In turn, the extent to which a bureaucracy is likely to be populated by staff who are affected by such considerations is in part a product of the character of the agency itself and the type of work that it performs. Wilson's (1989) survey of the literature on the US Federal bureaucracy, for example, suggests that professional agencies focused in 'activist' areas such as environmental protection, tend to attract staff motivated by an ideological commitment to the pursuit of agency mission, fuelling pressure for growth to a greater extent than in bureaux performing less politicised roles (for example street cleaning). Rowley (1992) makes a similar analysis of ideological bias and mission commitment in the US Legal Services Corporation. To use the terminology of Downs (1967), high profile politicised bureaux are more likely to attract 'zealot' personality types to their staffs.

In what follows, the framework outlined above is used to analyse the agencies of the British land use planning system. Each agency is categorised according to its bureaucratic profile, the nature of its clients and its expected behaviour examined against the available evidence. The final sections consider the implications of bureaucratic behaviour for the pattern of policy delivery within the planning system.

LAND USE PLANNING AS BUDGET MAXIMISATION

Bureaucratic control of land use change in Britain is divided between several agencies operating at both the national and the local scale. The Department of the Environment, Transport and the Regions (DETR) is the national sponsor body for the planning system as a whole but is not directly involved in the implementation of development control, except in a quasi-judicial function in the appeals procedure alongside the Planning Inspectorate. Rather, the DETR issues advice to local authorities in the form of Planning Policy Guidance Notes and occasional policy circulars. Planning is only a minor function within the overall DETR remit, accounting for less than 0.5 per cent of its £37 billion budget. Ninety-five per cent of this budget is allocated as transfer payments to local authority service provision and a variety of quasi-autonomous agencies operating in conservation, rural development, pollution control, housing and urban regeneration (DoE, 1995). The DETR is thus a Control bureau, but the planning directorate within the agency, for which no fully dis-aggregated budget figures are available is itself a regulatory agency (Pennington, 1997a, p. 112)

The vast bulk of policy implementation is controlled by bureaucratic organisations at the sub-national level through local authorities and quangos. Primary responsibility is held by planning bureaucrats in individual local authorities who administer the development control system and draft the local development plans, which lie at the core of the planning system. About 80 per cent of local authority finance is derived from central government grants (UK National Accounts) – channelled predominantly through the DETR, the Department for Education, the Department of Health, the Department of Transport and, the Home Office. The level of planning expenditure is thus dependent on the share of central government grants (obtained from the DETR), plus the 20 per cent of finance drawn from local taxes and charges which local authorities choose to allocate to these agencies.[4]

A secondary role is played by two quangos,[5] English Nature (formerly the Nature Conservancy Council /NCC) and the Countryside Commission (recently merged with the Rural Development Commission to form the Countryside Agency). Each of these bodies has its own budget voted through parliament, but the Secretary of State for the Environment, Transport and the Regions holds ultimate responsibility for their policy actions. A further role is played by a second central government department – the Ministry of Agriculture Fisheries and Food (MAFF). With agriculture as the dominant land use in the UK, through the various subsidy programmes of the European Common Agricultural Policy, MAFF has an important role in the land use system and often engages in consultation with local authorities, the conservation quangos and the DETR.

Table 4. 2 depicts the budget profile and agency classification of the major land use bureaucracies. With the exception of the DETR, which has a relatively small planning function, land use agencies predominantly take the form of regulatory bureaux. Local authority planning departments do not produce goods and services as such, but instead draft local land use designations and administer these through the granting or refusal of planning permissions. The CB for local authority planning at the District, County and Metropolitan levels accounts for over 90 per cent of the total program budget (£1.2 billion in 1991 – at 1993 prices) and with only minuscule transfer payments to the

Table 4.2 Land Use Planning – Budget Classification and Agency Types

	Staff	Admin. & Running Cost	Transfers to Private Sector	Transfers to Public Sector	Agency Type
	CB	CB	BB	PB	
DoE	2	2	1	95	Control
Districts	45	53	2	0	Regulatory
Counties	42	57	1	0	Regulatory
Metros	33	57	10	0	Regulatory
NCC/EN	40	35	25	0	Regulatory
CC	14	20	38	28	Reg/Trans
MAFF	20	20	40	20	Reg/Trans

Source: Computed from CIPFA Planning and Development Statistics, DoE, EN/CC/ MAFF Annual Reports.

private sector, especially in the Districts and Counties these bureaux may be classified as 'pure' regulatory agencies.

A similar though smaller regulatory function (total budget £56.7 million in 1991 – at 1993 prices) is carried out by NCC/EN, empowered under the Wildlife and Countryside Acts (1981 and 1985). EN may purchase or lease land as National Nature Reserves (a delivery function) and more important may regulate the behaviour of private landowners via the designation of Sites of Special Scientific Interest (SSSIs). The CB represents 75 per cent of the total budget with a subsidiary 25 per cent taken in transfer payments usually paid to land owning farmers who agree to practice ecologically sensitive farming.

The CC and MAFF are both 'mixed' regulatory/transfer bureaux. The CC is the statutory body responsible for countryside conservation under the 1968 Countryside Act and the Wildlife and Countryside Acts (total budget £47.7 million in 1994 – at 1993 prices). Its regulatory functions include the designation of Areas of Outstanding Natural Beauty (AONBs). The much bigger MAFF, meanwhile, supervises the transfer of agricultural subsidies under the Common Agricultural Policy of the European Union and domestic subsidies targeted at landscape conservation. It also performs a regulatory function in the designation of Environmentally Sensitive Areas (ESAs).

Given the theory of bureaucratic behaviour outlined in the previous section land use agencies would appear to conform to the theoretical types where budget maximisation may be a plausible utility enhancing strategy for bureaucrats. The planning directorate within the DETR is a regulatory bureau with an apparent incentive to maximise the length of the regulatory process and hence its budget, by drafting ever longer and more complicated planning guidance. Although as a control bureau and the major source of local government finance, the local government directorate of the DETR may have few direct incentives to maximise these internal transfers, local planning bureaucracies *do* have an incentive to gain as large a share as possible of the relevant grants. Similarly, local planning bureaucrats may have incentives to ensure that local authorities devote proportionally more time lobbying central government for grants which flow to their agencies, rather than those destined for other local services such as transport and housing, as well as maximising their share of locally raised finance.

Increases in land use budgets are spent almost entirely within the bureaux themselves on staffing, office equipment and administration. Moreover, to the extent that land use bureaucracies do engage in transfer payments (CC and MAFF), these are destined for a highly organised lobby group (farmers), well able to organise a flow back of benefits to senior officials in exchange for greater subsidy payments. Half the current policy team employed by the Country Landowners Association (CLA), for example, previously worked for MAFF (Pennington, 1997a, p. 115).

The incentives towards bureaucratic growth in planning would appear to be especially strong, compared even with other regulatory and delivery bureaux because of the high degree of professionalisation within planning agencies and a tendency towards an environmentalist ideology in planning staffs. Professionalisation in land use planning may be seen in the large proportion of agency personnel who are qualified planners. According to a survey by the Royal Town Planning Institute (RTPI, 1992), 60 per cent of local authority planning workers are in senior professional positions and 85 per cent of these have proceeded through formal training in town planning. Poole's (1975, p. 146) classic study of the local government system revealed that planning was second only to social work in the proportion of qualified graduates recruited and that only estate management and financial administration had a higher percentage (36 per cent) of staff in the top salary grades of principal officer/senior officer. These figures compared with only 6 per cent for education and 10 per cent for housing (Poole, 1975, pp. 206–7). Local authority planning departments appear, therefore, to exhibit a higher degree of professionalisation and staff seniority than the vast majority of the local government service.

In the case of ideology, although inner city planning has often been associated with a welfarist ideology committed to economic growth, numerous studies have documented the tendency for suburban and rural planners to be motivated by an environmentalist ethos and a commitment to the restriction of market forces (Hill and Bramley, 1986, Ch. 9; Reade, 1987; Shucksmith, 1990). Pennington and Rydin (2000) report a similar pattern of mission commitment within local planning departments and especially those dealing with countryside protection issues. In many cases planning bureaucrats in such agencies are actually members of prominent environmental interest groups. The conservation quangos, meanwhile, present a further set of agencies where there appears to be a tendency to draw disproportionately on the ranks of the 'environmentally committed' (Marren, 1993).

Together with the institutional form of planning agencies and the degree of professionalisation within planning staffs, all the incentives within these bureaux appear skewed towards bureaucratic growth and to a greater extent than in most other government agencies. In order to evaluate this theory, it is necessary to compare the fortunes of the major planning bureaucracies with general trends in bureaucratic growth across comparable agencies in the rest of the public sector. The illustrative data presented in Tables 4.3 to 4.9 are helpful in considering the relevance of the bureau-shaping perspective. In each case, the local government category which contains both delivery/regulatory bureaux and those which are less professionalised/ideologically motivated and are in a non-delivery/ regulatory format, acts as a control panel to enable comparison with land use planning.

Table 4.3 compares spending totals for local authority planning in England and Wales in the 1980s with overall local authority spending. The data do not contradict the view that planning agencies have a particular tendency towards bureaucratic growth.

Table 4.3 Revenue Expenditure for Town and Country Planning and Total Local Authority in England and Wales: 1979–1991

Year	Town & Country Planning		Total Local Authority	
	Spending	1979 Index	Spending	1979 Index
1979/80	959	100.0	63160	100.0
1980/81	1031	107.5	63285	100.2
1981/82	1013	105.6	63096	99.9
1982/83	993	103.5	62313	98.7
1983/84	1083	112.9	64288	101.8
1984/85	1085	113.1	64355	101.9
1985/86	1100	114.7	62892	99.6
1986/87	1017	106.0	63975	101.3
1987/88	1080	112.6	67041	106.1
1988/89	1159	120.9	68782	108.9
1989/90	1222	127.4	69293	109.7
1990/91	1246	129.9	69642	110.3
±%	+29.9	+29.9	+10.3	+10.3

Notes: All spending in millions (deflated 1993 = 100).
Source: Computed from Annual Abstract of Statistics. The Annual Abstract of Statistics does not publish full expenditure figures for local planning authorities after 1991.

Total local authority spending increased by 10 per cent in real terms but town and country planning fared considerably better with a real increase of almost 30 per cent, which was also far in excess of total public sector growth, 16 per cent (UK National Accounts) in the same time series. An 'ANOVA' test of variance was conducted on the Indexed data set to confirm whether the higher growth rate for planning was statistically significant. The results were as follows:

DF – Between Groups = 1   F Ratio = 10.6190
DF – Within Groups   = 22   F Prob =   0.0036

The F statistic is significant at the 1 per cent level – i.e. it is highly unlikely that the higher growth rate of planning was the product of random chance.

The increase in planning expenditure is particularly striking, given that much of the general rise in local expenditure was accounted for by the police force, which was a target for spending increases by the Conservative government at the national and local scale and by spending on social services, which may have increased due to the rise in unemployment and the effects of an ageing population.[6] Planning on the other hand was a target for deregulation, but by the end of the decade appears to have emerged in a stronger position than ever before.

Suggestive though these data are, they are not sufficient to confirm a consistent trend towards greater bureaucratic growth within planning agencies. It might be argued, for example, that the 1980s witnessed a substantial growth in the environmental lobby and the latter half of the decade, in particular, saw a substantial rise in the general electoral significance of the environment as a political issue (Robinson, 1992), which may have been a primary cause of increased expenditure. Moreover, since planning is subject to swings in the property market it could be the case that the buoyant market in the 1980s may have led to additional spending on the planning process. In order to confirm a consistent pattern of bureaucratic growth, therefore, a longer-term analysis of spending trends is required. The data reported in Tables 4.4 and 4.5 do indeed show that expenditure increases for town and country planning have consistently outstripped the average for other local authority bureaux.

Table 4.4 displays planning expenditure as a percentage of total local authority expenditure for both revenue and capital accounts over the 30-year period 1960/61 to 1990/91.

The percentage of revenue expenditure (spending on employees, running costs and transfer payments) accounted for by planning rose consistently throughout the period, from 0.67 per cent of the total budget in 1960/61 to 1.79 per cent in 1990/91, whereas the less significant capital expenses (spending on buildings) increased from 1.59 per cent to 5.58 per cent. These figures represent a substantial real gain for the planning bureaucracy, given that the percentage of Gross Domestic Product taken by local government revenue expenses also increased from 5.2 per cent in 1960 to 8.2 per cent in 1992 (UK National Accounts).

Table 4.4 Town and County Planning as a Percentage of Local Authority Expenditure: 1960/61–1990/91

Year	Revenue	Capital	Year	Revenue	Capital
1960/61	0.67	1.59	1976/77	1.46	3.11
1961/62	0.64	2.21	1977/78	1.45	2.97
1962/63	0.70	2.03	1978/79	1.40	3.13
1963/64	0.74	2.08	1979/80	1.52	3.68
1964/65	0.77	2.57	1980/81	1.63	4.57
1965/66	0.88	2.72	1981/82	1.60	4.07
1966/67	0.88	2.40	1982/83	1.59	4.87
1967/68	0.98	2.53	1983/84	1.68	4.68
1968/69	1.03	3.06	1984/85	1.69	4.97
1969/70	1.00	3.06	1985/86	1.59	6.07
1971/72	1.10	3.29	1987/88	1.68	5.58
1972/73	1.16	3.53	1988/89	1.69	na.
1973/74	1.19	3.23	1989/90	1.76	na.
1974/75	1.46	2.58	1990/91	1.79	na.
1975/76	1.54	2.72			

Notes: Change in percentage share for other major bureaux 1960/61–1990/91 – Education 37.3 to 33.8, Refuse 2 to 1.7, Highways 7 to 6.1, Buses 3.9 to 0.5 (1980), Libraries 1.1 to 1.2, Housing 15 to 16, Fire 1.4 to1.8, Parks 1.4 to 3.1, Police 6 to 8, Justice 0.6 to 1.1, Social Services 1.9 to 8.8, Environmental Health (1970) 0.8 to 1.7. *Source*: Computed from Annual Abstract of Statistics.

Table 4.5 presents the actual spending data from 1962 to 1991 (at 1990 prices). Although planning and the local authority category experienced a substantial real gain, the growth rate for planning was well in excess of the other local bureaux with a total real increase of over *600 per cent*. A test for variance on the indexed data set confirms that the difference in expenditure changes is highly significant (at the 0.1% level). The F statistics are displayed below:

DF – Between Groups = 1   F Ratio = 34.5502
DF – Within Groups = 56   F Prob = 0.0000

In short, planning bureaux have consistently gained a greater share of an already expanding pie. Of all the local authority bureaux (see notes to Table 4.4), only the highly professionalized social services showed a more rapid rate of growth and as suggested by the bureau-shaping model, the less professionalized areas such as refuse collection, highway maintenance, buses, libraries, fire, housing (a transfer bureau) and education (a mixed delivery/transfer bureau), all experienced a decline in relation to planning, as did the rest of the public sector as a whole.[7]

Table 4.5 Revenue Expenditure for Town and Country Planning and Total Local Authority: 1962/63–1990/91

Year	Town & Country Planning			Total Local Authority	
	Index of Applications	Spending 1990 Prices	1962 Index	Spending 1990 Prices	1962 Index
1962/63	100.0	160	100.0	23295	100.0
1963/64	103.6	181	113.1	24562	105.4
1964/65	116.2	201	125.6	25894	111.2
1965/66	111.6	248	155.0	28139	120.8
1966/67	104.5	261	163.1	29659	127.3
1967/68	106.3	313	195.6	31881	136.9
1968/69	107.3	342	213.8	32994	141.6
1969/70	101.4	393	245.6	39140	168.0
1970/71	104.3	450	281.3	42107	180.8
1971/72	116.6	481	300.6	44034	189.0
1972/73	154.8	539	336.9	46482	199.5
1973/74	156.7	615	384.4	51769	222.2
1974/75	104.4	786	491.3	53802	231.0
1975/76	114.3	849	530.6	55208	237.0
1976/77	112.3	794	496.3	54251	232.9
1977/78	111.2	743	464.4	51293	220.2
1978/79	126.0	761	475.6	54037	232.0
1979/80	na	854	533.8	56231	241.4
1980/81	93.6	933	583.1	57228	245.9
1981/82	103.4	906	566.3	56392	242.1
1982/83	108.2	891	556.9	56112	240.9
1983/84	106.0	965	603.1	57263	245.8
1984/85	108.7	967	604.4	55331	246.1
1985/86	134.4	974	608.8	57723	239.2
1986/87	150.5	919	574.4	57732	247.8
1987/88	171.9	963	601.9	59733	256.4
1988/89	158.0	1039	649.4	61666	264.7
1989/90	133.9	1097	685.6	62195	267.0
1990/91	128.6	1122	701.3	62678	269.1
% ±	+28.6	+601.3	+601.3	+169.1	+169.1

Notes: All spending in £ millions. Index of Planning Applications – base year = 397 301.
Source: Computed from Annual Abstract of Statistics and DoE Development Control Statistics.

The data on expenditure trends is particularly significant when controlling for demand side factors, such as the rise of environmentalism and property market cycles. It appears that the process of budgetary expansion was well underway years before environmental concerns reached the top of the political agenda in the late 1980s. Even as early as the beginning of the 1960s, the planning budget was expanding rapidly, well before the rise in the political significance of the environment as an election issue. Butler and Stokes' (1974) analysis of the most salient electoral issues in the 1960s and early 1970s, found unemployment, welfare services and health at the top of the political agenda with the environment scarcely registering a mention during this period of time. The rise of environmentalism in the 1980s, may thus account for some of the bureaucratic growth, but it seems unlikely that this can explain the sheer scale of the difference in the growth of the planning budget, which has consistently ran at *three times* the level of real growth in the rest of the public sector *over a period of 30 years.*

Neither does it seem likely that the scale of the expenditure increase can be accounted for by changes in the property market and in particular increasing demands for the processing of planning applications by the building industry. A reasonable indication of such demand side pressures can be derived from consideration of the number of planning applications submitted to local authorities, compiled in the national Development Control Statistics. The left hand column in Table 4.5 gives an index of applications from 1962 onwards, where it can be seen that the number of applications received increased by only 28.6 per cent over the period in question, compared to the 600 per cent increase in real expenditure over the same time period. Indeed, at one point in 1980/81, planning bureaucrats were actually processing fewer applications than in the early 1960s, even though real spending had increased by almost 500 per cent in the intervening years.[8]

Overall, the data do appear to offer support for the hypothesis that incentives within highly professionalised land use agencies are more heavily skewed towards bureaucratic expansion. Table 4.6, which compares the fortunes of the various theoretical agency types throughout the 1980s, offers additional, although relatively crude support for the public choice theory of bureaucratic behaviour.

It is apparent that of the major local authority bureaux those that remained in a delivery or regulatory bureau format fared best in terms of budgetary growth. The police force, administration of justice, fire services, libraries, social services, environmental health and town and country planning, all increased their share of the overall budget. The major local government transfer bureau – housing and those agencies which were subject to various forms of contracting out, by contrast (refuse-collection, highway maintenance and education, which in the late 1980s shifted into a control agency format), all witnessed a decline in their share of the overall budget.[9] The one exception to this pattern was parks and open spaces, which was subject to contracting out but nonetheless increased its budget share.

These data are, of course, open to different interpretations and cannot be taken as conclusive proof that bureaucratic incentives were the *cause* of the

Table 4.6   Local Authority Agency Types and Expenditure Shares: 1980/81–1990/91

| | | Percentage of Revenue Expenditure | | |
| | Agency Type | Year | | |
		1980/81	1985/86	1990/91
Non-Delivery				
Education	Del to Control	36.1	34.5	33.8
Refuse	Del to Contract	2.1	1.9	1.7
Highways	Del to Contract	6.9	6.4	6.1
Parks	Del to Contract	2.5	2.9	3.1
Housing	Transfer	18.0	18.2	16.0
Other*	Mixed	9.1	7.4	8.6
Other**	Mixed	5.2	6.4	6.2
Total Non Delivery		**79.9**	**77.8**	**75.5**
Del/Regulatory				
Police	Delivery	6.5	7.7	8.0
Justice	Delivery	0.7	0.9	1.1
Social Services	Delivery	7.1	7.5	8.8
Libraries	Delivery	1.1	1.2	1.2
Fire	Delivery	1.5	1.7	1.8
Planning	Regulatory	1.6	1.7	1.8
Env. Health	Regulatory	1.6	1.6	1.8
Total Del/Regulatory		**20.1**	**22.2**	**24.5**
Total Local Authority		**100**	**100**	**100**

Notes: There are no nation-wide data examining the variations in agency type throughout the whole country. The agency classifications used here are based on Ascher (1987) which notes the trend toward contracting out in refuse collection and highways and empirical work by Dunleavy and Biggs (1995) on the London Boroughs. *Other refers to unallocated general administration and transfer payments. **Other refers to unallocated services.
Source: Computed from Annual Abstract of Statistics.

observed expenditure patterns. Macro-political factors and in particular, the ideological hostility to public housing on behalf of the Conservative central government were probably more significant in this case than any effect that may be attributed to incentives within housing bureaux. Similarly, professional social services expenditure may well have increased because of the external demands brought about by rising unemployment and the effects of an ageing population, as opposed to budget maximising behaviour by professional social workers. The rise in police expenditure may also have resulted from macro factors associated with the rise in crime and the Conservative government's ideological commitment to law and order expenditures. Increasing central government controls over local expenditure through 'rate-capping' and the provisions of the Standard Spending Assessment also require that the role of bureaucratic incentives should not be overemphasised. What remains significant from the data in Table 4.6, however, is that all agencies which saw reductions in their share of expenditure were examples of less professionalised bureaux (refuse, highways and education) and were subject to some form of contracting out. None of the more professionalised services such as planning and social services saw the introduction of compulsory competitive tendering and a reduction in their share of expenditure. Whilst technical difficulties in the contracting out of services such as the administration of justice and less professionalised areas such as the fire service, might account for their exclusion from this process, no such difficulties exist in the case of planning and social services (Cullingworth and Nadin, 1994). This is at least suggestive that bureaucratic resistance to such processes, may have been a significant factor at play.

The data on staffing are also broadly in line with the analytical framework set out here. Planning bureaux did better in terms of staffing, experiencing no net change in numbers by 1993, compared to a substantial decline for the local authority category as a whole (Table 4.7). The difference between the two categories is not, however, statistically significant. Nonetheless, a closer analysis of trends within local authority staffing does lend some general support for the analytical framework. The indexed figures indicate that staffing in planning fell more or less in line with the local authority category during the early 1980s, but from the mid 1980s onwards, coinciding with the introduction of contracting out and compulsory competitive tendering (cct) throughout local government, a consistently widening gap opened up with the local authority category declining rapidly.

The impact of contracting out on staffing is significant given that highly professionalised agencies such as planning are expected to be more resistant of transfers to private contractors. Within this context, the Chartered Institute for Public Finance and Accounting (CIPFA) (1994) indicate that only 2 per cent of planning expenditure has been contracted out and significantly in the 1991 Department of the Environment Report recommending the extension of cct, planning services were excluded (Cullingworth and Nadin, 1994). The ability of planning, in particular, to escape the introduction of these procedures may be a reflection of the role of professionals within the planning directorate at the then DoE. These individuals are unlikely to have wanted to antagonise their professional Royal Town Planning Institute (RTPI) colleagues by recommending the introduction of contracting out into the local planning function. In general, it is the less professionalised bureaux, where the interests of top bureaucrats may depart from those of blue-collar staff, that have been subjected to cct. The services that have been exposed to cct, alongside education, have in

Table 4.7 Staffing Levels for Town and Country Planning and Total Local Authority: 1979–1993

	Town & Country Planning		Total Local Authority	
	Staff	Index	Staff	Index
1979	22.4	100.0	2086.6	100.0
1980	21.9	97.8	2056.4	98.6
1981	19.8	88.4	1891.3	90.6
1982	19.7	87.9	1873.9	89.8
1983	19.8	88.4	1881.7	90.2
1984	19.9	88.8	1876.5	89.9
1985	19.9	88.8	1877.1	90.0
1986	20.1	89.7	1894.1	90.8
1987	20.8	92.9	1915.3	91.8
1988	21.6	96.4	1920.6	92.0
1989	22.5	100.4	1890.8	90.6
1990	23.1	103.1	1894.0	90.8
1991	23.2	103.6	1866.5	89.5
1992	22.8	101.8	1834.4	87.9
1993	22.4	100.0	1691.3	81.1
±%	0	0	−19.9	−19.9

Notes: Staff figures in thousands.
Source: Computed from Monthly Digest of Statistics.

turn experienced the most dramatic decline in staffs. Those agencies, which have been considered for cct, but have largely resisted the trend are indeed the more professionalised agencies – planning, social services and environmental health. As Table 4.8 shows it is these agencies that have seen the smallest declines in staff.

Turning to the fortunes of the three remaining land use bureaucracies, these also offer broad support for the view that regulatory agencies are prone towards greater bureaucratic growth. In a decade when overall public sector growth was contained to 16 per cent in real terms and staffs were cut, the conservation quangos, in particular, experienced explosive growth in terms of expenditure and staffing (see Table 4.9) and both remained immune to any contracting out of the regulatory function. It is especially significant that both of these quangos fared far better than other agencies attached to the DoE in particular those transfer bureaux focused on housing where real spending barely increased at all throughout the 1980s (Pennington, 1997a, p. 129).[10] Some of the increase may be attributed directly to the provisions of the Wildlife and Countryside Acts (1981/85), but the sheer scale of the increase combined with evidence that

Table 4.8 Local Authority Staff Changes by Agency Type: 1979–1993

Agency	Agency Type	Staff 1993	% Change 1979–1993
Non-Delivery			
Education	Del to Control	698.6	−29
Construction	Del to Contract	69.3	−48
Refuse	Del to Contract	21.3	−58
Transport	Privatisation	1.4	−94
Parks/Leisure	Del to Contract	65.6	−14
Housing	Transfer	65.9	+29
Other	Mixed	224.1	−15
Delivery/Regulatory			
Police	Delivery	121.1	+6
Justice	Delivery	9.8	+36
Social Services	Delivery	231.9	+13
Libraries	Delivery	31.9	−3
Fire	Delivery	34.1	−16
Planning	Regulatory	22.4	0
Environmental Health	Regulatory	18.9	−13
Total Local Authority	Mixed	1691.3	−20

Notes: Staff figures in thousands. Staff declines for Transport are exaggerated by the impact of bus privatisation. Housing staffs increased due to the transfer of Housing Benefit responsibilities to local authorities.
Source: Computed from Monthly Digest of Statistics.

quangocratic salaries took a higher and higher proportion of total spending (Adams, 1993) is at the very least suggestive of self-interested bureaucratic behaviour.

In the case of MAFF, it is much more difficult to attribute bureaucratic growth directly to the actions of civil servants because spending decisions are made largely within the corridors of Brussels rather than in Westminster. Nonetheless, a 30 per cent real increase in CAP spending over the last ten years (Winter, 1996) is consistent with MAFF bureaucrats, maximising transfer payments to the highly organised farm lobby and at the very least there is no indication that senior officials have sought to resist this trend – real spending has actually increased following the so called MacSharry reforms which MAFF officials helped to negotiate (Pennington, 1997a, p. 130).

More important, domestic MAFF spending on conservation, where UK bureaucrats *do* exercise a much greater degree of clout, has also expanded rapidly, from nil expenditure in 1984 to £116 million in 1995. The new

Table 4.9 Expenditure and Staffing in the Conservation Quangos: 1980/81–1994/95

Year	NCC/EN		CC	
	Spending	Staff	Spending	Staff
1980/81	18.8	530	na.	na.
1981/82	19.2	535	18.9	90
1982/83	20.4	559	19.8	95
1983/84	22.3	550	21.3	98
1984/85	29.6	577	20.9	100
1985/86	36.0	689	23.8	100
1986/87	44.4	750	27.0	118
1987/88	46.7	780	32.3	120
1988/89	47.3	800	27.9	128
1989/90	49.6	820	27.5	150
1990/91	56.7	858	28.1	180
1991/92	*	*	32.6	230
1992/93	*	*	46.2	300
1993/94	*	*	48.7	310
1994/95	*	*	47.7	319
% change	+202	+62	+153	+254

Notes: All spending in millions (deflated 1993 = 100). All staffing in actual numbers.
Source: NCC/EN and CC Annual Reports.
* In 1991, the NCC was divided into three bodies, one each for England, Scotland and Wales. English Nature (the new body for England acquired 621 staff from the NCC in 1991 and by 1994/95 had recruited an extra 134 staff making a total of 755. Remaining NCC staff were transferred to the Scottish and Welsh bodies so the total employed in nature conservation is now over 1,000. EN spending increased from 32.6 million in 1991/92 to 39.6 million in 1994/95 (at 1993 prices).

agricultural regime of EU set aside payments combined with domestic conservation subsidies, as opposed to the previous policy of direct production support appears particularly amenable to bureaucratic interests. The new policies have reduced the level of surplus production which was becoming highly visible to politicians, yet at the same time have allowed an expansion of assistance to MAFF's major client group – the farm lobby. It might be suggested that these developments owe more to external pressure from the European Union than they do to any budget maximising behaviour in the MAFF. In actual fact, however, the very concept of ESAs appears to have been devised within the MAFF and then 'marketed' to the European Union (Cherry, 1996, p. 209; Winter, 1996).

BUDGET MAXIMISATION AND REGULATORY GROWTH

The apparent ability of the land use bureaucracies to secure greater budgets and to have largely resisted the major institutional reforms that have affected other parts of the public sector, is suggestive of a tendency for administrative incentives within these agencies to be skewed towards bureaucratic expansion. What is of particular significance, is that budget maximisation – if it occurs – appears to be synonymous with a strategy of regulatory maximisation, which in turn has implications for the policy focus of the planning system.

Local authority planning departments in England and Wales perform five main functions, four of which may be described as 'pure' regulatory activities. These are; planning policy, which involves staff in the drafting of local development plans; development control – the day to day procedure of reviewing planning applications; environment and conservation – the drafting of local conservation orders and other site designations; and enforcement, which includes the demolition of buildings erected without planning permission. The remaining function, economic development and promotion is predominantly a delivery activity. Planning staff employed in this area are responsible for the development of local authority owned land (a delivery or contract function), the collection of rents from local authority owned industrial sites, the marketing of development opportunities and the handling of regional development grants (a transfer function).

The overall significance of the regulatory function to local authority planning departments is illustrated in Table 4.10, which shows the proportion of staff employed in regulatory activities in relation to those in economic

Table 4.10 Budgeted Employees by Function in English Planning Authorities

	Regulatory Functions	Economic Development	Total	% Regulatory Functions
Non-Metro Districts	6602.8	608.1	7210.9	91.6
Counties	2208.0	526.0	2734.0	81.0
Metro-Districts	2093.5	696.5	2790.0	67.0
All Authorities	10904.3	1830.6	12734.9	85.6

Notes: The CIPFA data are not based on full returns from all local authorities, hence the lower staff totals than those indicated in Table 4.7.
Source: Computed from CIPFA Planning and Development Statistics 1991.

development. The table indicates that the vast majority of staff – especially in the non-metropolitan districts where the majority of planners are employed, are engaged in regulatory functions. The lower figure for the metropolitan districts (67 per cent) is a reflection of the greater role of these agencies in urban renewal programmes focused on inner city regeneration (see Chapter 6).

The *raison d'être* of non-metropolitan land use bureaux, therefore, is to create and to enforce land use regulations and in order to secure greater budgets, planning bureaucrats may be expected to offer differential support for those policies and interest groups, which will increase the level of regulation and the demand for staff and administrative expenses to enforce it. In support of this thesis, one need only reflect on the rapid growth of environmental site designations, the increasing complexity of the planning system and the low productivity rate of local planning authorities within the context of the sustained bureaucratic growth discussed in the previous section.

As noted earlier, it might be argued that the sustained growth in land use regulation is merely a response by the relevant agencies to increased demands for their services – the growth of the environmental lobby, for example – and that larger budgets have been incidental to meeting these demands. A glance at the behaviour of land use bureaucrats, however, reveals that they have not acted as passive respondents to these wider political forces but have, as public choice theory suggests, sought to stimulate the growth of their budgets and regulation. On the one hand, this has occurred through lobbying for additional controls – in some cases funding supportive interest groups. And, on the other, by bureaucrats escalating costs and lengthening the regulatory process.

With regard to the lobbying activities of planners, the District, County and Metropolitan Planning Officers Societies (D/C/MPOS) and the Royal Town Planning Institute (RTPI), joined with conservationists in the Council for the Protection of Rural England (CPRE) in the campaign for the 'plan-led' development control system, which was itself finally adopted following a parliamentary amendment drafted by the CPRE (Marsden et al., 1993; Pennington, 1997a). The Countryside Commission has, meanwhile, become one of the major financial donors to the CPRE following the group's successful campaign against a liberalisation of Green Belt policy in 1984 (Elson, 1986). Significantly, a recent chair of the CC, John Dower was the founder member of Rural Voice, an amalgam of rural interest groups including CPRE. The CC funded the conservationists during their national membership campaign throughout the 1980s and in the years 1991–1993 supplied subsidies to the tune of £120,000, which was the largest single contribution to the group (Pennington, 1997a, p. 134). Similarly, NCC/EN have close contacts with CPRE and with the Royal Society for the Protection of Birds (RSPB), the latter having been a frequent recipient of financial support in the management of its bird reserves (Dwyer and Hodge, 1996). There is, it would seem, a symbiotic relationship between land use bureaucrats whose budgets are dependent on regulation and those sets of interest groups demanding additional regulatory growth.

In addition to their lobbying actions, planning bureaucrats appear also to have played a role in the escalation of costs within the development control and plan preparation procedures. Figures produced by CIPFA (1992), for example, indicate that the net cost per capita of planning applications in the English non-metropolitan districts, increased from £4.90 in 1981/82 to £9.07 in 1991/92 (1993 prices) – a real increase of 85 per cent. Recall that real expenditure on planning increased by over 600 per cent between 1962 and 1991, but the overall number of planning applications increased by a mere 28 per cent in this same period of time. The difference between these two figures must be accounted, for at least in part, by cost escalation induced by planners, the increasing complexity of the planning system and a lengthening of the regulatory process, such as the increasing time to draw up structure and local plans. A similar pattern of regulatory expansionism is also apparent in the behaviour of the conservation quangos and in particular the NCC/EN. In the immediate aftermath of the Wildlife and Countryside Act (1981), the NCC estimated that its site designation duties would be completed within two years, but ten years later bureaucrats within these agencies were still designating additional sites (Marren, 1993; Adams, 1993).

Of course, the fact that planners and other land use bureaucrats may have lobbied for more regulation does not of itself *prove* that it is their actions that have been responsible for the expansion of the regulatory regime. A number of authors have, suggested that the power of local planning bureaucrats to influence policy outputs is heavily constrained by central government controls and edicts, an influence that is considered to have been particularly prevalent during the term of the Thatcher administration (Thornley, 1991; Montgomery and Thornley, 1990). Whilst it is must be recognised that local authority actors are indeed circumscribed by central government there is, however, sufficient evidence to confirm that local bureaucrats *are* able to exercise discretion, at least to some degree. A large body of research has developed in recent years that emphasises the significance of localities and their ability to shape central government policy objectives to their own ends (Cooke, 1986; Bagguley et al., 1990). Allmendinger (1997), suggests that this is particularly so where central government policy objectives are not clearly defined. As was noted in Chapter 2, (pp. 30–31) due to ideological divisions within the Conservative Party, this appears to have been the case with regard to planning in the 1980s. The lack of a clear policy commitment from the Thatcher administration to privatise the planning system or to introduce comprehensive de-regulation, provided an additional opportunity for local planning bureaucrats to shape policy to their own ends, including the growth of regulation and cost escalation.

The incentives that favour regulatory growth within the agencies of the planning system are particularly significant when considering the policy focus that planners are likely to support as a consequence of these incentives. Because planning budgets are dependent on the level of regulation it follows that planners may be inclined to offer differential support to those policies that are 'regulation intensive'. *Ceteris paribus* this is likely to mean that planners and especially those in non-metropolitan areas will be pre-disposed towards the urban containment and growth management policies discussed in Chapter 2 and more generally towards a stance that discriminates against new development.

The data in Table 4.10 indicate that these incentives are particularly prominent in the non-metropolitan districts and counties where as much as 90 per cent of the planning budget is devoted directly to the formulation and enforcement of planning controls. These bureaucrats would appear to have a strong interest in favouring the growth of controls that reduce the possibility of achieving planning permission in specific areas. In addition, planning bureau-crats may be likely to discriminate against development more indirectly, by lengthening the decision-making process and thus slowing the rate at which developers are able to respond to market conditions. This is not to say that planners will *always* rule against development – but that the structure of incentives indicates an *overall bias against development*. It would not, for example, be in the budgetary interests of planners to designate *all* land within their jurisdiction as Green Belt or *never* to accept a planning application. In these circumstances developers would cease to make planning applications and there would be proportionately less of a need for planners to enforce the relevant controls. So long as some planning permissions are granted, however, planners can be sure of a stream of applications, because the monopoly rents available to those who are successful are so huge that it is worth the risk of an application being turned down (see Chapter 3). It is not surprising, therefore, that Evans (1991) suggests planners are party to a Faustian pact with the big developers and the nimby lobby. Planning bureaucrats benefit in terms of budgets from an increasingly complex regulatory regime; corporate developers benefit from the monopoly profits derived from the occasional 'drip-feed' of planning permissions; and the nimby lobby benefits from the rise in property values and protection of local amenities that results.

In metropolitan and especially inner city authorities, the pattern of incentives and the attitude toward development may be somewhat different, owing to the higher proportion of the budget allocated to the economic development function in these areas. Even here, however, the 60 per cent share taken by the regulatory function suggests that planners have a powerful stake in creating a complicated administrative regime which is likely to stifle development or more specifically the *type of development which does not itself draw on the services of the local economic planners*. The most favourable budgetary strategy for metropo-litan planners, therefore, may be to lengthen and complicate the regulatory process, which discriminates against 'hum drum' projects carried out by small businesses, whilst at the same time lobbying for more resources to be spent on high profile re-development projects, managed by public/private partnerships, where the planning authority itself plays a central role (see Chapter 6). Within this context the current emphasis on a combined strategy of urban containment and brown-field redevelopment appears a particularly attractive option to urban planning interests. Non-metropolitan planning authorities, dominated as they are by regulatory functions have a powerful incentive to support a ratcheting up of the regulatory system and urban containment in particular. Metropolitan planners on the other hand, have a bureaucratic stake in supporting high profile brown-field reclamation schemes, especially where extra claims can be made on the public purse to fund these particular restoration projects.

Overall, it is not unfair to suggest that most aspects of the regulatory process act to discriminate against the transfer of land from agricultural to urban uses. Indeed, one of the most striking features of the contemporary British planning system is the virtual absence of any bureaucratic interests which would favour a greater level of urban and in particular residential development in rural areas. The only government agencies that have a direct stake in the provision of new developments are bodies such as the Housing Corporation and the Urban Development Corporations. Many of these bodies are, however, focused on urban regeneration rather than rural development. Within this context it is perhaps significant that the post-war decades to have witnessed the greatest amount of green-field development were the 1950s and 1960s, which corresponded with the highest levels of state involvement in the actual provision of new housing. In these circumstances, government housing bureaux were in a delivery/contract bureau format and their budgets were linked, in part at least, to the provision of new buildings (see Dunleavy, 1981). It has often been argued that government agencies have a tendency to be excluded from the controls governing the rest of the population (Di Lorenzo, 1987), a tendency which in the 1950s and 1960s may have acted as a counterbalance to the effect of growing regulation.[11]

As a parallel to this argument, consider the fortunes of the Department of Transport throughout the 1980s. The overall transport budget for this decade fared badly and the total programme was slightly smaller in real terms than under the Labour administration of 1979 (Cullingworth and Nadin, 1994, p. 233). The trunk roads budget element, however, where government contracts are destined for a highly mobilised lobby group (British Roads Federation), well able to secure post retirement positions and other perquisites for senior bureaucrats, fared disproportionately well, with spending on trunk roads 60 per cent higher in real terms for the year 1989 than a decade earlier. As Dowding (1995, pp. 114–15) reports, the then DoT, using highly dubious cost/benefit techniques, openly advocated the building of major roads projects such as the M3 extension which cut across designated AONB and SSSI and secretly promoted a strategy on behalf of the roads lobby of building 'bypasses' around towns, which often linked together to create major new roads. The overall effect on the rate of rural to urban conversion, however, was negligible, because transport planning permissions account for only about 3 per cent of total development proposals – compared to over 70 per cent (DoE Statistics of Planning Applications, 1994d) for residential developments where no such bureaucratic incentives appear to exist. In short, with the vast bulk of new housing development now supplied by the private sector, bureaucratic interests within the state are linked almost exclusively to the expansion of the regulatory regime. This is not to suggest that state provided housing should be seen as an answer to an institutionally biased planning system, but rather might be viewed as further evidence that state bureaucrats as a whole are far from selfless guardians of the public weal.

CONCLUSION

This chapter has sought to apply a public choice analysis to the behaviour of bureaucrats in the political market of British land use planning. Just as the operation of the planning system appears to reflect interest group incentive structures on the demand side, so too it would seem to be influenced by bureaucratic incentives on the supply side. It is implausible to suggest that planning bureaucrats have been wholly responsible for the growth of regulation, but it would be equally implausible to maintain that planners' actions have played no part in this process. A political response to the growth of the environmental lobby may account for some of the increase in regulatory expenditure, but the sheer scale and consistent nature of this growth, combined with evidence of rapid cost escalation, suggests that the peculiar set of incentives within land use agencies may be responsible for the enormity of this expansion.

In so far as these public choice conclusions represent the actual behaviour of public sector bureaucrats within the land use planning system they also challenge the normative foundations of contemporary planning theory. Public sector bureaucrats clearly have interests of their own, both material and non-material and it is the pursuit of these interests within the institutions of the planning system that may be responsible for the policy outputs, such as urban containment that are observed. The behaviour of bureaucrats within the British planning system does not seem to be based on the neutral evaluation techniques espoused by the cost/benefit theorists, or the impartial mediation of the collaborative planning enthusiasts. Planners clearly do consult with interest groups but these groups tend also to be the very interests that share the bureaucratic interest in expanding the regulatory regime. There is little evidence to suggest that planners seriously consider the interests of those groups, such as the consumers and small developers, who may have an interest in reducing the scope of regulation but for the reasons outlined in Chapter 3, have no effective political representation. There is, however, evidence to support the view that the actions of planners are based, in part at least, on the pursuit of individual self interest, manifested in an ongoing process of bureaucratic and regula-tory growth.

5

PLANNING AND THE
POLITICAL MARKET
Voter-Centred versus
Special-Interest Explanations[1]

INTRODUCTION

The previous two chapters have suggested that the development of the British planning system has owed much to the forces of special interest politics on the 'demand side' of the political market in planning and a tendency towards bureaucratic expansionism on the 'supply side'. That the evolution of land use planning has coincided with the interests of rent seeking groups and bureaucrats, however, is not sufficient evidence of a *causal* link between the actions of these groups and the policies that have been adopted. The surge of public interest in environmentalism that has occurred over recent years has undoubtedly played an important role in the British government's commitment to the further development of the land use planning system. Amidst growing public pressure for environmental protection the government has loaded additional responsibilities onto the planning system and has reinforced its commitment to long established policies such as urban containment. It may, therefore, be a mistake to attribute policy developments within the British planning system to the exercise of special interest power. Public choice theory is itself, divided over the relative degrees of power that are exercised by the general electorate and special interests within the political marketplace. 'Voter-centred' approaches based on the Downsian theory of electoral competition emphasise the significance of macro-electoral processes and in particular the power of public opinion to influence the processes of policy formation (Downs, 1957). Special interest theories reflected in the tradition of the Virginia school, by contrast, are sceptical of the ability of the general electorate to exert effective control over politicians, bureaucrats and special interest coalitions (Buchanan and Tullock, 1962, 1982).

This chapter seeks to evaluate the relative significance of macro-electoral and special interest forces in the political market of planning. Having outlined the major theoretical concepts, which inform the different branches of public choice theory, the chapter presents empirical evidence examining the politics of planning and in particular urban containment, through the lenses of the voter-centred and special interest schools. The analysis suggests that whilst macro-electoral shifts have provided the context for the continued growth of urban planning controls, there is sufficient evidence to suggest that special interest forces have been a key factor affecting the form and content of British land-use planning. In doing so, the chapter questions the extent to which the political process is subject to effective democratic control and offers additional support for the analysis of structural bias within the political market put forward in Chapters 3 and 4.

PUBLIC CHOICE AND LEGISLATIVE BEHAVIOUR: ACCOUNTABILITY OR GOVERNMENT FAILURE?

In public choice theory, politicians are viewed as self-interested actors who choose among alternative courses of policy action according to the relative set of rewards offered by each. These rewards may include such things as income, social status, patronage power, perquisites of office or the satisfaction derived from the implementation of a personal ideological project. Whatever the motivations of politicians the fulfilment of their goals is, to a significant extent, dependent on their maintaining a position in elected office. In order to secure re-election, therefore, politicians must 'supply' legislation to the electorate in exchange for a combination of votes, favourable publicity, campaign con-tributions and other forms of political support.

One of the major advances in political science in the last century was provided by Downs (1957) in his analysis of electoral competition. Downs was the founding father of voter-centred public choice theory and with his 'median voter theorem', offered a highly attractive view of the political process, closely in accord with pluralist conceptions of democratic accountability. According to Downs, assuming that voters' opinions are evenly spread out along an ideological spectrum, a party that wants to win an election should offer a policy platform which appeals to the voter with exactly as many voters on one side of her as on the other, i.e. the median position. In these circumstances, the best that another party can do in order to increase its electoral appeal is to come as close as possible to the policies offered by the opposing party. As a result, parties will converge in policy space, offering almost identical bundles of policies to the electorate in order to attract the maximum level of support. This simple analysis is, of course, appropriate under only very restrictive circumstances[2] but it does go a long way to explain the observed sensitivity of politicians to opinion polls (Forman, 1985; McLean, 1982, 1985; Kuran, 1991) and the tendency for parties to move towards the centre of the political spectrum, especially when an election is imminent (Forman, 1985; McLean, 1982, 1985).

More sophisticated voter-centred analyses, which draw on developments in social choice theory (Arrow, 1951; Black, 1958) also point to a similar logic. The basic Downsian account assumes that the policy space in which politicians operate is *uni-dimensional*, i.e. that the opinions of the electorate can be ranked along a single scale – from left wing to right wing, for example. In practice, however, policy space in most societies is *multi-dimensional* in nature. Of itself, this need not alter the view that politicians will converge on the position of the median voter – *assuming that a median position can be found* (Enelow and Hinich, 1984). Unless, however, opinion is distributed in an implausibly symmetrical way (so that every voter who stands on one side on each issue is matched by another who stands on the opposite on every single issue), then *no such median position exists*. A fundamental result in social choice theory (Arrow, 1951; Black, 1958) is that stable majorities typically exist when politics takes place over a single issue dimension, but majorities are almost always unstable when politics takes place over multiple issue dimensions (Riker and Ordeshook, 1973; Riker 1982, chapter 7). Under multi-dimensional conditions the set of winning platforms will be 'cyclical', where there is almost always the chance of a new set of policy bundles gaining support against the status quo.

Building on this analysis, Riker (1982, chapter 9, 1984) suggests that politicians, and especially those who are the current losers in the political process, have a constant incentive to seek out those issues which might be used to break up the existing winning coalition. The greater the number of issue dimensions, the more likely is cycling and as a result the greater are the opportunities to mobilise different bundles of policies to defeat the status quo. A primary implication of this theory ('heresthetics' to use Rikerian terminology) is that politicians will be eager to detect emergent trends in public opinion, seeking out new emphases in policy which will bring about increased support as the basis of a new winning coalition, without alienating their core supporters (Riker, 1982, 1984). As a result, elections are especially prone to agenda manipulation, with the winners being the politicians best able to promote those issues, which might break up existing coalitions.

In contrast to the rosy picture of democratic accountability painted by the voter-centred perspective, the Virginia school of public choice offers an account of the legislative process that is distinctly less optimistic about the prospects for effective voter control over elected representatives. According to this perspective, rather than seek support from the unorganised mass of the electorate, politicians cater to the demands expressed by majority coalitions of special interest groups. In Virginia public choice, a special interest issue is defined as one that generates substantial personal benefits for a relatively small number of constituents, whilst imposing a small individual cost on a larger number of other voters. Politicians 'supply' legislation, which concentrates benefits on special interest groups and attempt to win elections by putting together coalitions of such groups or 'rent seekers', by making promises in order to secure their support (Buchanan and Tullock, 1962, 1982; MacAvoy, 1965; Poole, 1985; Bartel and Thomas, 1987).

Seen through the lens of the Virginia school, there are structural reasons why the general electorate is unlikely to constitute an effective countervailing force and why political markets are less likely to be subject to electoral control than are private markets to the sovereignty of consumers. The first of these reasons is a direct consequence of the significant difference in the nature of private and of public choice – the 'bundle purchase' nature of voting in political markets (Aranson, 1990; Kuran, 1991; Tullock, 1989, 1993). Voters cannot shop around among an array of different policy options and political parties in the same way that private consumers may choose between different bundles of goods in the private market. Rather, voters must elect a politician who will represent them across the full range of issues occupying the political spectrum and there is little capacity for the voter to 'exit' from unwanted policies when compared to the availability of exit from unwanted products in the private market (Hirschman, 1970). Political parties, therefore, have considerable discretion to push through policies that are relatively unpopular because of the extremely limited choice of policy bundles and scope for 'exit' that is available to the electorate at large.

Second, most voters are 'rationally ignorant' of the specifics of policy implementation. An informed public is an essential prerequisite for democratic accountability, yet according to the Virginia school there are precious few incentives for the bulk of the population to invest in the acquisition of political information. Because the impact of any one individual on the policy process is so small, it is simply not worth the time and effort of becoming politically informed on other than the most superficial level (Aranson, 1990; Tullock, 1993).[3] This phenomenon applies equally to individuals who are 'civic minded' in their outlook as it does to those who are interested in purely material goals. From a Virginia school perspective, even an altruistic person would not rationally devote much time to acquiring political information for the sake of casting an informed vote, since in a large electorate the chance that her own vote will be decisive, is minuscule (Riker and Ordeshook, 1968). A rationally civic minded person may be better off spending time and effort where her own contribution can have a demonstrable effect – by helping an elderly neighbour, for example, rather than trying to become politically informed. It is as a result of such rational ignorance that most voters tend to rely on crude party identification strategies and ideological sloganising for the bulk of their political information.

Empirical research from both the United States and Western Europe suggests that even on relatively high profile issues, the vast majority of voters are ignorant of even the most basic political information (Campbell et al., 1960; Converse, 1964; Converse and Pierce, 1986; Graham, 1988; Page and Shapiro, 1992). In a survey conducted during the 1992 US Presidential Election, for example, Holbrook and Garand (1996, p. 361 quoted in Somin, 1998, p. 421) found that the overwhelming majority of respondents could not estimate the inflation or unemployment rate within 5 per cent of the actual levels. Similarly, some 70 per cent of the American electorate could not name either of their state's senators, and an average 56 per cent could not name *any* congressional candidate in their district at the height of an election campaign (Delli Carpini and Keeter, 1996, p. 94, quoted in Somin, 1998, p. 417 – for similar results in France see Converse and Pierce, 1986).

From a Virginia school perspective, such rational ignorance is crucial to the political market because the extent of political ignorance affects the ability of special interests to obtain wealth transfers from the public at large. Where voters are rationally ignorant and special interests supply misinformation then the electoral process may not be reflective of *underlying* voter preferences but of *manipulated* voter preferences. Special interests groups may disseminate biased information and may exploit the inability of a rationally ignorant public to discern the existence of rent seeking behaviour. If rational ignorance is extensive even on such high profile issues as unemployment and the rate of inflation then it is likely to be even more severe the more remote the issues are from the immediate public eye (Somin, 1998). Rents, which occur through the indirect mechanism of regulation, may be particularly prone to voter ignorance, as is the case when government controls restrict entry into a market increasing the profits of the incumbent firms. Whereas wealth transfers extracted directly from the electorate by way of taxation may eventually become visible to voters and may lead to an eventual reduction in taxes (Becker, 1983, 1985), it is difficult for the individual voter to attribute higher prices to the existence of regulation, because no direct transfer of wealth appears to have taken place (Tullock, 1989, 1993).[4]

The ability of special interests to manipulate the preferences of the electorate may also be aided by the absence of opposing groups within the political market. As chapter 3 showed, the logic of collective action suggests that competition amongst interest groups, introduces significant bias into political markets. This bias is a product of asymmetric access to political influence, reflective of the differential impact of the free-rider problem. Diffuse interests such as taxpayers, consumers and certain elements within the environmental lobby are often severely disadvantaged by collective action problems, where the contribution of the millions of potential members is so discounted by the irrelevance of an individual contribution to supply, that there is a powerful incentive to free-ride. (Olson, 1965; Tullock, 1989, 1993). According to the Virginia school, even if these interests do not remain completely latent as a result of selective incentives, legislators are less likely to respond to their demands because the high dispersion of benefits produces a low per capita stake, unlikely to be perceived as a major source of political support (Buchanan and Tullock, 1962, 1982; Tullock, 1989, 1993). Concentrated groups with a higher per capita stake may, therefore, be disproportionately influential because their members may be more likely to switch political allegiance over those issues that affect their personal wealth in a direct and substantial way.

Finally, the tendency towards special interest capture may be particularly pronounced where segments of the public bureaucracy have an economic stake in supporting special interests in their pursuit of favourable subsidies and regulations (Niskanen, 1971, 1975, 1995). Indeed, bureaucratic support for special interests may well be a more significant factor than their voting or financial strength to politicians alone. Bureaucrats are monopoly suppliers of regulation and services and may use this privileged position to push through policies favourable to special interests, irrespective of any wider political demand. In this case, politicians have comparatively little incentive to put downward pressure on expenditure and regulatory growth, or to monitor regulator 'capture' because any cost savings will be thinly dispersed across the voting population, minimising per capita gains and the associated electoral rewards (Niskanen, 1971, 1995).

PUBLIC CHOICE THEORY AND THE POLITICAL MARKET IN PLANNING

For public choice theory, the key to understanding political phenomena is to locate the incentive structures that face the key agents within the political market. In the specific case of the British planning system, what are the structures of costs and benefits facing voters, interest groups, bureaucrats and politicians from the continued growth of urban planning controls? In this section an attempt is made to evaluate the different branches of public choice theory in order to asses the extent to which developments in the British planning system are a response to macro-electoral and special interest forces.

From the perspective of voter-centred public choice, the major factor underlying the willingness of governments to expand the planning system is likely to have been the rising support within the general electorate for an increase in environmental regulation, of which policies such as urban containment policy have been a contingent part. This analysis posits an incentive structure that compels rival political parties to converge in policy space on a unique and stable equilibrium, which reflects the environmental preferences of the median voter.

Most accounts of British environmental politics stress the relatively recent arrival of environmental issues on the political agenda, with the late 1960s and early 1970s widely recognised as the period when environmental concern emerged as a potentially significant political issue. Indeed, it was not until the General Election of 1970 that the major political parties even referred to the term 'environmental policy' in their election manifestos and the creation of the Department of the Environment in that same year was the first time any kind of central responsibility for the environment had been established (McCormick, 1991, Chapter 1; Robinson, 1992, Chapter 1). Even so, there was little indication that environmental issues ranked significantly highly with the mass of the electorate, at least in relation to the more traditional electoral battlegrounds focused on the delivery of welfare services, unemployment, economic policy and defence (Butler and Stokes,1974).

Throughout the 1970s and up to the election of Margaret Thatcher's Conservative administration in May 1979, environmental issues maintained their position on the political stage but there was no indication that they might make a significant enough breakthrough to affect the general electoral support of the major political parties (McCormick, 1991; Robinson, 1992). In her initial period of office, Mrs Thatcher's government continued to show relatively little interest in environmental matters, but from the mid to late 1980s onwards and into the subsequent Major administration, this position was to change radically. McCormick (1991) highlights the now famous speech given by the Prime minister to the Royal Society in September 1988, in which she highlighted the potentially disastrous consequences of global warming, the emission of ozone depleting gases and continued population growth, as the turning point in the Conservative approach. Prior to this speech, the Thatcher administration had been preoccupied with economic policy and in particular its drive to stimulate economic revival through a policy of 'rolling back the state'.

The movement towards a more pro-active stance on the environment appears to have been stimulated by a series of events, which included public reaction to some of the government's own policies, the emergence of the environmental issue on the public agenda following high profile international environmental disasters and pressure from external authorities such as the European Union and the United Nations (Rawcliffe, 1998). All told, the combined effect of these internal and external forces was to shift the environment from its position as a relatively 'fringe' issue, to the very centre of the political stage. Evidence of this shift is apparent from a variety of sources. Opinion polls conducted in the summer of 1989, found that more people (35 per cent) rated the environment as the top political issue than concern for the National Health Service (29 per cent) and unemployment (24 per cent) (McCormick, 1991, p. 151). Similarly, attitudinal research published in the reports on British Social Attitudes show a rapid rise in public recognition of environmental concerns from the mid 1980s onwards (Robinson, 1992). The membership of environmental organisations also witnessed unprecedented growth in the late 1980s with the combined membership of groups such as Greenpeace and Friends of the Earth increasing by almost half a million (McCormick, 1991; DoE, 1994c). Most significant of all, however, was the unexpectedly strong performance of the UK Green Party at the European Parliamentary Elections in June 1989. Having previously never managed to achieve more than 4.7 per cent of the vote in any sort of election (Local, General or European) the party polled almost 15 per cent, illustrating most graphically the shift in public concern (Robinson, 1992, p. 209).

According to voter-centred public choice, therefore, the shift in political salience of environmental issues, which culminated in the surge of interest in environmental protection concerns at the end of the 1980s, reflected a shift in the position of the median voter. This movement in public opinion forced vote-seeking politicians to adopt a stance predisposed to a growth in environmental regulation. Thus, the increase in land-use regulation witnessed under the Thatcher administration in the 1980s, reflected the recognition by the Conservative Party of the emergence of the environment as a key election issue, which it sought to exploit in an attempt to 'neutralise' a threat to its majority coalition. It was, in effect, a strategic response by the Conservatives to the apparently more pro-environment stances adopted by the Labour and Liberal Democrat parties during the earlier part of the decade. More recently, faced with Conservative opposition to high profile development proposals, the new Labour administration has sought to maintain its public image as a pro-environment party, by bringing forward proposals to restrict development on green-field sites (The Times, 28 January 1998). In each of these cases, the growth of planning regulations such as green belts is a response to the logic of a choice situation, which reflects the electoral pulling power of environmental issues with un-mobilised sections of the voting population and the electorate at large.

Whilst this voter-centred interpretation puts emphasis on the need for politicians to respond to macro-electoral forces, a Virginia School perspective suggests scepticism over the extent to which public opinion has indeed been the driving force in the growth of urban planning controls. A principal weakness of the voter-centred theory is the assumption that politicians are likely to perceive *equal* advantage from the adoption of environmental regulations, *irrespective of the issue concerned.* From a Virginia School perspective, however, it is possible to accept the view that public concern for the environment has pre-disposed politicians towards greater regulation, but to note also a peculiar special interest logic, which suggests a particular emphasis on planning and especially the policy of urban containment.

According to this Virginia School account, a key element in the special interest logic is the local amenity interest as represented by the Council for the Protection of Rural England (CPRE). As was noted in Chapter 3, the CPRE lobbies for the extension of statutory planning controls such as Green Belts and Areas of Outstanding Natural Beauty (AONBs), to prevent the transfer of land from rural uses such as agriculture to urban uses such as housing. The membership consists of 46,000 individual members and 2,574 home-owners/ amenity groups (average membership 200 – total affiliated members 560,000) organised around the protection of local property and amenity values. With its national office involved in a much wider campaign remit, covering more diffuse issues such as species and wildlife conservation, it would be inappropriate to caricature the CPRE as a purely 'nimbyist' organisation. From the perspective of the Virginia School, however, the tendency for urban containment policies to concentrate benefits (in terms of property and amenity values) on the site specific amenity interests it represents, may give the CPRE a structural advantage in the political process, with planning issues of a 'nimbyist' nature more likely to be seen by politicians as a source of special interest support.

Empirically, it is notoriously difficult to trace *any* impact of individual issues on voting behaviour in Britain (McLean, 1982). Given conditions of rational ignorance, most people cast their vote according to ideology and relatively crude party identifications, rather than on the details of any specific policy (Tullock, 1989; 1993). This problem of party identification is particularly relevant to an examination of the significance of 'nimbyist' votes, where the stance of all the major political parties has remained almost identical and there has been no opportunity to judge whether a switch in policy would indeed affect electoral fortunes. It is useful, however, to assume that some votes would shift in order to gain at least a degree of insight into what a political party might stand to lose, should it break from the consensus position.

Table 5.1   Green Belt Marginals in England: 1992–1997

Constituency	Majority	%	Winner	Second
Warrington S	190	0.30	Lab	Con
Bolton NE	185	0.38	Con	Lab
Halifax	478	0.83	Lab	Con
Slough	514	0.90	Con	Lab
Hazel Grove	929	1.07	Con	Lib
Dewsbury	634	1.09	Lab	Con
Cambridge	580	1.10	Lab	Con
Bury S	788	1.46	Con	Lab
Bolton W	1079	1.80	Con	Lab
Chester	1101	2.07	Con	Lab
Thurrock	1172	2.17	Lab	Con
Batley & Spen	1408	2.31	Con	Lab
Cannock	1506	2.46	Lab	Con
Cheltenham	1668	2.60	Lib	Con
Basildon	1480	2.75	Con	Lab
Nuneaton	1631	2.75	Lab	Con
Stockport	1422	3.00	Lab	Con

Notes: Lab = Labour, Con = Conservative, Lib = Liberal Democrat.
Source: Dods Parliamentary Companion – cross-referenced with local Green Belt boundaries.

Table 5.1 provides a possible indication of the potential significance of 'nimbyist' votes following the 1992 General Election. The 560,000 members of the local amenity lobby account for approximately 1.3 per cent of the total electorate. This membership is not, however, evenly spread throughout the country, with a focus in the 311 English non-metropolitan constituencies.[5] Assuming that membership is evenly spread throughout the non-metropolitan areas then the average non-metropolitan seat is likely to have approximately 1,800 voters, or 2.6 per cent with a local amenity affiliation.[6]

Following the 1992 General Election there were 17 seats within the Green Belt where, had 50 per cent or less of the local amenity lobby switched political allegiance, they could theoretically have affected the result of the election. With a majority of only 21 for the Conservatives for the 1992 Parliament, these seats would appear to have been highly significant to the electoral fortunes of both the Conservative and Labour parties, an analysis confirmed by the 1997 general election when all but two of these seats (Hazel Grove and Cheltenham Lib–Dem) fell to Labour.

In addition, to the possible direct incentive provided by nimbyist votes a large number of other MPs from constituencies with highly organised and vocal nimbyist interests, may have been more likely to prefer a 'quiet life' to the concentrated storm of protest and the potential image of unpopularity, should the ire of these interests be raised. Such processes are often associated with lobbying by local party workers and councillors concerned with the impact of planning issues at the local authority level. Elected politicians at the local level may, if anything, be even more susceptible to nimbyist pressure than their Westminster equivalents, because of the greater frequency of local council elections. Within this context, pressure from local party workers appears to have been a determining factor in the recent mobilisation of 200 backbench MPs (from all parties) drawn from rural marginals and market towns, to lobby for a reduction in the predicted requirement of 4.4 million new homes in the next 20 years (The Times, 26 January 1998).

The electoral power of the agricultural lobby must also be considered as an element within the special interest logic. The continual reliance of the farm sector on agricultural subsidy payments has provided farmers and especially tenants, with a vested interest in restricting the transfer of land out of agri-cultural uses (Elson, 1986; Marsden et al., 1993; Murdoch and Marsden, 1994). Although accounting for less than 1 per cent of the total electorate, the concentration of farmers in key rural constituencies may have lent them a considerable degree of political clout. Including farmers, farm-workers and their respective dependants in the agricultural interest, Howarth (1990) found that in 1970 there were some 50 seats where the farm vote was potentially pivotal. The number of politically significant seats has, however, since declined markedly, mirroring the fall in NFU membership. At the 1983 General Election there were only eight constituencies where the farming vote was pivotal and with NFU membership having declined further by the 1997 General Election, there were only a handful of seats where the farmers held political significance.[7] Given the much smaller Conservative majority in the run up to this election, however, the overall importance of these seats may have been somewhat higher.

To supplement its electoral influence, the farming lobby may also have been able to rely on the economic interest of MPs themselves. Table 5.2 depicts the representation of farmers within Parliament following the 1992 general election. What is particularly striking is the number of Conservative members who have themselves been active farmers and in many cases actually members of the NFU. The 40 farmers on the Conservative side in 1992 represented 12 per cent of the parliamentary Conservative Party (6 per cent of parliament as a whole), whereas the farming population itself accounted for a mere 0.55 per cent of the total electorate. It should, however, be noted that some of these MPs also have commercial and financial interests, so it is not clear that they would offer unswerving support for pro-containment policies. None the less, with such a high representation of farming interests in the legislature there may have been opportunities for Conservative members to support policies, which were not only in the economic interests of the farm lobby, but to their personal economic advantage as well.

Similarly, those Conservatives who are NFU members may have been more likely to prefer a quiet life to the antagonism that might have arisen should they

Table 5.2 Agricultural Interests in the House of Commons: 1992–1997

	Con	Lab	Lib Dem	Total
General*	28	10	2	40
Special Interest**	40	1	1	42
Total	68	11	3	82

*All members who list an unspecified interest in the agricultural industry.
**Includes all active farmers/large landowners, directors of agricultural firms and registered NFU members.
Source: Dods/Roth/Times/Vachers Parliamentary Companions and The Guardian, 8 May 1996.

have sought to shift the emphasis of policy away from urban containment and agricultural protection.

Construction interests in the house building industry and especially the larger corporate developers in the House Builders Federation (HBF) (3,500 members) represent a third group in the special interest coalition. They have relatively little incentive to lobby against the growth of planning controls, but rather seek to gain control of the regulatory process in order to restrict entry into the land development market (Rydin, 1986; Evans, 1988; 1991; Simmie, 1993). The electoral power of construction interests is, however, minimal given the relatively small number of member firms in the industry. It should, in theory be possible to include the construction workers unions in this category, but in practice, there would appear to be little in the way of benefit to building workers from any relaxation of planning controls. The major beneficiaries from a partial liberalisation would be the larger corporate firms able to realise the capital gains on their land banks.

Although the electoral power of building interests is limited it should be noted that construction interests have been major sources of financial contributions to the Conservative Party. Empirical research on political donations in the UK suggests that only a minority of business organisations supply campaign contributions, but of those that do, Mitchell and Bretting (1991) discovered that over 50 per cent were concentrated in either property and construction or in the tobacco industry. At present, however, the building lobby appears to be in a relatively weak position with respect to the conservation and agricultural lobbies and has been unable to achieve even the modest release of controlled land that its members would prefer.

The planning bureaucracy itself represents a further and perhaps crucial element in the special interest logic. As was shown in Chapter 4, the vast majority of expenditure on the land-use planning system is spent on the drafting of planning guidance, plan preparation and the enforcement of statutory regulations. The greater the number of land-use designations and the tighter and more complicated the regulatory regime the greater is the demand for staff and administrative expenses to supervise these regulations. Land-use planners, therefore, may have a powerful incentive to join with groups such as the CPRE in campaigning for additional regulation in order to boost their job security and budgets.

A final factor that may reinforce the position of the special interests is that there may be insufficient incentive for the losers from policies such as urban containment to mobilise within the political market. As Chapter 3 showed, the mass of consumers of new housing who accept higher priced, poorer quality and denser residential developments and the taxpayers who continue to pay the subsidies which keep land in agricultural production, are a large and diffuse set of interests who are often absent from the realm of organised politics. Moreover, it is very likely that these 'losing' interest groups are not even aware that rent-seeking activity is actually taking place. The transfer of benefits derived through the land use planning system is virtually invisible to the average voter, occurring as it does through the mechanism of regulation. Academic research may indicate that urban containment policies produce higher housing costs and other potentially negative effects, but given that such correlations are not immediately obvious to the voter, there may be little incentive to trace the source and magnitude of rent seeking exploitation.

From the perspective of the Virginia School, the structure of incentives within the political market continually pushes in the direction of tighter urban planning controls. More important, the elements making up this particular incentive structure are *often not present in many other environmental protection issues*. On the one hand, many environmental regulations might produce highly dispersed benefits. This would appear to be the case in areas such as air pollution control, or in attempts to control the environmental side-effects of subsidised farming, e.g. water pollution and loss of species diversity. In such cases the per capita benefit from regulatory growth is relatively small and may be less likely to be seen as a potential source of support than nimbyist issues, which concentrate benefits on identifiable groups (Webster, 1998). On the other hand, there are often concentrated economic lobbies who seek to resist regulation. The farming lobby, for example, may be willing to accept regulations that prevent the transfer of land from rural to urban uses, but it has vigorously resisted any attempts to introduce controls which limit the environmental impact of subsidised agriculture itself (Lowe et al., 1986; Winter, 1996; Pennington, 1996).

In addition, the economic interests of public sector bureaucrats are often not so unambiguously tied to the growth of controls. This may be especially so where bureaucrats have a stake in the expansion of activities with serious environmental side-effects, or where there is a regular exchange of staff between the bureaucracy and regulated industries. The welfare of bureaucrats in the Forestry Commission and the Ministry of Agriculture, Fisheries and Food (MAFF) is, for example, partly linked to the expansion of the forestry and agricultural industries (Pennington, 1996). According to the Virginia School, it is this difference in the logic of the choice situation that is likely to dispose politicians and bureaucrats towards a greater emphasis on land use planning and urban containment in particular, than other aspects of the environmental agenda where the special interest logic is missing.

CHOOSING BETWEEN VOTER-CENTRED AND SPECIAL INTEREST THEORIES

In order to evaluate which of the public choice perspectives best captures the underlying logic of the political market in planning, some empirical issues must be addressed. First, have politicians and bureaucrats indeed been more pro-active in the field of urban planning than other areas of environmental policy where the hypothesised special interest coalition is absent? And second, if politicians and bureaucrats have shown a greater willingness to enforce urban planning controls, has this merely reflected the focus of public opinion (as the voter-centred theory would suggest) or have other environmental concerns been more significant in the public mind? If the focus on containment reflects special interest power then it must first be established that public opinion has been focused to a lesser (or no greater) extent on containment than other environmental issues.

Turning to the first of these questions, a variety of evidence indicates that politicians and bureaucrats *have* been more eager to support urban planning controls than other areas of environmental regulation. Throughout the 1980s and 1990s there was a substantial growth in land-use planning controls. The area of Green Belt, for example, more than doubled from 1.7 to 4.2 million acres between 1979 and 1994, to account for 14 per cent of the land area of England (Cullingworth and Nadin, 1994). Similarly, by the early 1990s the Conservative government had announced a moratorium on the construction of new settlements in rural areas, committed itself to the building of at least 55 per cent of new homes on so-called brown-field sites in existing urban centres and introduced stringent controls on the construction of out-of-town shopping developments. Correspondingly, legislation contained in the 1990 Town and Country Planning Act and the 1991 Planning and Compensation Act, laid down a framework of a 'plan-led' development control, widely believed to have strengthened the regulatory hand of planners against development pressure (Healey, 1992; Cullingworth and Nadin, 1994). This ongoing push towards ever more restrictive urban land-use regulation was reflected, in part at least, by the 1980s recording the lowest level of rural to urban land conversion at any time since the war – 5,000 ha between 1980 and 1990 compared with a rate of 30,000 ha in the 1960s (Cullingworth and Nadin, 1994). Statutory designations, such as Green Belts and Areas of Outstanding Natural Beauty, now account for almost 50 per cent of the land area of England and Wales, and with refusal rates for planning applications in these areas running at between 85 and 100 per cent it has become increasingly difficult for developers to obtain planning permission to develop housing in the countryside (Simmie, 1993, p. 112). Between 1986 and 1990, for example, over 200 planning applications were submitted for the construction of 'new settlements' in rural areas, but only seven of these were finally granted with planning permission (Pennington, 1997a, p. 186).

The growth in land-use regulations highlighted above reflects a longer, historical focus on statutory regulation in the field of urban planning with the British planning system effectively nationalising the rights to develop land for urban uses (Cullingworth and Nadin, 1994). Whilst there has undoubtedly been a more general growth in environmental regulation in recent years (Gray, 1995), there is evidence to suggest that this growth has been more uncertain and less rigorously enforced than in the case of urban planning controls and specifically the policy of urban containment. There has, in particular, been a tendency to rely on a 'voluntary' approach to regulation with a lesser emphasis on statutory controls. The most striking example of this 'voluntary' approach can be seen in the continued reluctance of the British government to regulate the environmental consequences of subsidised farming, in spite of evidence that this is one of the most environmentally destructive forms of land-use. Young (1995) has described policy developments in this area as akin to 'running up the down escalator'. Following the Wildlife and Countryside Acts (1981; 1985) and the 1986 Agriculture Act, government policy has remained a hotch-potch of subsidised voluntary conservation programmes, such as the Environmentally Sensitive Areas Scheme, paid for with additional outlays of tax revenue, leaving most forms of agricultural development, (such as the drainage of wetlands and water pollution), outside the scope of statutory planning controls. Environmental campaigners have complained of the continuing damages wrought by agricultural production to Sites of Special Scientific Interest (SSSIs) and have repeatedly argued for the introduction of statutory regulation over agricultural uses. Successive governments, including the new Labour administration have, however, continued to resist such pressures preferring instead to rely on a 'voluntary' approach. Rather than introduce planning controls on farm operations politicians, under pressure from the farm lobby and the MAFF, have sought to pay additional subsidies to 'persuade' farmers not to damage wildlife and habitats (Lowe et al., 1986; McCormick, 1991; Winter, 1996; Pennington, 1996).

A similar pattern is discernible in other areas where the environmental interest is diffuse and where bureaucratic interests within the state have an economic stake in resisting regulation. Pennington (1996, pp. 37–9), for example, has noted the continued ability of the Forestry Commission and other forestry companies to resist the imposition of planning controls on industrial forest plantations, in spite of their well known environmental side-effects. The Forestry Commission as a part of the state bureaucracy, is itself one of the largest landowners in the country with a budgetary interest in avoiding regulation. In addition, there has traditionally been an extremely close relationship between the Commission and corporate forestry interests with a continual transfer of staff between the major firms and the bureaucracy (Stewart, 1987; Winter, 1996).

Turning to the area of pollution control, Skea (1995) argues that the UK government's position on the reduction of sulphur dioxide emissions has continued to be driven by the cost considerations of the major economic actors and in particular the electricity generating companies (a concentrated interest); the government has been reluctant to increase targets for sulphur dioxide reductions for fear of closing down the remaining coal-fired electricity generators. Writing in a similar vein, Jordan (1993) highlights the haphazard and incremental implementation of integrated pollution control and the pronounced tendency toward regulatory capture by industrial interests. This continues a longer tradition of 'arms-length', or 'voluntary' regulation by bodies such as Her Majesty's Inspectorate of Pollution (HMIP) where there has been a regular exchange of staff with the regulated industries. In these cases, even when regulatory controls have been increased (as with the 1995 Environment Protection Act and the creation of the Environment Agency), the record of enforcement has tended to be poor (Jordan, 1993; Smith, 1997; Gouldson and Murphy, 1998).

In the area of urban air pollution, Barde and Button (1990), and Button (1995), examine the lack of a coherent strategy to reduce the emission of transport related pollutants. According to these authors, UK transport policy continues to be dominated by short-term policy solutions aimed at localised problems such as noise (where there is a local amenity/ nimby element), to the neglect of a broader approach aimed at the reduction of transport externalities such as the introduction of road pricing (where there is not a local amenity/ nimby element). Rydin (1998a), who highlights the reluctance of policy makers at both the national and the local level to act in order to improve urban air quality, has confirmed this analysis. In so far as there have been movements to curtail excessive road use – as with the apparent death of the roads programme in the last years of the Major administration – these appear to have been driven by the inability of the then Department of Transport to secure funds from the Treasury and the existence of the very sort of concentrated 'nimbyist' activity against road building that has arguably contributed to the more general emphasis on urban containment (Cherry, 1996).

From the perspective of the Virginia School, the continued growth of urban planning controls compared with the more 'voluntary' approach to regulation elsewhere, confirms the suspicion that urban containment exhibits a special interest logic, absent from other environmental protection areas. In order to strengthen this argument with respect to the voter-centred alternative, however, it is necessary to examine whether public opinion and concern for environmental protection has itself focused on the land-use planning system and the reinforcement of urban containment.

Whilst the surge of interest in 'the environment' witnessed towards the end of the 1980s appears to have now waned, environmental issues continue to rank well above the levels of public concern registered in the early 1980s (Jordan and

Maloney 1997). It is also apparent that public opinion as a whole is, to a large extent, opposed to any relaxation of containment policies. Indeed, during the last decade, opposition to development on green-field sites appears to have strengthened. The British Social Attitudes surveys conducted in 1986 and 1996, specifically asked members of the public for their opinion on the development of new housing on green field sites. In 1986, 64 per cent of respondents suggested that such development should either be discouraged or stopped altogether. By 1996, this figure had risen to 70 per cent. These findings were confirmed in the response to similar questions for the 1992 British Election Study, the results of which are reported in Table 5.3.

It should be noted, however, that public perceptions of rural urbanisation and the loss of countryside to housing may themselves have been manipulated by special interests taking advantage of the rational ignorance effect. Thus, as Cullingworth (1988, p.184) notes, survey evidence also indicates that two thirds of the population believe that 65 per cent or more of the UK is now devoted to

Table 5.3 Attitudes to House Building in Rural Areas

Response	Number	Percentage
New house building in the countryside should be:		
Stopped Altogether	155	10.0%
Discouraged	829	54.0%
Don't Mind	349	22.7%
Encouraged	199	13.0%
Don't know	5	0.3%
No Answer	0	0.0%
Total	1537	
Britain Has Gone Too Far/Not Far Enough, Building New Houses in Rural Areas?		
Gone Much Too Far	81	5.1%
Gone Too Far	542	35.1%
About Right	612	39.6%
Not Gone Far Enough	257	16.6%
Not Gone Nearly Far Enough	33	2.1%
Don't Know	17	0.3%
No Answer	2	0.0%
Total	1544	

Note: Percentages may not sum to 100 due to rounding.
Source: Computed From 1992 British Election Study Panel Survey, ESRC Data Archive, University of Essex.

urban land-uses, when the actual figure is a mere 11 per cent. The data presented in Table 5.4 would certainly appear to confirm that the views of special interests and especially the CPRE lobby are disproportionately represented in terms of coverage in the printed media. As Chapter 3 suggested, this is not at all surprising given the severe collective action problems facing many of those who would stand to gain from a more liberal policy stance. This raises the possibility that were members of the public to be better informed of the current position they may have a preference for higher levels of new development.

Setting aside the possibility that environmental preferences have been manipulated by special interests, the available survey evidence would appear to indicate a clear public preference in favour of urban containment. Significantly, however, it *does not* suggest, that the public rates this issue as highly as other aspects of the environmental agenda which have received less political and bureaucratic attention and which continue to be governed by a voluntary approach to regulation. As Table 5.5 shows, in both 1989 and 1996 urban containment/ loss of green belt land, ranked well down the top 20 environmental issues which most worried members of the public. Other issues and in particular those focused on various aspects of atmospheric and water based pollution consistently rated above the loss of green belt land as the issues at the centre of public environmental concern. Indeed, 'urban' environmental issues, such as concerns over traffic fumes and congestion (which may have been exacerbated by containment policies), appear to have ranked more highly than those focused on the loss of green-field sites yet these have historically been the areas where policy action has been minimal. Similarly, the loss of trees and hedges associated

Table 5.4 Interest Groups, The Media and Urban Containment

Interest Group	No. of articles on Containment	Coverage A	Coverage B	Coverage C
CPRE	50	16	31	3
HBF	12	3	8	1
FoE	10	3	6	1
RTPI	5	0	5	0
TCPA	5	1	4	0
NFU	4	0	4	0
CLA	4	0	5	0
RICS	2	0	2	0
BEC	2	0	2	0

Notes: A = article with no spokesperson presenting contrary views.

B = article with discussion of contrary views.

C = article with no spokesperson to defend the groups' views.

Source: Financial Times Media Database (FT Profile), May 1992–February 1995.

Table 5.5 The Distribution of Public Environmental Concern 1989 and 1996
Percentage of People Who Were Worried About:

		1989	1996
1	Chemical Pollution of Rivers & Seas	64	65
2	Sewage on Beaches	59	61
3	Toxic Waste	–	60
4	Radioactive Waste	58	60
5	Oil Spills	53	56
6	Traffic Fumes	33	48
7	Ozone Depletion	56	46
8	Loss of Plants & Animals	–	45
9	Traffic Congestion	–	42
10	Fumes & Smoke From Factories	34	41
11	Loss of Trees & Hedgerows	34	40
12	Drinking Water Quality	41	39
13	Loss of Green Belt Land	27	38
14	Global Warming	44	35
15	Fouling by Dogs	29	34
16	Effects of Livestock Methods	–	33
17	Acid Rain	40	31
18	Litter and Rubbish	33	30
19	Over-fishing of the seas	–	30
20	Smoking in Public Places	–	28

Source: Attitudes to the Environment Survey: Department of Environment, Transport and the Regions (1997), London, HMSO.

with subsidised farming has rated at least as highly as concerns over urban development, but this area too has remained largely exempt from regulatory control.

It might be suggested that it is the previously rigorous enforcement of urban planning controls that explains the relative lack of concern over containment in relation to those areas which have seen a historically weaker policy stance. This does not explain adequately, however, why it is that containment has remained a focus of regulatory growth over the last decade, when areas such as urban air pollution and the effects of subsidised farming have tended to receive relatively less political attention and continue to rely on a 'voluntary' approach. Macro-electoral forces may indeed have provided a favourable context for the continued growth of urban planning controls, but from a Virginia School perspective it is the presence of the special interest logic, which provides the *critical* spur to political and bureaucratic action.

Overall, the evidence is supportive of a Virginia school interpretation, but to complete the analysis it is necessary to consider whether the elements of the special interest coalition do indeed have the capacity to exert political influence. The evidence presented earlier suggested that special interests in the nimbyist and agricultural lobbies have had at least some potential to supply benefits, electoral or otherwise to politicians. Given the overwhelming role of party identification in determining electoral behaviour, however, it seems unlikely that it is the ability to sway a few additional votes or other benefits over the containment issue, which is the only factor at play. This is especially so, because in 'British style' parliamentary systems, policy change is initiated almost entirely by the government (cabinet) and by the bureaucracy, rather than by individual MPs (Jordan and Richardson, 1987; Dowding, 1995). A more complete explanation of the peculiar emphasis on containment, therefore, would also point to the coincidence of special interest demands with those of the planning bureaucracy itself.

Under conditions of rational voter ignorance, politicians within the government have relatively little incentive to scrutinise the actions of their bureaucratic agencies, because voters tend to be informed about the content of policy at the level of political rhetoric only (Niskanen, 1975, 1995; Tullock, 1989, 1993). Beneath senior politicians' environmental sloganising, therefore, bureaucrats have considerable discretion to support those interest groups and policies, which are favourable to their own preferences and budgets, irrespective of whether these accord with the underlying distribution of public environmental concern. Bureaucrats may also use their monopoly position to inflate the political significance of those interest groups which will aid their pursuit of higher budgets, whilst resisting pressure from those who threaten bureaucratic turf. This may often occur where bureaucrats are themselves responsible for the drafting of policy documents. Rather than monitoring rent seeking behaviour, politicians themselves may fuel the tendency towards bureaucratic and special interest capture by seeking to ensure that resources are devoted towards their most influential constituent groups. In these circumstances, institutional 'checking' mechanisms, such as scrutiny committees, may become dominated by representatives of the groups they are supposed to be monitoring (Spiller, 1990; Alston and Spiller, 1992; Shepsle and Weingast, 1987; Weingast and Marshall, 1988).

Evidence of the relative failure of politicians to scrutinise the behaviour of bureaucratic agencies in Britain and of special interest penetration is apparent in the House of Commons Select Committee System. The twelve parliamentary select committees were established in 1979 in order 'to examine the expenditure, administration and policy of the principal government departments and associated public bodies.' Compared with the US Congressional system, the British select committees are relatively weak bodies – they are devoid of law making powers and unlike their American counterparts, cannot attach amendments to proposals emanating from the executive. In so far as they do have powers of scrutiny, however, these appear to reflect the principal agent problem between politicians and the bureaucracy and the tendency towards special interest control.

As Drewry (1985) discovered in the most comprehensive study of the committee system to date,

> 'Committees have not used their financial powers to undertake regular and systematic inquiries into public spending and ... have made it clear that they are not prepared to undertake regular and complete scrutiny of the main public spending estimates each year as a matter of routine. (Robinson, 1985, in Drewry, p. 307).

Indeed, far from seeking to provide an institutional check on public expenditure, according to Robinson (1985) eight out of the 12 committees could be categorised as 'unremitting spenders' of public money. This failure of the select committees to monitor bureaucratic behaviour effectively is not surprising given the pattern of committee membership. Studies suggest that the system is dominated by MPs representing special interest groups with a substantial stake in the deliberations of the relevant committee. Judge's (1991) analysis of the Trade and Industry Select Committee, for example, showed that membership was drawn disproportionately from industrial constituencies or those sponsored by manufacturing trades unions. In the specific case of land use planning there is evidence to suggest a bias in the membership of the relevant committees towards the special interest coalition representing the nimbyist and agricultural lobbies. Table 5.6 and 5.7 display the membership structures of the environment and agriculture select committees respectively.

The DoE/DETR has a much wider policy scope than environmental protection, including matters such as local government finance and with so many policy areas encompassed within this jurisdiction it is difficult to detect any systematic trend towards the selection of particular economic or electoral interests. Nonetheless, a general bias in favour of non-metropolitan or rural con-stituencies is detectable on the environment select committee. MPs representing English metropolitan constituencies – defined by the Times Parliamentary Companion as those seats falling within the boundaries of the old metropolitan authorities – accounted for an average 28 per cent of members on the environ-ment committee throughout the period in question, ranging from a high point of 36 per cent in 1991 and 1993, to a low of 10 per cent in 1995. This compares with a 41 per cent (213 out of 523) representation of metropolitan constituencies in the House of Commons as a whole, the remaining 59 per cent being non-metropolitan, shire county seats.[8] At no point in the decade 1985–1995,there-fore, were the metropolitan areas accorded a degree of representation in line with their parliamentary numbers.

This same pattern is discernible on both sides of the party divide. With the exception of 1985, when two Conservative members were drawn from metro-politan seats, Conservative representation in terms of these constituencies has been below the average for the parliamentary party as a whole. Metropolitan representation was 16.6 per cent, 14.2 per cent, 14.2 per cent, 0 per cent and 0 per cent for the years 1987, 1989, 1991, 1993 and 1995 respectively, whilst

Table 5.6 Membership of the House of Commons Environment Select Committee

1985	1987	1989
Rossi (C) *M*	Rossi (C) *M*	Rossi (C) *M*
Alexander (C)	Bellingham (C)*	Bellingham (C)*
Chapman (C) *M*	Holt (C)	Holt (C)
Jones (C)	Jones (C)	Jones (C)
Mackay (C)	Hunter (C)*	Hunter (C)*
Miscampbell (C)	Mans (C)	Mans (C)
Pike (C)	Squire (C)	Squire (C)
Roberts (L)	Pendry (L) *M*	Pendry (L) *M*
Mark-Taylor (L)	Pike (L)	Pike (L)
Smith (L) *M*	Cummings (L)	Cummings (L)
	Boateng (L) *M*	Boateng (L) *M*

1991	1993	1995
Rossi (C) *M*	Jones (C)	Ainsworth (C)
Bellingham (C)*	Clifton-Browne (C)*	Clifton-Browne (C)*
Holt (C)	Field (C)	Dover (C)
Hunter (C)*	Streeter (C)	Elletson (C)
Mans (C)	Pickles (C)	Patnick (C)
Steen (C)	Thomason (C)	Thomason (C)
Pendry (L) *M*	Raynsford (L) *M*	Stephen (L)
Lewis (L) *M*	Jackson (L) *M*	Gerrard (L) *M*
Pike (L)	Barron (L) *M*	Olner (L)
Howells (L)	Bennet (L) *M*	Taylor (LD)
Summerson (L) *M*		

Key: C = Conservative, L = Labour, LD = Liberal Democrat.
* = Active Farmer, *M* = Metropolitan Seat.
Source: Dods/Times/Vachers Parliamentary Companions.

the percentage of the Conservative parliamentary party accounted for by such seats in the equivalent years was 28 per cent, 26 per cent, 26 per cent, 21 per cent and 21 per cent. On the Labour side, meanwhile, metropolitan seats accounted for over 70 per cent of the parliamentary party throughout the period, but only in 1993 was a comparable level of representation achieved (when all Labour members were from metropolitan seats). In short, the membership of the environment select committee appears to have exhibited a distinct bias towards the non-metropolitan shire counties.

In the case of the agriculture committee, the direction of membership bias is even more clear. Between 1985 and 1995 there was consistently a 25–30 per

Table 5.7   Membership of the House of Commons Agriculture Select Committee

1985	1987	1989
Spence (C)*	Wiggin (C)*	Wiggin (C)*
Body (C)	Body (C)	Alexander (C)
Harris (C)	Alexander (C)	Boswell (C)*
Hunter (C)*	Hunter (C)*	Marland (C)*
Spicer (C)	Winterton (C)	Winterton (C)
McQuarrie (C)	Torney (L) *M*	Martlew (L)
Maynard (L) *M*	Maynard (L) *M*	Morley (L)
Nicholson (L)	Nicholson (L)	Jones (L)
Torney (L) *M*	MacDonald (L)	MacDonald (L)
Strang (L) *M*		

1991	1993	1995
Wiggin (C)*	Wiggin (C)*	Wiggin (C)*
Alexander (C)	Alexander (C)	Alexander (C)
Amos (C)	Browning (C)	Moate (C)
Bradley (C)	Winterton (C)	Winterton (C)
Winterton (C)	Marland (C)*	Marland (C)*
Marland (C)*	Gill (C)*	Gill (C)*
Gill (C)*	Pickthall (L)	Pickthall (L)
Martlew (L)	Stevenson (L)	Stevenson (L)
Morley (L)	Corston (L) *M*	Corston (L) *M*
Jones (L)	Campbell (L)	Campbell (L)

Key: C = Conservative, L = Labour, * = Active Farmer, *M* = Metropolitan Seat.
Source: Dods/Times/Vachers.

cent representation of active farmers on the agriculture committee and these typically accounted for at least half of the majority Conservative group. Given that farming interests are already over-represented in the House of Commons (12 per cent of Conservative members), the data are consistent with the view that the committees are likely to be dominated by the representatives of special interests. The metropolitan areas, by contrast, have never accounted for more than 30 per cent of the committee membership and for the vast majority of the period numbered 10 per cent or less, even though these constituencies account for over 40 per cent of seats within parliament (Times Guide, 1983–1995).

From the perspective of the Virginia school, the membership biases evident on both of these committees are suggestive of special interest politics in operation. Although the committees themselves do not possess significant powers, their membership patterns may be indicative of the underlying incentive structures within the wider political market. The planning bureaucracy has, for example, frequently joined with groups such as the CPRE (in some cases actually funding them – see Chapter 4) in campaigning for additional urban planning controls and a lengthening of the regulatory process. This appears to have been the case when the then DoE drafted the legislation for the 1991 Planning and Compensation Act – a major source of the recent growth in planning regulation. The membership of the environment committee, meanwhile, suggests that politicians have relatively little incentive to put downward pressure on bureaucratic growth in the planning system. Membership of the committee is biased towards those parts of the country where additional regulation will concentrate benefits on nimbyist interest groups, whilst diffusing costs across under-represented metropolitan taxpayers and consumers. Indeed, far from providing a check on bureaucratic action, the committee has actively lobbied for more regulation and stronger containment policies as with its 1984 report on Green Belts (HC 275 1984) and more recently, proposals to halt the construction of 'out of town' shopping developments (HMSO, 1997).

It is the lack of bureaucratic and political quiescence to environmental interests in other government agencies, when compared to urban containment that may also explain the different policy stances adopted in these areas. The MAFF and Forestry Commission, have, for example, repeatedly fought attempts to introduce planning controls over agricultural and forestry operations – the subsidies to which provide the major source of their budgets. Indeed, it was only with the prospect of additional budgets for so called 'agri-environment' subsidies that these agencies even began to consult the environmental interest groups at all (Cherry, 1996; Pennington, 1996; Winter, 1996). The high representation of active farmers or representatives of rural seats on the Agriculture Select Committee, suggests there have been few incentives for politicians to provide a check on any expansionist tendencies in the domestic MAFF budget and to resist the continual transfer of resources to the farming sector. Farm subsidies concentrate benefits on readily identifiable constituent groups, whilst diffusing the economic and environmental costs across an unidentified public.[9]

The ability of the Department of Transport to maintain a commitment to new road building – the major source of its budget, power and political prestige – and to resist the demands of the environmental lobby until very recently, may also reflect the influence of such bureaucratic and special interest power (Dowding, 1995; Pennington, 1997a, p. 104). The Transport committee of the House of Commons was for many years dominated by representatives of the road and rail lobbies and according to Ganzs (1985, p. 258)

acted as a pressure group asking for more public expenditure, untrammelled by the responsibilities of government to suggest cuts elsewhere'.

A similar pattern of bureaucratic resistance to regulation or propensity for 'capture' by industrial interests has been discernible in the area of pollution control. In this case, government agencies such as the former HMIP, have been heavily reliant on regulated industries for their staffing and technical expertise and preferred as a result an 'arms length' approach to the regulation of air and water pollution (Jordan, 1993; Smith, 1997; Gouldson and Murphy, 1998). Since the benefits of pollution control are thinly dispersed across a largely unidentified public there is relatively little incentive for politicians to monitor examples of regulator capture.

CONCLUSION

This chapter has sought to examine the politics of the British planning system and in particular the emphasis on urban containment policy, through the lenses of both voter-centred and special interest public choice theory. There continues to be a relative paucity of research in comparative environmental policy to fully establish the argument presented here, but there is sufficient preliminary evidence to treat the public choice account as a serious working hypothesis. Within this context, the clearest strength of voter-centred public choice lies in linking the developments in the planning system to the apparent eagerness of politicians to present themselves as 'green'. To explain the development of land use planning as purely a response to such macro-electoral factors, however, is to oversimplify the analysis. That politicians have changed their rhetoric to cater to the emerging environmental agenda does not imply that each area of environmental policy has developed in equal accord with public green concerns. The great weakness of voter-centred public choice is the assumption that individual voters are well informed and can exert effective control over politicians and bureaucrats with respect to the specific content of environmental policy. As the Virginia school has emphasised, however, the tendency towards voter ignorance allows considerable discretion for politicians and bureaucrats to implement policies, which do not necessarily reflect the distribution of public preferences. Special interest public choice, therefore, appears to offer a more complete explanation of policies such as urban containment. By highlighting the greater concentration of benefits that are available to special interests and bureaucrats from this policy, the Virginia school offers a plausible explanation for the support given to greater regulation in this area, compared to the reliance on a more voluntary approach in other environmental policy fields.

This argument is not to imply that *more* regulation is necessarily an appropriate policy response in all the areas that have continued to rely on a 'voluntary' approach (though this may sometimes be appropriate). In the case of agri-environmental policy, for example, perhaps the most effective environmental policy would be to abolish agricultural subsidies, rather than introduce additional regulatory controls (Howarth, 1990; Ridley, 1996). As public choice theory suggests, however, there are insufficient electoral benefits available for politicians to adopt such an approach because the benefits of maintaining subsidies are highly concentrated on the farm lobby, whilst the costs in terms of taxes are dispersed across a tax-paying populace with insufficient incentive to overcome the collective action problem. Neither does the analysis necessarily support the development of urban containment, as a reflection of the popular will. On the contrary, the structure of incentives within the planning system highlighted in this and the previous chapters is suggestive of a pronounced tendency towards 'over-regulation' and considerable rational voter ignorance in this particular field. What the analysis *does* suggest, however, is that the *incidence of regulation* and the *type of regulation* adopted may often be a product of special interest capture and the differential effect of this phenomenon within the different branches of the political marketplace. The experience of land use planning in Britain, therefore, would appear to support the Virginia school of public choice theory in suggesting that the outputs resulting from the inter-action of political demand and political supply may often be a product of government failure.

6

PLANNING AND THE POLITICS
OF GROWTH

INTRODUCTION

The political economy of the British planning system appears to be characterised by a pattern of government failures that biases decision-making incentives towards the growth of restrictive land use regulation and the interests of what might be described as an 'anti-growth' coalition. Whether it is at the local level in the formulation of development plans, or at the national level, which has created and maintained the broader policy framework, incentives on both the demand and supply sides of the political market have tended to reinforce the restrictive regulatory regime. The experience of planning in Britain, however, is not always and everywhere associated with an anti-growth agenda. There are a number of exceptions to the general emphasis on anti-growth politics and urban containment, where both planners and politicians have sought to promote various forms of new development. In general, though not exclusively, these have been based around attempts to revive the fortunes of the older urban areas, which have suffered a prolonged period of economic decline.

Growth oriented planning in the British context tends to be the exception rather than the rule, but no analysis of the land use planning system would be complete without an account of the political and institutional factors that have produced these exceptions. Understanding the circumstances that may affect the politics of growth in Britain is also important in helping to gain potential insights into the workings of planning systems outside of the British institutional context. In the United States, for example, a different planning system and government structure has witnessed an approach to the practice of land use control that has often appeared more sympathetic to a growth-oriented agenda.

This chapter uses public choice theory to develop an account of planning and the politics of growth. Focusing on both the demand and supply sides of the political market it presents an analysis of the political and institutional factors that may produce a more growth oriented approach to planning and to understand the types of growth that tend to be favoured by such regimes. Just as incentive structures and government failures may lead to the capture of the political process by anti-growth lobbies, so different institutional and political conditions may structurally bias incentive structures towards the demands of groups demanding *inappropriate* forms of growth. Understanding the underlying incentive structures that produce examples of pro-growth planning, therefore, is central to an evaluation of the policies that result.

The aim of the chapter is not to provide an exhaustive account of *all* the specific factors that may have contributed to the development of particular growth promotion schemes – these are far too complex to be considered in a single chapter. Rather, the intent is to highlight some of the most important factors which public choice theory suggests may explain in *general* terms the most salient characteristics of these planning regimes. In doing so, the chapter argues that pro-growth planning is often structurally biased towards policy outputs that are neither economically efficient or socially equitable and which are frequently driven by the twin demands of special interest rent seeking and bureaucratic expansionism.

THE DEMAND SIDE: COLLECTIVE ACTION AND THE POLITICS OF GROWTH

The structural biases towards an anti-growth agenda and to the policy of urban containment within the British planning system owe much to the existence of an influential coalition of interest groups on the demand side of the political market. More specifically, the combination of nimbyist environmental group-ings and the agricultural lobby appears to be a critical factor, which continues to drive the growth of restrictive land use planning. If the existence of anti-growth coalitions is a key factor in the support given to urban containment policies, so one would expect the presence of pro-growth coalitions to be a significant element in the political equation where more development oriented planning regimes have been adopted.

Growth Coalitions and the Politics of Planning

In recent years increasing attention has been paid to the significance of urban growth coalitions within political science. Molotch (1976) and Logon and Molotch (1987) developed the concept of 'urban growth machines' to explain the practice of urban development and redevelopment schemes within the United States. Subsequently, a growing number of authors have utilised this concept in an attempt to account for the incidence of growth oriented or 'boosterist' planning outside of the American context and especially in the UK (Bassett and Harloe, 1990; Harding, 1991, 1994).

Central to the concept of growth machines is the role of property interests within the development process. According to this perspective, the practice of growth promoting planning owes much to the entrepreneurial and political activities of property owning or *rentier* groups within the political economy. The economic interests of rentiers lie in the constant attempt to maximise the value of their holdings by intensifying the uses to which they are put or by developing higher value alternatives. Rentiers have investments that cannot be moved from place to place, i.e. they are 'place bound' and so have a substantial

stake in attracting economic investment into particular localities in order to raise
the value of their assets. Landowners, for example, are always likely to be on the
lookout for ways of increasing the rental value or sale price of their holdings and
will be inclined towards political campaigns supporting policies that maximise
their income stream. According to Logon and Molotch (1987), such interests
are the driving force in pro-growth planning schemes and have been in large
part responsible for shaping the pattern of urban growth within the United
States. Rentier inspired growth machines were a key player in the competitive urbanisation of the United States during the nineteenth century, where
coalitions of landowners sought to attract investment capital to develop particular localities. More recently, property interests have been central to a large
number of urban regeneration schemes and in the development of so-called
'place marketing' strategies, which attempt to market development opportunities in a particular area by creating a favourable economic image of place
(Ashworth and Voogd, 1990; Sadler, 1993).

In addition to rentiers, successful growth machines may include a range of
other economic interests. Foremost amongst these are the businesses that stand
to profit directly from the process of urban development. Examples include
construction interests such as house builders, property developers, architects,
and local financiers who are responsible for the actual process of development
and derive profits from the increased demand for their services. To these groups
may be added a further range of interests who benefit in a more indirect way
from the adoption of a growth oriented agenda. These may include local
retailers, the local media, utility companies, labour unions, professional sports
clubs and universities, all of whom may experience a boost in the demand for
their services as a consequence of economic growth (Harding, 1991, 1994).
Finally, successful growth coalitions may broaden out beyond these core economic interests to encompass a range of charitable, 'not for profit' and community organisations who support a pro-growth agenda in order to reduce
unemployment and more generally to improve the living standards of disadvantaged groups.

Growth Coalitions and the Logic of Collective Action

The presence of organised groups lobbying for additional growth is the central
concern of the theory of urban growth machines but the concept of growth
machines itself says relatively little about the specific circumstances where such
coalitions may be expected to arise. Theorists following Logon and Molotch
(1987) have been criticised for presenting an overly descriptive account of the
political economy of growth. There has been a tendency to describe particular
instances of the growth machine phenomena without providing enough of an
analytical framework to explain *why* growth coalitions are able to form in some
localities but not in others (Harding, 1991, 1995: Clarke and Goetz, 1994;
Clark and Gaile, 1994). As a consequence, the growth machine notion may
have over emphasised the significance of growth coalitions because theorists

have focused on examples where pro-development coalitions *have* arisen rather than the (perhaps more numerous) examples where they *have not*. In response to these difficulties a growing number of authors have developed the concept of 'urban regimes' to account for the different practices of planning and the institutional and political factors that contribute to the formation of pro, or anti-growth planning systems (Harding, 1994; Stoker and Mossberger, 1994).

One of the reasons for the overly descriptive account of growth machines is a neglect of the collective action problems facing interest groups that have been emphasised by public choice theorists. Much of the literature on pro-growth planning draws on an elitist or neo-pluralist perspective (Lindblom, 1977), which assumes that organising an effective interest group coalition is a relatively straightforward matter and that business interests, because of their superior access to monetary resources, are privileged within the political economy. From a public choice perspective, however, the organisation of a growth promoting coalition is far from a straightforward matter (Cheshire and Gordon, 1996). Economic growth exhibits many of the characteristics of a collective good. The beneficiaries of growth in a given area may include the owners of sites, commercial developments and all other business and labour interests who derive benefits from an increase in the general level of economic activity. If an area develops as a result of pro-growth planning policies, then the beneficiaries will include not only those who lobbied for the relevant policies but *all* other earners of economic rents in the place concerned (Cheshire and Gordon, 1996). The formation of growth coalitions may thus be problematic because the potential members may find themselves in the prisoners' dilemma situation. All the potential members of the growth coalition would be better off if they contributed to the provision of the collective good, but each individual may have a powerful incentive to free-ride. Within this context, public choice theory, suggests a number of possibilities where the collective action problem may be more easily overcome and thus offers an account of the political conditions that may prove more fertile for the development of growth promoting regimes.

One factor that may be a key determinant of the capacity to organise growth coalitions is the scale of the benefits to be derived by potential members of the coalition. *Ceteris paribus* the larger the potential benefits to individuals and firms, the more likely it is that there will be a sufficient number of actors prepared to bear the costs of collective action. Higher per capita stakes are more likely to occur where business investments are closely tied up with the rate of growth in a particular locality. The place bound property interests or rentiers referred to by Logon and Molotch (1987) may fall into this category as may other business interests with substantial local investments or those heavily dependent on other locality specific factors, such as a specialised skills base (Cheshire and Gordon, 1996). The greater the proportion of actors who are economically dependent on the fortunes of a given locality, the more likely is growth promoting collective action to occur because the costs of inaction may be deemed too great. Within this context, growth coalitions may be especially prone to develop if a proportion of the members constitute a privileged group.

In this situation the potential gains for some actors may be such that they will be prepared to bare a disproportionate share of the costs of organising a pro-growth campaign. Again, the presence of land owning and other property interests may be a significant factor here, as was earlier seen. to be the case in Britain with the house building lobby (Chapter 3). These interests may avoid the problem of free-riding behaviour because any member firm defecting from the coalition will fail to have its own sites identified for development and will thus be unable to appropriate the gains from growth.

Another variable that may affect the robustness of growth coalitions is the number of individuals and firms who may benefit from the boosterist agenda. The smaller the number of potential beneficiaries the lower are the transaction costs of monitoring and penalising free-riding behaviour and the collective action problem may be more easily overcome. Where a few large firms dominate the local economy or local land markets are relatively concentrated then it may be easier to form and sustain a pro-growth campaign. Monitoring costs may also be reduced where there are pre-existing business networks. If the potential member firms are well known to one another then there may be scope for the development of co-operative behaviour through strategic interaction. The presence of strong local chambers of commerce and other business groupings may, for example, be an important source of business networking, helping to reduce monitoring costs. Firms are much less likely to be free-riders if they are engaged in ongoing relationships and where they may, in the future, need to seek the assistance of other local businesses.

Areas characterised by an homogenous economic structure may also be more likely to witness the rise of pro-growth lobbies. More heterogenous economies, by contrast, may be less inclined to this phenomenon, because business hetero-geneity reduces the likelihood that member firms are known to one another (Cheshire and Gordon, 1996). Where business interests are heterogenous, it may be especially difficult to monitor free-riding behaviour because it may be hard to detect whether those failing to contribute to a pro-growth campaign are genuinely free riders or are actually opposed to the groups aims.

The ability to mobilise non-material selective incentives is often not considered to be a significant factor in the development of business coalitions, the primary purposes of which are pecuniary. Nonetheless, the presence of such incentives may be a further stimulant that may help to create the appropriate conditions where a growth coalition may arise. Areas exhibiting a strong sense of cultural/political identity may be better able to rely on such incentives. A combination of solidary and expressive benefits may help to broaden out of the base of a coalition to include individuals and groups with less of a personal economic stake but who are keen to derive other benefits associated with lobbying activity (Miller, 1992). These could include the sense of achievement derived from being involved in a successful growth promoting project, or the social approval value of being seen to campaign for the economic success of a locality with a strong sense of local pride or 'place patriotism'. Similar processes may operate in areas demonstrating severe unemployment problems, where individuals may wish to gain social approval and status from an outward display of 'social responsibility'. Where business interests appear to be involved for such purposes it is difficult to disentangle such motives from underlying financial incentives, but the significance of non-material benefits should not be entirely discounted.

Notwithstanding the considerable theoretical interest in the concept of growth coalitions, there continues to be a relative shortage of empirical studies to examine in full the capacity of public choice theory to explain the incidence of this phenomenon. In so far as there is empirical evidence, however, it does lend some general support for the theoretical analysis sketched above. The existence of high per capita stakes has clearly been a significant factor in a number of important British growth coalitions. Simmie's (1981) account of the role of University land owning interests in Oxford is a useful example in point. In this case, the high degree of land ownership by University institutions was a significant factor in the development of a growth coalition as the University sought to reap the substantial profits from the sale and development of its landed assets within Oxford. More recently, Shaw (1993) has highlighted the role of property interests in a number of 'place marketing' and urban redevelopment strategies such as the Newcastle Initiative set up in the North East of England. According to Shaw, (1993) a key element in these strategies has been the existence of a small coterie of business and property interests with substantial local investments highly dependent on the economic regeneration of the city region around Newcastle upon Tyne.

Most examples of growth coalitions in Britain have been centred around urban regeneration programmes in cities such as Manchester, Liverpool, Newcastle, Leeds and Sheffield, but there are some notable examples where coalitions have sought to develop green-field locations and have lobbied for a relaxation of the commitment to urban containment policy. Pennington (1997a, Ch. 6), for example, examines the significance of a growth coalition on the development plan process within Chester in a controversial attempt to relax Green Belt restrictions in the late 1980s. In this case, the pro-growth lobby consisted of a consortium of house builders and local landowners that pushed for the release of over 400 hectares of Green Belt land for a combination of housing and business park developments. The coalition was also joined by a retail interests in the local chamber of commerce and employed a team of marketing consultants and surveyors in a campaign to market the city of Chester as a new 'regional growth pole'. So great were the stakes concerned that the house building consortium proceeded to take the then Secretary of State for the Environment to the High Court, following his decision to 'call in' the Chester Local Plan and the Cheshire Structure Plan to block the release of the Green Belt land.

The examples of growth coalitions given above appear to confirm that a relatively small number of potential participants with high per capita stakes is often a key factor that facilitates the mobilisation of pro-development lobbies. Harding's (1991) case studies of public/ private partnerships in UK urban redevelopment projects provide further confirmation of this analysis. Evidence suggests that private sector interests are more likely to play a prominent role in growth coalitions where land markets are characterised by a more concentrated pattern of ownership. Where land markets are characterised by a fragmented ownership structure – as they are in many British cities, the role of business-led growth coalitions has been less significant (Harding, 1991, pp. 308–10). This pattern would seem to explain the more general phenomena of growth coalitions dominated by 'big business' and large landowners to the neglect of smaller firms and landowners which are often far too numerous and diffuse to overcome the collective action problem.

The local business networks that may also help growth coalitions to overcome the collective action problem have historically been much weaker in the United Kingdom than in countries such as the United States and it is the relative lack of such networks that may in part explain the less significant role played by private sector growth coalitions in this country. In places such as Newcastle, the ability of pro-growth lobbies to overcome the collective action problem does seem to have been aided by the existence of a tightly knit local business elite with substantial local property and financial investments (Shaw, 1993). In Britain as a whole, however, the greater significance of national business interests appears to have prevented the more widespread development of local business networks, when compared with countries such as the United States, where there is a much stronger representation of locally owned 'big business' (Harding, 1991, 1994).

Basset and Harloe's (1990) account of the development of pro-growth interests in Swindon during the post war era, points to the significance of business homogeneity in facilitating collective action. The roots of the successful pro-growth lobby that developed between the 1950s and 1970s may have resulted, in part at least, from the strong consensus of interests derived from the homogenous economic structure of what was essentially a one-industry town. (Cheshire and Gordon, 1996). Ironically, however, according to Cheshire and Gordon (1996, p. 396), it was the initial success of this growth coalition, which was to precipitate its eventual downfall. As the industrial structure of Swindon diversified and the number of firms in the vicinity multiplied dramatically, so the base of the original coalition collapsed. A similar phenomenon may help to explain the more general absence of growth coalitions in economically diversified regions such as south-east England. Whilst individual business interests, such as house builders, with a high per capita stake are frequently able to mobilise, it is relatively rare to find broader business coalitions mobilised around a more general growth promoting agenda.

Turning finally to the significance of non-material incentives, the example of Newcastle provides perhaps the clearest indication within the UK that such factors may come into play. The strong tradition of regionalism in the North East of England based around labourist politics, trade unionism and sporting identity is such that solidary or expressive benefits may well have been a significant factor in helping to mobilise a broader coalition for growth (Shaw, 1993; Newman and Thornley, 1996). Outside of Britain, there is considerable evidence that the existence of a strong cultural or political identity is an important variable. The development of a powerful growth coalition in the Barcelona region, centred around the cultural politics of Catalan nationalism and the campaign to host the 1992 Olympic Games is perhaps the most famous example in point (Cheshire and Gordon, 1996). The ability of growth coalitions in such cities to draw in a broader range of actors beyond the business core may also have been aided by the existence of expressive benefits associated with the economic conditions in these areas. In Newcastle, for example, the Newcastle Initiative project brought in a number of quasi-charitable organisations such as Business in the Community to push the case for growth promoting policies. High unemployment and other social pathologies in such cities may have provided opportunities for the members of such groups to obtain the social approval value from a public display of concern for the unemployed and other dis-advantaged groups.

In general, however, it is the relative absence of such non-material incentives that would appear to explain the apparent difficulty of mobilising more broadly based growth coalitions on a much wider scale. For the most part, Western Europe and the United States are characterised by highly mobile and transient populations with relatively little sense of cultural identity. In these circumstances, it is unlikely that solidary and expressive benefits can be mobilised in favour of a politics of growth, an explanation that may account for the failure to mobilise growth coalitions in cosmopolitan regions such as South East England (Cheshire and Gordon, 1996). Similarly, the lack of social approval value associated with membership may explain why the majority of more broadly based growth coalitions have been centred on urban regeneration rather than suburban or rural development schemes. It is much more difficult to mobilise expressive benefits associated with displaying one's concern for the plight of the unemployed in the more affluent suburban and rural areas where unemployment is not such a significant social issue. As was argued in chapter 3, in so far as expressive benefits are a factor in much of the United Kingdom, these seem to be based around anti-growth politics and public displays of 'environmental consciousness' rather than a growth supporting agenda.

The above account of collective action in growth coalitions, whilst far from comprehensive, provides some important insights into the factors that may contribute to or constrain the development of a politics of growth on the demand side of the political market. In doing so, at the most general level public choice theory highlights the chronic difficulty of mobilising growth coalitions in terms of collective action problems and may thus account for the failure of such coalitions to be a more widespread phenomenon in the political economy of planning. More significantly, however, in pointing to the conditions that *do* allow growth coalitions to mobilise the public choice approach suggests that there are pronounced biases within the political market that are likely to favour a very *particular type of coalition*.

First, the importance of high per capita stakes and a small number of actors points to the domination of growth coalitions by big business and property interests to the neglect of the small business sector which is often too diffuse to overcome the collective action problem. The interests of the urban poor and of taxpayers are also unlikely to be considered in such coalitions. From a public choice perspective, the former are a large and heterogenous interest prone to free riding and with little time to devote to organised politics given their immediate requirement to secure the basic essentials of life. The latter are a similarly large and diffuse group who may also find themselves in the logic of the prisoners' dilemma. In turn, it is the relative absence of such groups in the political market that may create a structural bias in favour of large-scale property interests. Property-based coalitions do not tend to favour growth based on open and competitive markets, but on *regulated growth*, which restricts market entry and reduces competition. Growth coalitions demand a strong regulatory framework frequently backed up by substantial subsidy payments to provide certainty in the process of urban development (Harding, 1991). 'Certainty' in this context, however, may often be little more than a euphemism for the exercise of monopoly privilege obtained through special interest rent seeking.

Second, the significance of tightly knit business networks to the formation of growth coalitions confirms the possibility of structural bias towards anti-competitive rent seeking policies, which stems from the underlying logic of collective action. Tightly knit business groupings may be highly exclusionary in terms of the growth agenda that they seek to promote. Consequently, there may be a pronounced bias towards policies that favour politically connected firms (subsidies and exemptions from regulations) to the neglect of potential market entrants who might threaten the existing players and the urban poor who have limited access to social networks of this sort.

Finally, in so far as expressive benefits are a factor in the formation of growth coalitions, these may bias the incentive structure still further in favour of high profile development projects driven by the rent seeking demands of large scale property interests. Expressive benefits associated with a strong sense of cultural/ political identity or the desire to demonstrate one's commitment to the cause of the disadvantaged are often dependent on the *scale* and *visibility* of the projects concerned. There seems little prospect of mobilising expressive support for less visible development strategies, which may require a longer period of time to display their positive effects. Low profile alternatives to large-scale urban redevelopment, therefore, are likely to be discarded (Woodlief, 1998a, 1998b). These could include market liberal proposals to relax the urban land use regulations that may hamper the formation of businesses amongst low-income groups (Gordan and Richardson, 1997) or the community based redevelopment schemes favoured by the 'New Left' (Montgomery and Thornley, 1990).

Critics of property led urban redevelopment and in particular advocates of collaborative planning have long complained of the failure of successive urban redevelopment programmes to address broader economic and social concerns. Although there have been some signs of greater efforts being made to accommodate wider community interests in recent years, these have often been dismissed as examples of tokenism and there continue to be calls for greater community participation in order to provide a more balanced decision-making process (Brownhill, 1990; Keating and Krumholtz, 1991; Healey et al., 1992; Imrie and Thomas, 1993). From the perspective of public choice theory, however, it may be naïve to expect such plans to remain impervious to the corporatist, rent seeking agendas of powerful interests. Inequalities of access to the political process are frequently not the result of insufficient opportunities for public participation in decision-making. Rather, they may be a product of underlying incentive structures that favour the concentrated interests who are able to overcome the logic of collective action to the neglect of those too numerous and with too small a stake to act collectively to challenge the status quo.

THE SUPPLY SIDE: BUREAUCRATS, POLITICIANS AND THE POLITICS OF GROWTH

The analysis of the incentive structures that have helped to produce examples of pro-growth planning, presented thus far, has concentrated on the role of interest groups on the demand side of the political market. Empirical evidence on the incidence of boosterist planning initiatives, however, suggests that the involvement of public sector agencies on the supply side is often a crucial factor in the development of growth coalitions. In the United Kingdom and Western Europe more generally many such schemes have been actively *led* by public sector agencies, which have sought to bring together a range of private sector actors (Harding, 1991, 1994; Shaw, 1993). Even in the United States, the leading role of rentier groups on the demand side may well have been over-emphasised. Most urban redevelopment schemes in America have not simply involved the relaxation of local land use regulations to facilitate growth but have required substantial injections of public subsidy (Mollenkopf, 1983; Gordon and Richardson, 1997). It is necessary, therefore, to develop a supply side per-spective. More specifically, what are the factors that lead bureaucrats and politicians to favour growth and how do incentive structures in the political market influence the form that this growth is likely to take?

Bureaucrats, Politicians and Growth Coalitions

From the perspective of public choice theory the extent to which bureaucrats may be expected to support pro-growth planning will be dependent on the benefits that they themselves may receive from the pursuit of such an agenda. Following the account of bureaucratic behaviour outlined in chapter 4 one would expect planning bureaucrats to be sympathetic to growth promotion where a high proportion of their Core Budget (CB – expenditures on staff, administration and general running costs) is devoted to growth related functions and where the CB itself represents a high percentage of the total plan-ning budget. In this situation a budget maximising strategy would require the expansion of growth promoting functions and thus one would expect planners to play an active role in seeking to encourage pro-growth schemes.

Bureaucrats might also be expected to engage in growth promoting activities where the Bureau Budget element (BB – subsidies and contracts to the private sector) of their agency enables them to develop closed or corporatist relationships with the special interest groups who may be lobbying for additional growth. Planners pursuing their economic self-interest might seek to pursue a growth oriented agenda if this will involve the supply of payments or contracts to highly organised lobbies able to supply a flow-back of benefits in exchange for greater subsidies.

A further factor that may also incline planners to the support of pro-growth policies is the extent to which these policies accord with their professional ideology. Planners driven by a welfarist ideology committed to the pursuit of economic growth in order to reduce unemployment and other poverty related problems may be more sympathetic to pro-growth concerns. Related to this may be the desire of planners to use their bureaucratic role to obtain expressive benefits. These could include the possibility of deriving public and political praise from *being seen* to have played a role in a successful growth-promoting project and in being publicly associated with the physical development or redevelopment of a particular area.

If the interests of bureaucrats in promoting growth are dependent on the budgetary consequences of such strategies, the interests of elected representatives are closely associated with the political and electoral consequences of pursuing a pro-growth agenda. Elected politicians must consider a number of potentially decisive arguments in their utility functions when deciding whether to promote growth and the particular form that such an agenda should take.

From a public choice perspective, the primary concern of the politician is the necessity of maintaining a position in elected office, so the extent to which votes can be mobilised in support of a pro-growth initiative is likely to be a key element in determining the political stance adopted. The benefits of economic growth to society as a whole are, however, spread very widely and it is unlikely that a large number of votes could be swayed on the basis of any particular scheme. Due to the collective action problems discussed in the previous section active support for growth may be confined to the business interests involved in the process of development itself. These groups are unlikely to be significant in terms of direct voting strength but may have the capacity to supply other benefits including campaign contributions and other forms of political support. In these circumstances the decision to pursue a pro-growth agenda may be affected by the more general ideological attitude to growth promotion. Where the macro-political climate is generally favourable to growth and where politicians seem unlikely to lose support as a consequence of growth promotion then the benefits provided by business interests may be sufficient to tilt the incentive structure in favour of development. It may also be the case that a favourable ideological climate may allow politicians to obtain expressive benefits such as the approval value from being seen to 'take action to reduce unemployment' or to 'reverse urban decay'. Action of this type may be especially significant in a context where voters are rationally ignorant and dependent on such crude symbolism for the bulk of their political information.

The experience of boosterist or growth promoting planning in Britain, Western Europe and the United States offers a variety of empirical support for these supply side propositions. The significance of a strong bureaucratic stake in the formation of pro-growth planning regimes would certainly seem to be an important factor in the British case. As was shown in Chapter 4 what is most noticeable about the institutional structures of the British land use planning system is the relative *absence of economic development functions*. The vast majority of expenditure in British planning agencies is devoted to regulatory activities such as the development control and plan preparation procedures, with only a tiny minority of staff employed in delivery functions associated with economic development. In the non-metropolitan English district councils where the majority of planners are employed, a mere 8.4 per cent of staff time is allocated to economic development and promotion. Within this context, it is not surprising that for the most part the British planning system is characterised by 'anti-growth' regimes, supportive of nimbyist interest groups and institutionally committed to urban containment and other regulation intensive policies.

The exception to this general pattern occurs in the metropolitan local authority areas where a much higher proportion of planning staffs (33 per cent) are employed in delivery functions related to economic development and promotion. These include the development of local authority owned land, the collection of rents from local authority industrial sites, the marketing of development opportunities and the handling of regional development grants obtained from central government departments such as the Department for Trade and Industry and increasingly in recent years, from the European Union. The expansion of these activities does not discriminate against new development but would appear to imply the active promotion of new building and economic activity. If bureaucrats employed in such functions are to expand their budgets and to improve their job security and status this would appear to imply that more local authority owned land is developed, more rents and charges are collected from firms locating in the areas concerned and additional marketing and promotion of development sites occurs.

Given this pattern of bureaucratic incentive structures, one would expect the incidence of growth promotion approaches to planning to coincide with the local authority areas with the highest proportion of staff employed in the economic development function. In those areas with the lowest proportion of such staff, by contrast, one would expect planners to rely almost exclusively on the expansion of the regulatory regime for their bureaucratic well being. The evidence from Britain would seem to confirm this pattern of behaviour. The majority of empirically documented pro-growth planning regimes have been drawn from the metropolitan local authorities. In Harding's (1991) analysis of growth coalitions, for example, seven out of the nine English examples cited were located within metropolitan areas with only two drawn from the non-metropolitan districts/shire counties. Planning bureaucrats were actively involved in the marketing of development opportunities and in land acquisition and servicing and in most cases played the lead role in bringing together business and property development interests to form a variety of public/private 'partnerships'. Far from being demand driven phenomena many growth coalitions in the UK appear to have been aided in their attempts to overcome collective action problems by an activist planning bureaucracy.

The coincidence of bureaucratic incentive structures with the pattern of support for growth coalitions does not, of course, prove the direction of causality i.e. that it is the exercise of bureaucratic power that has been the driving force in the support given to such coalitions. One alternative explanation for the more pro-growth stance adopted by the metropolitan authorities might point to demand side factors and in particular the relative lack of nimbyist opposition in these areas. Nimbyism is a phenomenon found more frequently (though not exclusively) in the affluent rural and suburban parts of the country (Chapter 3). Metropolitan politicians, therefore, may be more inclined to support a growth-based agenda and it may be their willingness to do so as opposed to planners' power that has been the key factor at play. On a related point, it might be suggested that to equate the incidence of pro-growth planning regimes with the metropolitan local authorities is simply to state the obvious. One would expect that those urban authorities that have suffered heavily from economic decline over recent decades would be those most actively involved in the encouragement of new development. Moreover, in so far as these authorities have pursued such policies they may have done so as a consequence of pressure from central government rather than the immediate pursuit of their own bureaucratic interests.

The above explanations have considerable merit, but there is evidence to suggest that they do not adequately capture the story. On the one hand, there are a number of examples where local planning bureaucrats have sought to push through growth promoting schemes *even in the face of nimbyist opposition*. On the other hand, even where boosterist planning has occurred against the backdrop of a political climate, which is generally more favourable to growth, there is evidence to suggest that bureaucratic incentive structures have been a determining factor in affecting the *shape of that growth*. This would appear to confirm a wider body of empirical work, which has suggested that notwithstanding central government controls on local authorities, planning bureaucrats have been able to exercise a considerable degree of autonomy in shaping the implementation of policy in accordance with their own objectives (Cooke, 1986; Bagguley et al., 1990; Allmendinger, 1997).

Turning to the first of these issues, there are several examples of local authorities that have sought to pursue a boosterist planning agenda that have not simply been based on inner urban regeneration but have sought to secure the development of Green Belt land and a selective relaxation of the commitment to urban containment. Pennington (1997a, Ch. 6) highlights the examples of Newcastle and Chester as the most significant cases in point. In the former instance, Newcastle Upon Tyne City Council, in addition to its plans for inner city regeneration, played a leading role in seeking to secure the release of almost 10 per cent of the city's Green Belt. In the latter case, Chester City Council and Cheshire County Council, in conjunction with a consortium of private developers, were the driving force in the plans to release 400 ha of the Greater Chester Green Belt and the promotion of Chester as a 'regional growth pole'. The example of Chester is particularly intriguing because both the city and county councils fall into the non-metropolitan authority category and throughout the 1980s and 1990s were almost unique amongst such authorities in pursuing an apparently growth oriented approach. The proposals for the release of Green Belt land in both Newcastle and Chester generated vociferous opposition from nimbyist and other environmental groupings. Indeed, so vigorous was this opposition that the local plans of both authorities were 'called in' by the then Department of the Environment (DoE) and were eventually overturned by a Secretary of State, eager to minimise controversy over the security of Green Belt policy on a national scale (Pennington, 1997a, pp. 224–5).

That planning bureaucrats in Newcastle and Chester have pursued a growth promoting approach in the face of such opposition may be explained, in part at least, by the structure of the planning function within these authorities. Table 6.1 illustrates bureaucratic staffing arrangements in these areas when compared to the non-metropolitan and metropolitan categories as a whole. The contrast in terms of staffing structures is very marked indeed. In the metropolitan category the economic development function employs a far higher proportion of the total planning staff than in the non-metropolitan equivalent, a figure reflected in Newcastle (a metropolitan authority), which employs almost 43 per cent of its staff in promotional functions. Chester District Council and Cheshire County Council also employ a far higher proportion of their staff in economic development than is the norm in the non-metropolitan areas. The primary reason being that Chester and much of the rest of Northern Cheshire

Table 6.1 Budgeted Employees by Function in English District Planning Authorities: 1991

	Economic Development	Other Planning	Total	% Economic Development
Newcastle	53.0	71.0	124.0	42.7%
Chester City	8.0	24.0	32.0	25.0%
Cheshire County	46.0	81.0	127.0	36.2%
Metro-Districts	696.5	2093.5	2790.0	33.0%
Non-Metro Counties	526.0	2208.0	2734.0	19.2%
Non-Metro Districts	608.1	6602.8	7210.9	8.4%

Source: CIPFA Planning and Development Statistics/ Chester City Council 1991.

has been included in the central government's Assisted Areas Scheme (AAS). This scheme makes both the city and county council eligible for a range of central government (Department of Trade and Industry – DTI) and European Union regional development grants aimed at the promotion of development opportunities. As Figure 6.1 shows, the Assisted Areas Scheme is, for the most part, restricted to the metropolitan conurbations of the north and to Scotland and Wales.

The implications of these bureaucratic structures in explaining the support for a pro-growth agenda in areas such as Newcastle and Chester would appear quite clear. Put simply, a significantly high proportion of bureaucratic interests in these authorities have an economic stake in the pro-development functions within their budget the expansion of which may require the release of land from the usual planning constraints. Access to AAS funds and to economic development grants from the European Union and hence bureaucratic job security and patronage power are linked to a more growth-oriented approach. Whereas, the majority of non-metropolitan authorities are almost devoid of economic functions and hence rely on regulatory activities that are often biased against new development, the metropolitan authorities have a *wider range of options* in seeking to expand their agency budgets, some of which may result in the active promotion of pro-growth schemes.

The contrast in bureaucratic forms is especially stark when comparing the Newcastle and Cheshire examples with non-metropolitan planning authorities such as Buckinghamshire, Berkshire, Hampshire and Surrey, all of which, are especially known for pursuing a highly restrictive planning regime (Murdoch and Marsden, 1994). Table 6.2 illustrates the staffing structures for the English non-metropolitan county councils, where it is apparent that the size of the economic development function is closely related to coverage by the Assisted Areas Scheme. Throughout most of the country where there is no AAS, and especially in southern England, the economic development function is minimal, with some counties such as Oxfordshire and Berkshire employing no staff in this area at all. The county of Cheshire, on the other hand, has one of the highest proportions of development related staff and employs the highest number of such staff in absolute terms.

The examples of Newcastle and Chester suggest that the incidence of pro-growth planning regimes cannot simply be explained with reference to demand side factors such as the relative absence of nimbyist interests in economically depressed areas. Rather, the willingness of planning bureaucrats to pursue a growth-oriented approach in spite of high profile opposition may confirm the significance of bureaucratic interests on the supply side in determining the character of the planning regime. The Chester example is particularly suggestive because unlike many of the metropolitan and especially inner city areas that have a similar proportion of economic development staff, Chester is a relatively prosperous district with an unemployment rate close to the national average. Its ability to secure AAS funding stemming purely from its close proximity to the Merseyside Development Area (Pennington, 1997a, p. 211).

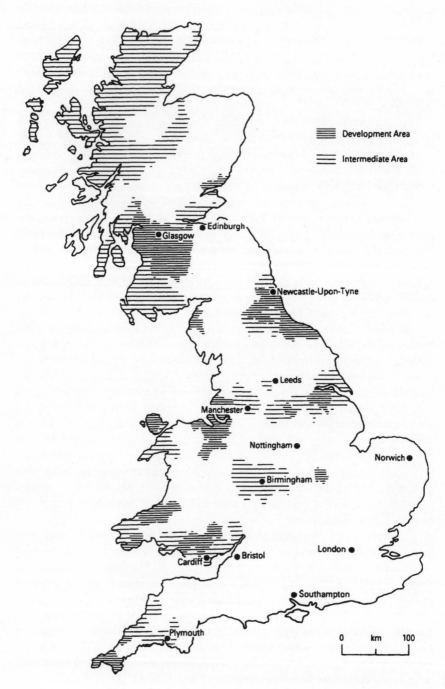

Figure 6.1   *The Assisted Areas Scheme 1992*

Table 6.2 Budgeted Employees by Function in English County Planning Authorities: 1991

	Economic Development	Other Planning	Total	% Economic Development
Cheshire	46.0	81.0	127.0	36.2%**
Durham	41.0	61.0	102.0	40.2%**
Nottinghamshire	40.7	98.0	138.7	29.3%
Lancashire	33.2	62.8	96.0	34.6%**
Humberside	31.6	55.9	87.5	36.1%**
Staffordshire	27.5	107.0	134.5	20.4%*
Leicestershire	26.6	50.6	77.2	34.4%**
Kent	26.6	110.4	137.0	19.4%
Cleveland	24.9	55.5	80.4	30.9%**
Essex	23.0	157.0	180.0	12.7%
Cornwall	20.5	41.1	61.6	33.3%**
Warwickshire	18.6	38.3	56.3	33.0%*
Shropshire	17.0	28.8	45.8	37.1%*
Northumbria	16.8	46.2	63.0	26.6%
Cumbria	13.5	52.5	66.0	20.4%**
Devon	11.2	66.9	78.1	14.3%
E. Sussex	11.0	56.0	67.0	16.4%
Lincolnshire	9.0	26.0	25.0	36.0%**
Bedfordshire	9.0	69.0	78.0	11.5%
Gloucestershire	8.3	41.3	49.6	16.7%
North Yorks	8.0	46.5	54.5	14.7%
Hereford	8.0	38.0	46.0	17.4%
Derbyshire	7.6	89.4	96.0	7.9%
Northants	7.4	30.7	38.1	19.4%
Somerset	7.0	45.0	52.0	13.5%
Wiltshire	6.0	22.5	28.5	21.0%
Suffolk	5.8	39.8	45.6	12.7%
Norfolk	5.5	52.5	58.0	9.5%
Surrey	4.6	86.4	91.0	5.0%
Cambridgeshire	4.0	30.0	34.0	11.8%
W. Sussex	4.0	50.0	54.0	7.4%
Hampshire	1.1	125.9	127.0	0.9%
Isle of Wight	1.0	10.5	11.5	8.7%
Hertfordshire	0.5	80.0	80.5	0.6%
Berkshire	0.3	59.7	60.0	0.5%
Dorset	0.3	54.2	54.5	0.5%
Oxfordshire	0.0	18.5	18.5	0.0%
Buckinghamshire	0.0	33.0	33.0	0.0%
All Counties	526	2208.0	2734.0	19.2%

** = DAS within county * = IAS within county.
Notes: Figures for Berkshire and Buckinghamshire are 1992.
Source: Computed from CIPFA Planning and Development Statistics 1991.

Broader support for this theory can be found in a number of other British studies of growth coalitions. Harding's (1991) analysis, for example, confirms the significance of a high percentage of local authority land-ownership as being a central factor in explaining the existence of a growth-oriented approach. The Newcastle and Chester growth coalitions also corroborate the importance of a high bureaucratic stake in development land ownership. In the former case the local authority were keen to reap a substantial capital gain from the sale of land to Newcastle United Football Club for the construction of a new stadium to replace the ageing St James Park. In Chester, meanwhile, the local authority was in receipt of European Union funding to redevelop council owned land for the pursuit of business park developments (Pennington, 1997a, p. 211).

It would appear that where planning budgets are linked to the expansion of development then such proposals may be more likely to be pushed through, *even in the face of opposition*. In general, it is the metropolitan planning authorities that exhibit the highest percentage of local authority owned land and it is these same authorities that have also proved the most fertile territory for the development of pro-growth planning regimes. Where the state itself has an active role in the development process and where planners are essentially *regulating themselves* then development seems much more likely to proceed. The figures on the percentage of public sector development applications that are granted with planning permission when compared with the private sector equivalent offer confirmation of this institutional bias. Approval rates for public sector managed developments have consistently run at a higher rate than for those generated and managed exclusively by the private sector (Loveless, 1983; Goodchild and Denman, 1989).

Outside of Britain the examples of planning regimes in other parts of Western Europe may confirm the importance of bureaucratic stakes in determining the attitude towards new development. In countries such as France and Sweden where the state itself plays a more active role in the actual process of construction there appear to be fewer obstacles to new development with building rates proceeding at a considerably higher rate than in the UK (Barlow and Duncan, 1992). In Sweden, most new housing production is built directly by local authorities or contracted out to one of the few corporate giants that make up the private house building industry. Local authority bureaucrats, therefore, may have a powerful incentive to push through building projects irrespective of any opposition because their budgets and the exercise of patronage power are dependent on the development process.

That bureaucratic incentive structures are a key determinant in growth machines is given further weight when considering the *character* of the pro-development schemes that planners have supported. In Britain, even in the authorities that have a relatively high proportion of their expenditure in the area of economic development, *regulation based activities* are still by far and away the most important bureaucratic function. In the English metropolitan planning authorities as a whole 67 per cent of planning staffs are employed in direct regulation as opposed to economic development. From a public choice perspective, therefore, one would not expect planners' to support *any* growth-related agenda, but to have a strong preference for a *particular type of pro-growth policy*, that requires a substantial bureaucratic input from planners themselves. More specifically, planners may have an incentive to support development schemes, where the expansion of economic functions represents *an addition to existing regulatory budgets*.

In the 1970s the favoured bureaucratic option was large-scale land acquisition, the promotion of slum clearance programmes and the mass development of high rise public housing projects as documented by Dunleavy (1981). Although working from a neo-Marxist frame of reference, Dunleavy's account of the behaviour of local authority housing, planning and architects departments can easily be squared with a public choice approach. The pursuit of large scale re-development projects based on the construction of high rise public sector housing was the product of a closed relationship between bureaucrats and private sector construction and design professionals who pushed through these schemes at highly inflated costs, irrespective of public opposition. In public choice terminology, the relevant local authority agencies were in a delivery or contract bureau format and bureaucrats stood to gain from the resultant increase in budgets either directly in terms of staffing or from the potential patronage benefits derived from the big construction firms in exchange for the granting of monopoly contracts. More recently, with the change in the macro-political climate against large scale public housing and more generally against public sector redevelopment, pro-growth planning has shifted towards an 'entrepreneurial' or 'property led' approach. The emphasis has again been on high profile redevelopment projects but with local authorities adopting an 'enabling' role. Through 'place marketing', land assembly and the provision of 'leverage' grants and subsidies planning authorities have sought to attract private investment capital to redevelop urban areas in 'partnership' with the public sector (Harding, 1991).

Given the structure of metropolitan planning budgets, the most favourable bureaucratic maximisation strategy may lie in lengthening and complicating the regulatory process, whilst at the same time lobbying for more resources to be spent on growth related schemes *where the planning authority itself plays a central role* – either directly in the development of local authority owned land or indirectly through the provision of grants to corporatist interests. As a consequence, planners may have an incentive to discriminate against self-financing, 'low profile' projects carried out by predominantly small businesses and to favour instead high profile redevelopment projects, managed by subsidised public/private 'partnerships'. Seen in this light, it is not surprising that supposedly 'pro-growth' metropolitan authorities, especially those in the inner urban areas, have an equally poor record in terms of the productivity of the development control procedure as their non-metropolitan equivalents. In some of the most economically depressed inner urban authorities, where one might think that planners would be most sympathetic to new development, the productivity rate is remarkably low. In authorities such as Lambeth in London, for example, as little as 19 per cent of planning applications are processed within the DETR target period of eight weeks (DETR, 1997). As was shown in Chapter 4, the substantial increase in planning expenditure that has occurred over recent years does not seem to suggest that such figures can be put down to a lack of resources.

The pattern is repeated in many of the other urban local authority areas that have simultaneously sought to promote public/private growth coalitions in the recent past, with the 'most productive' of authorities scarcely able to process 60 per cent of applications (many of which are for trivial household developments) within two months. In the supposedly 'pro-growth' cases of Newcastle and Chester discussed earlier, for example, the productivity rate is a mere two planning applications processed, per month, per worker (employed specifically in development control) – a rate which does not appear to suggest that the promotion of enterprise *per se* is the dominant motive at play (authors calculation from DETR Planning Applications Bulletin, September 1997). On top of these delays must also be considered the dampening effect on economic activity of the plan preparation process itself with many Unitary Development Plans taking up to three or four years to complete.

Whether it is for increases in job security, the exercise of patronage power or the expressive benefits of being seen to have played a part in urban renewal, bureaucrats have little incentive to relax the myriad regulatory controls that may stifle the formation of local businesses. On the contrary, improving productivity, shortening the length of the planning procedure and simplifying the regulatory process, however beneficial for the fortunes of the economy, may be counter to the interests of planning bureaucrats. Bureaucratic objectives it would seem may be less concerned with 'enabling' growth than enabling high profile developments involving corporatist relations with big business where local economic planners are often influential brokers of power. In this sense, the structure of incentives on the supply side of the political market would appear to reinforce the in-built bias towards policies based on the anti-competitive rent seeking that stems from the logic of collective action and inaction on the demand side.

Notwithstanding the significance of these bureaucratic incentives, it is important not to overemphasise the extent of planners' power on the supply side of the political market. The electoral strategies of politicians have undoubtedly played an equally prominent part in determining the character of the politics of growth and to a considerable extent have actually shaped the institutional environments in which bureaucratic actions have been played out. Foremost amongst these has been the desire of politicians at both the national and local levels *to be seen* to be 'taking action' to reverse the process of urban decline that has afflicted many British cities since the 1960s. In order to create a favourable public image, politicians from both left and right have had a powerful incentive to support high profile regeneration projects, whether of the state dominated model favoured by the Labour Party of the 1970s or the public/private partnerships favoured by the Conservatives in the 1980s and early 1990s and 'New Labour' in the late 1990s.

This pattern of political incentives has been an important factor in explaining the concentration of pro-growth planning regimes in the older metropolitan areas and the tendency for non-metropolitan rural and suburban areas to be characterised by an anti-growth approach. It is much more difficult for politicians to generate broader support for a pro-growth coalition in these more affluent areas than it is in the inner cities where jobs are often in short supply. Bureaucratic incentive structures at the local authority level, therefore, have been determined, in part at least, by the policy framework laid down by central government and in particular the provision of finance in the form of economic development grants such as the Single Regeneration Budget and the Assisted Areas Scheme. The geographical discrimination exercised by programmes such as the AAS has been an important factor in determining the incentive structure facing planners. Throughout the last thirty years central government policy has been driven by the desire to revive the economic fortunes of inner city areas and the bulk of the funding for economic development has been concentrated within these areas. The inability of the majority of non-metropolitan planning authorities to secure such funds may thus have skewed incentives towards an exclusive emphasis on regulatory expansion.

Changes in the macro-electoral context have also played a fundamental role in determining the character of the regeneration programmes adopted. In the 1960s and 1970s the ideological support given by the national Labour government and by many Labour local authorities, was a key factor in securing political backing for the mass public housing projects and public sector re-developments that were the principal approach to urban policy at that time. Similarly, in the 1980s and 1990s, it was in large part the ideological hostility towards such schemes exhibited by successive Conservative administrations that was responsible for the shift towards the property led form of urban redevelopment that has been the defining feature of more recent growth coalitions. The threat to replace local authority planning departments with Urban Development Corporations and other centrally appointed bodies, unless they were more willing to co-operate with private sector actors, was a fundamental determinant of planners' policy options throughout this period of time (Harding, 1991).

The institutional arrangements for the funding of planning and other local services represent a still further macro-political variable that has shaped politicians incentive structures. In the post-war period the funding of local government services in the United Kingdom has seen an increasing proportion of service provision funded through central government transfer payments (now approximately 80%) rather than through locally raised property taxes. The increasing role played by central government control has in turn enabled the British State to pursue a policy of financial equalisation. This has involved the redistribution of resources from the wealthier local authorities that have a relatively large tax base to authorities, which are relatively poorer. The underlying rationale behind this policy has been to ensure a measure of equality in the level of local service provision between those areas, predominantly in the inner cities that have suffered economic decline and thus have a smaller tax base and the generally wealthier suburban and rural areas (Bailey, 1999).

The dominant role of centrally raised taxation in the financing of UK local government may have been a key factor in explaining the general tendency towards anti-growth planning regimes. Where the delivery of local services, such as education and policing, is dependent on the receipt of locally raised finance then politicians have an incentive to favour a pro-growth agenda in order to finance service provision and to keep tax rates down. This is an especially pertinent constraint where the population is highly mobile and where the so-called Tiebout effect comes into play (Tiebout, 1956). Politicians that fail to allow sufficient development and as a result raise taxes face the threat of lost population and revenues as local taxpayers 'shop around' between different locations according to the balance of services provided and the taxes charged (Fischel, 1985; V.Ostrom et al., 1988; see Dowding, John and Biggs, 1994, for a survey of the empirical literature in this regard). The higher the proportion of central funding, therefore, the lesser is the link between the level of local economic development and the provision of local services and tax rates, as politicians can lobby for increased transfers in order to make up for any shortfall.

The reliance of British local authorities on central government transfers may have further reduced the incentive for politicians to keep a downward check on the regulatory expansionism of planning bureaucrats and may thus explain the general prevalence of anti-growth regimes. It may not, therefore, be a coincidence that as the dependence of local government on central government transfers has increased throughout the post-war period, so the emphasis on anti-growth/ urban containment policies has also increased. More general support for this proposition may be derived from the comparison of British and American experience. The tradition of 'fiscal federalism' in the United States has meant that local authorities are much more dependent on taxes raised from local residents and businesses for the provision of local services and have until relatively recently been constrained in their ability to obtain Federal funding. Seen through a public choice lens, this may explain the apparently greater frequency of pro-growth planning regimes in the United States than in the UK. Even in the United States, however, it should be noted that local authorities have increasingly transformed themselves into 'demand side' interest groups lobbying for Federal transfer payments as a response to failed planning policies and falling revenues. As the relative share of locally raised finance has declined so the frequency of anti-growth regimes appears to have risen (Foldvary, 1994).

The macro-institutional environment of local government finance in Britain may also help to explain the character of the 'pro growth' planning regimes that have tended to emerge. Even in the areas that have sought to promote development, the relative absence of the Tiebout effect and the ability to obtain central transfers has meant that local authorities have opted for strategies that are commensurate with bureaucratic and political interests but are not necessarily *economically self-sustaining*. The clearest manifestation of such processes was the massive land acquisition programme carried out by urban local authorities throughout the 1960s and 1970s and the subsequent construction of mass public housing projects. Throughout this period, a large number of urban local authorities were pursuing a growth-based agenda centred explicitly on a political preference for heavily subsidised public sector schemes. So much so that many inner urban authorities deliberately set out to discourage private sector activity in their jurisdictions, whether it be for housing or commercial uses (Jones, 1982; Loveless, 1987; Goodchild and Denman, 1989). Urban authorities acquired enormous land banks and ran up substantial debts in the process. Much of the land, however, was never developed as local authorities held onto these assets, refusing to sell in a declining market in the hope of obtaining additional central government transfer payments to fund their development schemes. It was partly (and still is to a significant extent) as a result of such processes that large tracts of land in the cities were left derelict with as much as 90 per cent of vacant land held in public sector ownership (Loveless, 1987). With the somewhat tighter public expenditure constraints introduced under the Thatcher administration, the incentive for urban local authorities to release some of these land banks and to enter into growth based partnerships with private sector actors was undoubtedly increased (Harding, 1991, 1994).

The macro-political factors discussed above have clearly been important in shaping the overall structure in which the bureaucratic strategies discussed earlier may have been exercised. Within the confines provided by this political context, however, planners have been extraordinarily effective in defending their bureaucratic interests. Allmendinger's (1997), account of the implementation of the Thatcher government's 'Simplified Planning Zones', for example, shows how local planning bureaucrats in places such as Birmingham, Derby and Slough, were able to subvert supposedly 'de-regulatory' initiatives to conform to bureaucratic objectives and in many cases to *increase* the level of regulation and the complexity of decision-making. Within this context, the desire of politicians to favour high-profile, 'quick fix' solutions to problems of urban decline appears to have provided an opportunity to expand budgets not only through active involvement in such schemes, but by simultaneously increasing the level of regulation, often on lower profile forms of enterprise. In turn, there appears to have been relatively little incentive for politicians to put serious downward pressure on such activities because the benefits of removing the controls that constrain the growth of small and medium sized businesses would be delivered over the longer term and in a more gradual, less politically visible way.

The processes discussed above would seem to provide a possible explanation for the failure of the Conservative administration of the 1980s/1990s to de-regulate the planning system in other than a superficial way and to opt instead for the corporatist policy of promoting public private 'partnerships'. The costs of such policies are widely spread across the mass of a tax paying populace that continues to fund high profile, heavily subsidised programmes of urban renewal. Correspondingly, this position has not been aided by the lack of a clear ideological opposition to such policies from the major political parties. The Thatcher administration lacked a clear commitment to privatisation in this field due to internal party divisions and the need *to be seen* to pursue a high profile attempt to regenerate the inner cities (Allmendinger, 1997). Both Labour and Conservative governments have been committed to strongly interventionist urban policies, though the character of this intervention has changed with the colour of the administration concerned. It is arguably this ideological context of interventionism that has helped to provide an environment in which rent seeking and bureaucratic expansion, have been able to thrive.

CONCLUSION

Throughout the last thirty years the experience of pro-growth planning and in particular programmes of urban renewal has been heavily criticised for their failure to reverse the processes of economic decline that have afflicted the major urban areas within many western democracies. In Britain, urban development schemes have been characterised by high profile projects heavily dependent on big business interests and by huge levels of state subsidy that have been required to secure their completion – the London Docklands programme alone having received in excess of £1 billion in government aid (Rydin, 1998b, p. 347). In the United States, meanwhile, urban renewal projects have a similar record, often characterised by the destruction of neighbourhoods and the small businesses that support them. The subsidised construction of luxury hotels, civic centres and highways has often paid little attention to the fate of the people and businesses that have been 'relocated' to make way for such politically high profile schemes. The principal beneficiaries of such policies have been large scale land owning interests and property developers, often to the neglect of the employment and housing interests of the local population (Logon and Molotch, 1987; Brownhill, 1990; Mills, 1991; Keating and Krumholtz, 1991). Within this context, there are few, if any examples of growth-based policies driven by the small business sector or small-scale property owners (Raco, 1997). Supposedly 'free market' policies, such as the declaration of 'Enterprise Zones', 'Simplified Planning Zones' and 'Urban Development Corporations' have been nothing of the sort. These policies have tended to be based on the *selective* exemption from regulations and taxes for politically favoured business and property interests and massive state intervention by way of land acquisition and subsidy (Brownhill, 1990; Harding, 1991; Imrie and Thomas, 1993). Despite substantial injections of public money there is little to suggest that these projects have succeeded in halting the economic decline of the inner cities. With the possible exception of London, which has continued to benefit from broader economic trends and its position as an international finance capital, urban redevelopment programmes have failed to halt the ongoing loss of population from the major metropolitan areas (Gordan and Richardson, 1997; Woodlief, 1998a, 1998b; Hall, 1998).

This chapter has sought to explicate some of the processes on the demand and supply sides of the political market that may have led to these policy outcomes.

The analysis is by no means exhaustive and cannot account for all of the various complexities that characterise the political economy of growth. The public choice approach is, however, able to explicate some of the most salient features of pro-growth planning regimes as they have developed in Britain and a number of other western democracies over recent years.

On the demand side, the privileges granted to the rent seeking interests of big business at the expense of market efficiency and of the urban poor may be explained, in part at least with reference to the logic of collective action. In the absence of a major ideological shift against corporatist methods of intervention, there seems little prospect of mobilising a coalition for alternative models of growth because the potential beneficiaries are often too numerous to overcome the collective action problem. On the supply side, meanwhile, there is little incentive for bureaucrats or politicians to opt for longer-term, though lower profile 'bottom up' solutions to urban decline, when electoral and budgetary interests continue to point in the direction of high profile schemes, which can be manipulated for political and bureaucratic ends. It is difficult to determine the precise weight of these demand and supply side forces, which may vary with the specific context involved. What is clear, however, is that the structure of incentives on both sides of the political market often pushes in the direction of a form of urban planning, which is simultaneously characterised by 'over-regulation' on the one hand and subsidised, corporatist redevelopment on the other. It would appear, therefore, that pro-growth planning might be equally inimical to the goals of both social equity *and* market driven efficiency.

7

LAND USE PLANNING: PUBLIC OR PRIVATE CHOICE?

INTRODUCTION

In recent years and in particular following the Earth Summit in Rio de Janeiro (1992) an academic consensus has emerged that stresses the central role of land use planning in the pursuit of sustainable development (Healey, 1992, 1997; Blowers, 1994; Thornley, 1994). The contemporary orthodoxy is that land use planning should act as a strategic device, acting to ensure an appropriate balance between environmental protection and economic development goals and to reflect public preferences in this regard. Planning is seen to have a central role to play in ameliorating the environmental deficiencies of the market system and to act as a vehicle for democratic empowerment, especially for those on low-incomes. The theoretical and empirical analysis presented throughout this book, however, has sought to question the validity of such arguments and would appear to suggest that the contemporary environmental policy literature, may be misguided in placing the emphasis on market rather than government failure.

Market failure is undoubtedly an important problem in the environmental sphere, especially with regard to the management of externalities and collective goods problems, where private actors are often not held sufficiently to account for the consequences of their actions. Yet, as this book has demonstrated, it is far from clear that planning is capable of providing adequate solutions to such deficiencies. The institutions of British land use planning *do not* operate in such a way that encourages the internalisation of externalities, but appear to allow the externalisation of costs onto those actors whose interests are not sufficiently represented within the planning system. Whether it is the influence exerted by nimbyist interests and planning bureaucrats in urban containment policy, or the power of corporatist interests in strategies for urban regeneration, there is little to suggest that the planning system balances the interests of *all* the different groups that are affected by the regulatory regime. It is not, of course, possible to offer conclusive proof that the costs imposed on those that lose from the practice of land use planning outweigh the gains obtained by the holders of political power since these costs are subjective. From the perspective set out in this book, however, there are strong theoretical and empirical reasons to believe that land use policies are *structurally biased* towards a process of special interest capture and bureaucratic expansion. As such, the experience of land use planning in Britain may represent an example of government failure.

On the demand side of the political market, the interest groups that gain the most from the planning system are those sufficiently small in number or with the capacity to deploy selective incentives that they are able to overcome the logic of collective action. The losers, by contrast, are the groups too numerous and with too weak an individual stake to act collectively in order to challenge the status quo. On the supply side, meanwhile, planning appears to be driven by pressures within the public bureaucracy that point to the continual expansion of the regulatory regime and the propensity for politicians to concentrate benefits on organised groups whilst simultaneously dispersing the costs across the unorganised mass of the electorate.

If the account presented in the preceding pages is accurate, then the practical experience of planning may be viewed as a product of institutional deficiencies that have been the focus of more general public choice critiques of the regulatory state. These critiques suggest that the mere identification of 'market failures' is not a sufficient condition to warrant government intervention. On the contrary, it is to commit the 'nirvana fallacy' to suggest that the alternative to 'imperfect' markets is a government immune from similar, if not more serious institutional deficiencies. The normative implications of these analyses should not, therefore, be overlooked at a time when still greater levels of government regulation in the field of land use planning are currently being proposed (DETR, 1998). Given the evidence of government failure presented in this book, perhaps it is time to challenge the view that only through the continual growth of government regulation can the goals of environmental improvement and individual empowerment be achieved. It is to these normative implications of public choice analysis that this final chapter turns.

The first part of the chapter sketches out the theoretical basis for a property rights approach to land use problems, focusing on the greater possibility for contractual arrangements within the private market to internalise costs and to empower individual actors. The second and concluding part examines the more specific contribution that such approaches might make to internalising the external costs which have been associated with the political market of land use planning. The analysis suggests that a market system based on private property rights, may have a greater capacity than statutory land use planning to generate the necessary information and incentives that are needed to internalise costs and to reflect public preferences for environmental protection. In making this case the chapter aims to highlight the advantages of a classical liberal agenda and to nudge the terms of the contemporary debate towards a greater recognition of the deficiencies of public planning.

MARKETS AND PROPERTY RIGHTS IN THEORY: THE CASE FOR PRIVATE PLANNING

In order to appreciate the case for a private system of land use control, it is necessary to return to the informational advantages of markets and the deficiencies of public planning as emphasised by the Austrian/Hayekian school. As was argued in Chapter 1, the primary advantage of using markets rests primarily on their ability to convey information that it is highly dispersed and to facilitate a degree of co-ordination between the diverse preferences and expectations of the millions of different individuals within society. Market prices do not, by any means, provide a 'perfect' reflection of public preferences, but they do provide a useful guide to decision-makers when choosing how to allocate resources amongst competing ends and provide for a degree of co-ordination, which may not be possible under a centrally planned alternative. Government planners lack the direct informational feedback provided by the account of profit and loss and have no easy way of knowing how much and what type of environmental protection that the public actually desires. It is as a direct result of the difficulties of 'planning' in this sense that planners cannot act as impartial calculators of social welfare, but may respond instead to public choice pressures, which as this book has shown, may not provide an effective mechanism to reflect the general welfare.

If markets provide a useful means of generating information with respect to public preferences then it follows that the most appropriate way to reveal such preferences for environmental protection may be to establish a functioning market. Within this context, the Coasian tradition in economics has suggested that defining and enforcing an adequate system of property rights so that people can capture the benefits from 'making a market' in externalities, may obviate the need for government intervention (Coase, 1960). In its initial formulations this approach has been heavily criticised as irrelevant to many environmental problems because it assumes the absence of transactions costs in the definition and enforcement of property rights (see, for example, Turner et al., 1994). As his subsequent followers have pointed out, however, it was not the intention of Coase to claim that transaction costs do not present obstacles to market exchange, but to note the presence of these costs in *any institutional setting* (Dahlman, 1979; see also Lai, 1997; and Webster, 1998, for some recent land use examples). As this book has shown, the alternative to 'imperfect' markets is not a cost-less nirvana where all externalities are internalised, but the reality of a political market where high transaction costs and their associated incentive structures may result in chronic examples of special interest and bureaucratic capture. The case for relying on markets, therefore, stems from the argument that given the informational problems of planning and the public choice problems of government administration, markets may be *more likely* to internalise costs and to reflect public preferences than the alternative of statutory planning.

The Coasian approach suggests that the presence of externality and collective/public goods problems, which are the most frequently cited causes of market failure, are a product of the high cost of enforcing property rights. Market failures are indeed a product of high transaction costs, but the market process itself does offer at least some incentives for individuals to devise ways of *reducing* these costs and to *internalise externalities* by developing new methods of converting what are currently collective/public goods into private marketable commodities. The ability of individuals to capture the full benefits and to bear the full costs from resource use is not, therefore, a static phenomenon (Anderson and Leal, 1991). As Anderson and Leal (1991) note, *any* case of external benefits/costs may provide fertile ground for an entrepreneur who can define new sets of property rights. A land owner or property developer, for example, who can devise ways of excluding non-payers from the benefits of a scenic view may reap a profit by attempting to the define the appropriate set of rights. If there is no demand for such views or other environmental amenities then few will attempt to internalise the relevant externalities, but if people are willing to pay for these goods, profits will reward those who are most successful at marketing the relevant environmental values (Anderson and Leal, 1991).

The private property rights approach suggests that the market system may provide an effective, if imperfect way of allocating environmental resources. Seen through this lens, the role of government should be confined to the provision of a legal system, which can ensure the enforcement of contractual bargains struck between private individuals. Instead of acting in the role of planner and regulator, government should confine itself to the maintenance of a supportive institutional setting of secure property rights. The former role implies that the state concerns itself with discovering the wants and desires of the public in order to bring about central planning, an informational impossibility according to the Austrian/Hayekian school (Hayek, 1948; Buchanan, 1969; Lavoie, 1985; Cordato, 1992). The latter involves government acting merely as a facilitator of voluntary exchange, strengthening rather than supplanting the market system in its vital information generating role (Buchanan, 1986; Kwong, 1990; Anderson and Leal, 1991; Shaw, 1994).

From the perspective of public choice theory, not only do property rights solutions generate more information than government planning, but they also encourage the development of institutions where individual agents bear more of the opportunity costs of their actions by bringing decisions within the realm of the market system. One of the key advantages of markets is that they allow individuals with disparate and inconsistent plans to co-ordinate their activities through a process of mutual adjustment as market prices indicate the relative value placed on goods and services by other members of society. Under market institutions, consumers pay directly for the resources they use and have an incentive to become well informed and to monitor alternative suppliers of goods in order to make the best choice possible. Entrepreneurs, meanwhile, who succeed in satisfying consumer preferences may reap the rewards of so doing.

Private individuals operating in the market are, of course, limited in their ability to process information and to monitor the behaviour of other market participants, but from the perspective of Virginia public choice theory, there are strong theoretical reasons to believe that such problems are likely to be *more severe* in the realm of collective, political decision-making. Foremost amongst these are the relative ease of linking product quality to product performance in markets, compared to the great difficulty of linking social outcomes to public policy decisions; the greater ease of finding disinterested (non-political) advice on market transactions (e.g. consumer guides); and the existence of enforceable contract and tort remedies against deception by private producers of a sort that are not available against deceptive politicians (Somin, 1998). Within this context, analysts since Schumpeter (1950) have repeatedly noted that most individuals are far more knowledgeable about their private affairs than about politics because of the insurmountable information and monitoring costs involved in the latter. In the private sector the gains to an individual from seeking out a cheaper or better product are confined to the individual concerned. In the public sector, by contrast, the costs of decisions made by voters, politicians and bureaucrats are dispersed across the electorate as a whole. If poor decisions are made, the costs are not confined to the individuals who make such decisions but are spread across the entire population. Under these conditions there is little incentive to seek out an appropriate level of political information.

When property rights are well defined, the market process acts to internalise costs because the prices paid by consumers for different bundles of property rights, are reflective of the relative value placed on these resources by other members of society. The political process, by contrast, tends in its very nature to *externalise* costs through the mechanism of collective decision. The 'all or nothing' nature of political decision-making means that once a majority coalition has been assembled resources can be extracted from the rest of the population without their express consent. From a public choice perspective, therefore, there are strong grounds for limiting the role of the state to the enforcement of private contracts (Buchanan, 1986).

A further advantage of private markets is that they tend to allow a greater degree of social experimentation, which may reduce the relative significance of errors in decision-making. In the market place, if the value of land in a particular use to future consumers is greater than to those in the present, private property owners may have a financial incentive to conserve. Because the future is uncertain, subjective considerations are inevitably involved in analysing the future profitability of alternative uses and it is because of this uncertainty that errors will be made and markets will be prone to failure. Markets, however, although manifestly imperfect may allow for a wider range of forecasts to be made, *at least some of which, may prove to be accurate*. Government planning, by contrast, tends to be less polycentric in its decision-making form and should an error occur, the negative consequences may be correspondingly more far-reaching (Lavoie, 1985; Gray, 1993). Thus, as chapter 2 of this book showed, in Britain the blanket emphasis on urban containment, appears to be preventing experimentation with a range of different urban forms that could deliver as yet unforeseen environmental benefits.

Given the potential for government failure in the political market, what makes the continued adherence to the nirvana fallacy all the more unfortunate is that there may be much greater scope for harnessing the positive aspects of private markets than is commonly recognised. Theorists in the Coasian tradition have presented numerous examples that demonstrate the ability of market institutions to overcome transaction costs in response to rising environmental demand and to supply many of the goods which it is often thought should be the monopoly preserve of the state.[1] This approach is of particular relevance to many of the questions which have traditionally been the focus of land use planning, given that there are a variety of relatively low cost transaction measures which can bring environmental values within the realm of the market.

One of the most frequently cited examples of the property rights approach is the use of private covenants and deed restrictions in contracts. In these circumstances, developers specify in contracts the particular activities which are to be permitted with respect to a set of properties for sale, in order to internalise external effects and capture the returns through higher asset prices (Ellickson, 1973; Siegan, 1974; Veljanowski, 1988; Anderson and Leal, 1991). Prior to the advent of land use planning, restrictive covenants had a long history of use in the United Kingdom. One of the earliest examples of these privatised-planning arrangements was at Victoria Park near Manchester. Originally laid out by a private developer in 1837, the park was operated privately until 1954 and the sale of its lots carried with them 'certain conditions, the "laws" of the Park, which protected its open spaces' (Spiers, 1976, p. 13). Similarly, many of the most beautiful urban developments in Westminster, Bloomsbury, Chelsea, Hampstead, Oxford and Cambridge have been preserved through private restrictive covenants. These covenants have included restrictions on noise, chimney smoke and permitted alterations to exterior design in order to inter-nalise external effects (West, 1969).

The case of restrictive covenants provides useful clarification of a key element in the property rights approach, which is often misinterpreted by critics of market alternatives to land use planning. Sagoff (1994), for example, uses a famous illustration from Pigou. Suppose a firm wishes to build a factory in a quiet residential area; from a Pigovian perspective, the residents will have to grin and bear the ugly face of the factory or pay the owners not to build in their neighbourhood. Sagoff argues (1994, p. 225) that a free market would require residents to express their wishes by compensating the factory owner for the marginal advantage between building in their neighbourhood and going to the next best location. Environmentalists, he points out, would then see the possibility of a developer having received a 'bribe' not to build in one area, proceeding to extort payments from other communities by threatening to build there as well. According to Sagoff, therefore, statutory land use planning is called for, in order to eliminate similar 'market perversities'.

Sagoff's argument, however, illustrates a common misrepresentation of what the adoption of a property rights approach would actually mean in practice. Under a market system of land use control there would be incentives for *developers of quiet residential areas* to supply restrictive covenants in the *initial terms of contract*, which forbid noxious land uses within particular neighbour-hoods. These covenants would increase the sale prices of such developments, assuming that people would not purchase a house in an area where their neighbours could convert their property into a factory site. Those individuals choosing to live in an area where such controls were absent would already have expressed a preference for lower house prices and a higher level of environmental risk and so would not experience a breach of their property rights if the factory was built in the area. Where covenants exist, the factory developer would *not* be able to threaten the community because the *residents would own the relevant rights.* It is not the factory owner who receives compensation in this case, but the initial developer who marketed the covenants and hence defined the relevant set of property rights. There is no prospect of 'market perversities' under such a system because any breach of the restrictive covenant as any other breach of property rights (e.g. theft) would be punishable through the courts.

In a more recent theoretical development, Foldvary (1994) advances the idea of the 'private proprietary community' as an effective way to deal with the problem of externalities and collective goods. According to this perspective, many collective goods often categorised as non-excludable are in practice 'territorial goods' and are thus excludable by definition. The benefits of a scenic view or open space, for example, can often be 'tied in' to the provision of other goods, such as leisure or the purchase of residential environments. So long as the relevant area is privately owned by an individual or group/co-operative, people must reveal their preferences to access the territory in question and the free rider problem can be resolved (see also Buchanan and Stubblebine, 1962 and Demsetz, 1964, for a similar approach). Privately owned settlements, therefore, provide the opportunity to capture amenity values through real market trades and to subject this provision to market competition on a range of territorial scales.

The collective facilities provided by private shopping malls provide a small-scale example of the 'tie-in' concept. Shopping centre merchants provide an array of collective goods through the market, such as malls, security forces, parking lots and a pleasant shopping environment, tied-in to the purchase of private merchandise. Whilst competitors could in theory enter the market offering comparable private goods at a lower price, by not 'tying in' a surcharge for the collective goods (Varian, 1994), there are many goods whose value is *contingent* on being provided as part of a package deal (Schmidtz, 1994). Thus, shopping centre merchants who do not provide car parking or a litter collection service might well be able to charge less for food – but they will also lose the custom of those who value these services (witness the trend from town-centre to 'out of town' shopping in Britain). Likewise, a housing developer who fails to provide a package of restrictive covenants to protect amenity values will lose custom to those competitors who do. As Schmidtz (1994) proceeds, 'One does not have to be a visionary to realise that market forces can in theory provide shopping malls. But the point is that there is no a priori reason why similar structural tie-ins could not lead to the provision of a variety of other public goods as well,'(see also Brubaker 1975; Cowen, 1985, 1988; Boudreaux, 1993).

A useful illustration of the larger scale provision of collective goods through contractual ties-ins is provided by the concept of garden cities, envisaged by the very founder of the town planning movement, Ebenezer Howard. The first settlements proposed by Howard were to be developed and owned entirely by a private corporation or co-operative, which would plan the design features of the town, including open space provision, parkland and landscaping and then collect the associated revenues in the form of ground rents. Before the advent of statutory planning and the subsequent nationalisation of 'new towns', the first garden city in Britain, Letchworth, was developed on precisely this basis (see Foldvary 1994, for a collection of American case studies). Similarly, in the United States, the town of Reston, Virginia was modelled on the garden city ideal. The development of the town was financed entirely by the Reston Corporation, a private company, which bought the site and financed the project including the provision of roads and parks through the collection of rent. The town has a population of 50,000, housed in 18,000 residential units on a 7,400 acre site. The grounds are landscaped with thickly wooded areas separating the main residential districts, all of which are covered by restrictive covenants.

The property rights approach set out above is not dissimilar to the proposals for 'common property regimes' outlined by authors such as Ostrom (1990). In the proprietary community model individuals are, in effect, contracting into a set of *collective or shared private property rights* (Nelson, 1977; Weiss, 1987; Foldvary, 1994).[2] There is, therefore, nothing in advocating a market system of land use control that need minimise the significance of 'community'. Advocates of planning and especially 'collaborative' planning often denigrate market competition as 'atomistic', and as encouraging non-co-operative forms of behaviour, with the implicit assumption that only the state can foster a spirit of social co-operation (Healey, 1997). Market competition is not, however, antithetical to co-operative endeavour. In a world of uncertainty and imperfect knowledge, what the market process involves is competition between *different types of co-operation*, allowing social experimentation and a discovery process to unfold, that can reveal which particular ways of organising production work best. It is precisely this process of entrepreneurial experimentation and discovery, which is thwarted by attempts to force allegedly 'co-operative' endeavours into a single plan. The necessity for competition results in large part from the insuperable limits to individual human knowledge and the subsequent need to try out a wide array of *different* 'plans' (Hayek, 1948, 1982). As voluntary worker co-operatives, such as the Mondrogon have illustrated so well, there is nothing in the market system that precludes the development and growth of more collective ownership forms, alongside conventional models of economic organisation (Steele, 1992; see also Nozick, 1974; Di Zerega, 1993). All that is required is that individuals should be able to contract into such collective arrangements on a voluntary basis and that they should be subject to a market test through the account of profit and loss.

In the proprietary community model people *agree* to sacrifice complete control over decisions relating to their property to the principles of community governance laid down in the proprietary contract. The communities examined by Foldvary (1994), for example (Reston, Virginia; Fort Ellsworth, Virginia; Arden, Delaware), marketed 'constitutional provisions' for the settlement of neighbourhood disputes and laid down a set of rules and procedures (voting rules etc.), by which the members of the community could change the terms of collective control (see also Beito and Smith, 1990).[3] The great advantage of the proprietary community model, therefore, is that it facilitates competition and experimentation between different communities and lifestyles offering various bundles of collective and individual private property rights and different rules for community management on a range of territorial scales. Which particular mix of individual and common property rights works best cannot be known in advance, but may be discovered over time through a process of competitive trial and error in the market.

There are clear similarities between the proprietary community model and Tiebout's (1956) public goods theory of local taxation. Tiebout suggested that citizens could select the communities which best satisfied their preferences for collective goods by choosing in which areas to live on the basis of local service provision and that competition between local authorities for citizens would prevent the exercise of monopoly power. From a property rights/public choice perspective, however, the fundamental difficulty with the Tiebout approach is that local authorities are not private, profit making entities and as result cannot go bankrupt if they fail to deliver the services which consumers desire. As was noted in Chapter 6, the trend in Britain and in many Western democracies has been for local authorities which have lost revenues over time, to turn into 'demand side' interest groups lobbying for central government transfer payments to make up for financial deficits and therefore to externalise costs. In the proprietary community model by contrast, all the rewards and penalties from community management accrue to the relevant developers removing the potential for such rent seeking behaviour (Foldvary, 1994).

A further deficiency of the Tiebout theory, it should be noted, is the implicit assumption that local authorities themselves provide the ideal jurisdictional units for the management of land use problems an assumption that is also common to the advocates of collaborative planning. There is, however, little reason to believe that such an assumption is warranted. In the vast majority of cases local authority boundaries have been effectively imposed on communities in an essentially arbitrary way, for political reasons which have little to do with their efficacy in delivering local services and improving environmental quality (Foldvary, 1994). The great advantage of a property rights approach, therefore, would be to facilitate the formation of proprietary communities or common property regimes on a voluntary, contractual basis, with competition between developments allowing for a process of entrepreneurial discovery to reveal the scale of community governance best suited to the management of land use externalities. Seen from this perspective, just as the optimum size of a firm is not something that can be known in advance of competition, so the optimum scale of a proprietary community or common property regime cannot be known but must be discovered and rediscovered through a process of organisational trial and error within the market.

One important objection to the property rights approach is that it fails to take into account the effect of distributive inequalities within the market system and the likelihood that lower incomes groups will be unable to gain access to a sufficient level of environmental quality under such a system. Public planning is justified, therefore, as a means of 'empowering' low-income people and ensuring a more equitable level of access to environmental goods. From a property rights/ public choice perspective, however, given the informational problems of planning outlined earlier, public intervention in the allocation of land uses may be an inappropriate way of seeking to empower those on low incomes. If the goal is to ensure such a measure of equality, a more appropriate mechanism might be to redistribute resources *directly* through the tax system. In this case, greater equality in material resources would allow the subjective values of those individuals with previously low incomes to be given greater weight in an otherwise free market, rather than to rely on an arbitrary planning process. Perhaps more important, by re-distributing resources in a direct and transparent way, rather than rely on complex regulatory systems (which so often discriminate against low-income groups – see, Goodin and Le Grand, 1987), the problems of special interest capture and bureaucratic expansion described in this book, are more likely to be avoided.

A further criticism often raised against market solutions is that property rights advocates who distrust the powers of administrative bureaucracy in general, appear to have undue faith in the ability of the state judicial system to enforce property rights without similar examples of government failure. In this view, property rights 'solutions' would simply transfer the incentive for over-elaboration and the expansion of costs associated with administrative regulation to the legal professions and the courts, which would necessarily have to enforce the relevant contractual arrangements (Weale, 1993). This line of critique is not without merit, but it does miss the significance of the wider framework in which property rights, market solutions are advocated. The Virginia school of public choice theory suggests that many of the problems associated with government failure stem primarily from the sheer enormity of contemporary state intervention across the full spectrum of economic and social affairs. Rational voter ignorance, the power of special interests and bureaucratic inefficiency all result from the impossible information and monitoring costs facing voters when the state intervenes in so many areas of modern life. What is needed, therefore, is a fundamental withdrawal of the state from the vast bulk of the responsibilities it now assumes and the installation of constitutional limits to the scope of government power (Buchanan, 1986). Seen in this broader context, if the state confines itself to the maintenance of a legal system and other minimalist functions, such as the provision of a minimum income and basic environmental standards, then the problem of excessive monitoring costs in the political process is reduced, if not removed altogether. There are always likely to be some government failures in the legal system, but there is a fundamental difference between a government limited to the *enforcement* of property rights, from a system based on the *continual redistribution of property rights* through rent seeking and bureaucratic control (Buchanan, 1986; Somin, 1998).

Seen through the lens of Virginia public choice theory an interesting irony emerges for the advocates of collaborative planning who propose a form of deliberative democracy (Dryzek, 1996). Far from constraining the scope of the state, theorists such as Healey (1997) advocate a public sector even larger than it is today, by extending the scope of deliberative, collective decision-making at the expense of private markets. These writers do recognise the existence of government failures but contend that their incidence can be reduced by an extension of 'greater democracy' to even more areas of social life. In doing so, however, collaborative planning theorists appear to ignore the enormous *increase in voter information/monitoring costs* and hence rational ignorance that would inevitably ensue. A case can be made, therefore, that it is only by *reducing the size of the public sector* to a minimum set of functions, and by *focussing public debate on a more circumscribed set of concerns* (such as the provision of a set of minimum environmental standards and a safety net for the disadvantaged), that the *quality* of public discourse may actually be improved. As Somin (1998, p. 441) points out, by failing to recognise that the roots of deliberative incapacity reside in rational ignorance, deliberative democrats end up proposing cures for government failure that might actually spread the disease.

Perhaps the most far-reaching criticism of the property rights approach is that there are clearly some externalities, which for technical reasons simply cannot be subject to contractual solutions. Webster (1998), for example, argues that planning may be in the best position to organise and deliver collective goods, because high transaction costs prevent the development of voluntary market solutions, especially in large urban areas where externalities are diffuse and the number of bargaining parties is too great. According to this approach, attention should turn instead to institutional redesign *within the public sector* so as to minimise the instances of government failure.

Defences of planning on these lines do indeed constitute a marked improvement on orthodox Pigovian welfare economics (which assume zero transaction costs and the presence of perfectly informed and benevolent bureaucrats) and present some awkward problems for those who seek to justify a position which approaches laissez faire. It must surely be accepted that there is always likely to be a large range of external effects, which simply do not lend themselves to market solutions and might in principle suggest a quite extensive role for the state. There are, however, some important issues, which transaction costs theories of planning have tended to neglect.

First, transaction costs theories have still to provide an account of how government planning can overcome the informational problems exposed by the Austrian/Hayekian school, as outlined in Chapter 1. It is certainly true that in the case of trans-boundary effects there is likely to remain an important category of 'market failures' (this is always likely to be the case in terms of 'global effects' such as climate change and the preservation of bio-diversity). It is *not* possible, however, to say that planning will result in the *correction* of these failures. How, for example, is one to know whether the 'benefits' of seeking to reduce green house gas emissions through the use of the land use planning system will outweigh the 'costs', when planners may not know the subjective cost/benefit trade-offs of the many different individuals within society? It is precisely because of the informational problems of 'planning' in this sense that planners respond to public choice stimuli, which as this book has shown may not necessarily be a reflection of community interests as a whole. Policies with questionable environmental benefits might well be introduced if these can be put to the benefit of special interest coalitions. In the British case, for example, as argued in this book, the emphasis on reducing transport emissions through an intensification of urban containment policy – a far from proven strategy – appears to reflect the political power of the interest groups and bureaucrats that benefit most from these policies and who have sought a new rationale to maintain the status quo. In these circumstances, there may be grounds to be wary of intervention, even in the absence of a viable market alternative.

Second, it is debatable the extent to which one can rely on the redesign of public sector institutions in order to overcome such government failures. Whilst there is undoubtedly some potential to move in this direction, for example by making decision-making more transparent and providing easier access to information, it may also be the case that there is an important category of government failures, which may be endemic to public sector decision-making *per se*. The key determinant in evaluating market and public sector alternatives is their relative capacity to *correct for errors over time* and to facilitate learning and innovation. Market institutions are highly imperfect, but they do provide an error correcting mechanism through the account of profit and loss, which may ensure the reallocation of resources away from those who make consistently bad decisions. In the public sector, by contrast, there is no obvious mechanism to correct for errors in institutional design. Although the processes of democratic accountability are not totally without teeth, they may be an inadequate substitute for market competition. Should errors occur in designing the initial regulatory framework, public choice forces may lead to institutional sclerosis, 'locking in' erroneous decisions as special interests coalesce around a given set of arrangements within the political market (Olson, 1982; North, 1990, p. 73). In these circumstances, the gains to those who would benefit from institutional reform may be too diffuse to prompt corrective action and inefficient institutions may survive thorough a process of 'path dependence'. It would appear to be precisely such a process that has typified the practice of land use planning in Britain as documented in this book.

Finally, what is neglected in transaction costs theories of planning is the capacity of markets, however imperfectly, to evolve solutions over time and to develop technologies which can lower transaction costs in response to rising environmental demand. Where transaction costs problems in the market are extreme, as with the more diffuse sources of air pollution, there may indeed be a case for the state to lay down a general framework of minimum environmental standards within which market forces should operate. In these situations the relevant standards would have to be determined in the political rather than the private market. For the reasons outlined earlier, the process of democratic deliberation is likely to work more effectively if it is paired back to such minimalist functions.

Within this context, it should also be remembered that even if there is *no* market 'solution' to a particular problem this *does not* provide an *automatic* rationale for public intervention. By intervening and effectively supplanting the market, public choice processes may thwart the development of new markets for environmental goods. In Britain, for example, prior to the 1947 Town and Country Planning Act, the use of covenants and other contractual solutions was an evolving market response to the growing demand for the protection of environmental amenities. The nationalisation of development rights, however, effectively supplanted the growth of this system which could, over time have developed into an effective means of marketing amenity values (Walters et al., 1974; Veljnaowski, 1988). Moreover, by thwarting the development of private solutions to localised land use problems regulation may in turn, have prevented the development of property rights approaches to more intractable issues where bargaining costs are considerably higher. The development of restrictive covenant and proprietary community models could, for example, have acted to lower the transaction costs of coping with trans-boundary externalities as contractual communities reduce the number of contracting parties and facilitate market exchange at the *inter-community* level. In short, private property rights approaches do not offer definitive solutions to all land use planning problems, but they do suggest that one should not overlook the ability of markets to bring forth more innovative approaches than a public sector faced with the institutional deficiencies that have been the focus of this book.

MARKETS, PROPERTY RIGHTS AND PRIVATE LAND USE PLANNING: A THOUGHT EXPERIMENT

The first part of this chapter has sketched out in theoretical terms the case for a free market, property rights alternative to the provision of goods, which it is often thought, may only be provided by government land use planning. The fundamental purpose of adopting such an approach as an alternative to state regulation is to *change the structure of incentives* so that decision-makers are *more likely* to face the opportunity costs of their actions and are *less able* to transfer costs to other sets of actors. How then might a *change in the incentive structure* resulting from the move to a property rights model, be reflected in the *outcomes* that have been associated with the practice of land use planning? In what follows an attempt is made to answer this question. The aim of the analysis is not to outline a comprehensive 'blueprint' for policy change, but to present a theoretically informed thought experiment, concerning the likely consequences of a liberal market system for the land use planning issues that have been the concern of this book.

House Prices and Property Rights Approaches

As was noted in Chapter 2, planning designations such as Green Belts restrict the supply of land for housing so that house prices are considerably higher than might otherwise be the case. In turn, the evidence presented in this book suggests that the interest groups that lobby for such planning controls and the bureaucrats who enforce them, are not faced with the full opportunity cost of such actions within the political system. The members of 'nimbyist' groups, for example, who gain in terms of increased property values and the preservation of amenities, have no incentive to take into account the costs imposed on prospective consumers of housing who must pay higher prices. Planning bureaucrats, meanwhile, who obtain additional job security through the growth of the administrative system, have little incentive to consider the costs imposed on consumers and on other groups such as small developers. From a public choice perspective, these diffuse groups are largely absent from the political process due to their inability to overcome the logic of collective action. Regulations, therefore, are 'supplied' in the political market at a 'price' which does not reflect their full opportunity cost and the political demand for land use regulation is likely to be *too high*.

Some commentators regard planning controls such as Green Belts or restrictive zoning classifications as essentially the same thing as the private covenants proposed in the property rights approach outlined in the first part of this chapter, because they are directed towards the same sorts of issues. As Fischel (1985) observes, however, the *crucial* difference is that under a private system a *financial price must be paid for the exercise of controls over other peoples' property*. This position is equally the case when a developer imposes covenants on buyers of new residential lots. The price paid by the developer is the opportunity cost of allowing the land to be used for some activity not permitted by the covenant. Since it is developers/ landowners who are attempting to maximise the value of their assets under such a system they are led to at least consider the alternative uses to which their land might be put – housing development without covenants, for example (Fischel, 1985, p. 28 and 138). Under a restrictive covenant or private communities/common property model, therefore, people seeking to restrict development in order to preserve amenities would have to *compete directly in the market for land* with others who value the land in alternative uses. Consumers of residential amenity would have to pay developers directly for the provision of land use controls via contracts and would thus be faced with more of the immediate cost associated with the level of regulation that they are demanding.

From a property rights perspective, a key feature of such a system would probably be a *reduction in the overall level of restriction,* because those people no longer able to obtain regulations at a subsidised level through the state may cease to demand the equivalent level of control (Fischel, 1985, p. 138). As a result, a more diverse and flexible pattern of land management may emerge. Covenanted developments, common property regimes or proprietary communities might prevail where individuals are still prepared to pay the full price for preventing additional development, but a more permissive system is likely elsewhere. Siegan's (1974) classic study of the land use system in Houston, for example, the one American city which has operated without a comprehensive system of land use planning, found that restrictive covenants were less comprehensive than land use controls in comparable cities with statutory regulation.[4] The increased flexibility brought about by this system facilitated greater levels of new residential development and substantially lower land and house prices than in comparable American cities.

It should be noted at this point that a property rights approach would not necessarily result in a sudden and dramatic fall in property prices, as might occur if all planning controls were removed overnight. The point of the property rights approach is not to remove *all* controls, but save for some minimum environmental standards laid down by the state, to have *the level of restriction determined in the market*, by way of covenants or contractual equivalents, rather than by a system of administrative regulation. The major effect of a property rights approach, therefore, would be to bring about a more flexible approach, allowing a greater level of new development and a slow but steady fall in house prices and other property values over a longer period of time. Seen through a public choice lens the principal beneficiaries of this approach would be the consumers of new housing development whose interests are more likely to be accounted for by the price system than by a system of political control.

In addition to the price reductions brought about by the elimination of nimbyist activities, there are other reasons to believe that prices would be lower under a private property rights regime. One of the causes of high house prices under the British planning system is the cost of delay brought about by the complicated administrative procedures associated with planning. As chapter 4 showed, bureaucrats have little incentive to minimise such costs because their job security and budgets are partly a function of administrative load. Neither do the larger construction companies have an incentive to seek a reduction in regulation, because it is these costs, together with the discretionary granting of planning permissions, which restrict market entry and reduce competition. A property speculator or developer holding a site with planning permission has little incentive to bring land forward for development safe in the knowledge that prices are likely to go on rising because of the scarcity of alternative sites brought about by planning restrictions. Under a property rights approach developers would be freed from many of the administrative costs and delays and would have more of an incentive to bring land onto the market because they would no longer be assured the monopoly profits associated with the *discretionary* granting of planning permission.

In a market free from statutory planning entry into the house building industry would be eased considerably and the ability of developers to make profits would be more a reflection of their ability to supply housing types (with or without covenants or equivalents) which match consumer preferences (Veljanowski, 1988).

One area that might, for example, provide a source of new competition in the housing market would be the rejuvenation of the 'self build' sector. Attempts by individuals to build their own homes or to contract directly with small developers have been virtually eliminated in Britain because the complicated bureaucratic procedures of attaining planning permission prevent most people from entering into this type of arrangement, leaving the field wide open for the larger corporate concerns (see for example, Hardy and Ward, 1990).

For the potential benefits of this free market approach to have their full effect, especially for low-income groups, property rights solutions would have to go hand in hand with the removal of many other controls within the housing market, such as rent controls and security of tenure legislation, which continue to discourage the letting of previously owner-occupied homes (Minford et al., 1987; Tucker, 1990). A sufficiently generous welfare safety net would, of course, be required to protect those individuals still unable to purchase adequate housing in the market. From a public choice perspective, however, the aim should be to move towards a system, which subsidises people to make purchases in the market and not to have land use and housing space allocated by bureaucratic means.

Amenity Values, Dwelling Densities and Property Rights Approaches

Turning to the questions of amenity provision and the density of development, there are a number of reasons to believe that the change of incentive structures brought about by a property rights approach might bring forth significant improvements in the allocation of land uses. One important benefit of a free market system is likely to be an overall rise in the quality of amenities provided as a consequence of the likely reduction in land prices discussed above. Under land use planning the artificially scarce supply of housing land has meant that the profitability of obtaining a planning permission for developers, is far higher than the profits to be made from the design of attractive developments. Given the absolute shortage of development land due to planning, the value of a house, or any building *per se* is now exceptionally high, but the marginal profitability of that building being well designed is very low (Evans, 1988). Increases in the total supply of housing which would be brought about under a market system would increase the relative profitability of well designed and carefully landscaped developments. Similarly, by lowering barriers to entry in the private house building market and increasing competition, a market system of land use control would encourage developers to seek a competitive edge by improving design quality and the range of amenities available such as the provision of parks and open spaces.

In Britain, where urban containment policies have reduced the amount of land taken for development, the overall effect of adopting a property rights approach might be a lowering of average dwelling densities. The primary reason for this would again be the removal of the nimby effect. As argued throughout this book, Nimbyist groups lobbying for Green Belts and other designations are able to impose costs on those consumers who have a preference for lower density forms of living but whose voice fails to be heard in the political marketplace because of the collective action problem. Under a market system individuals who have a preference for land use controls, which raise dwelling densities overall, would have to pay developers for the provision of such controls and to compete directly in the market with prospective residents seeking a greater level of new building. Because the *de facto* subsidy to nimbyist interests represented by government planning controls would be removed, the overall level of control is likely to be reduced and with it the level of new residential densities.

In countries such as the United States, where restrictive growth controls have encouraged a more *low density* pattern of development, a free market system is likely to *raise* the density of new building as developers would no longer need to comply with large lot zoning ordinances, unless consumers are prepared to purchase something similar in the market. Average urban densities in the United States are, however, always likely to be lower than in countries such as Britain, where the relative scarcity of land is higher and where the point at which agriculture becomes more profitable than residential uses is closer to the major urban centres (Evans, 1985; Fischel, 1985).

Within this context, it is important to recognise that adopting a free market approach *does not* imply support for *any particular level of residential density*, but rather implies that the market should be left free to respond to consumer preferences in this regard. The contemporary environmental planning literature is characterised by a polarised debate between various 'urban design experts' some of whom are champions of high density dwelling (see, for example, the Report of the Urban Task Force, 1999) as the best environmental option and others who favour a more low density approach (Crane, 1996). In Britain, at present, it appears to be the advocates of high density, 'compact city' policies, supported by a nimbyist/bureaucratic coalition, which is in the ascendancy. As the debate between planning experts itself illustrates, however, the environmental costs and benefits of different density developments remain highly uncertain. *None* of the relevant commentators may genuinely be in a position to judge the 'social' costs of different developments and must instead rely on their own *subjective* preferences to define what type of development would constitute an improvement in environmental quality.

One of the great advantages of a market driven system, therefore, would be a far greater level of experimentation with competition between a wider range of potential urban forms, which could then be subject to the verdict of the consumers through a market test. Some proprietary communities, condominium associations and common property regimes might seek to promote the development of 'compact' settlements, with other organisations opting for a more low-density approach and still other areas operating without any controls. Consumers of urban environments under such a system would then have a wider variety of options from which to choose and would be able to express their own subjective preferences for the type of development that they believe is commensurate with an improvement in the quality of life. The resulting competitive market discovery process may throw up a range of options for different mixes and densities of development, some of which may deliver unforeseen environmental benefits. Land use planning, by contrast, precludes such experimentation and the discovery of new information as the forces of special interest capture and bureaucratic expansionism documented in this book, effectively lock the entire land use system into a single pattern of development.

Transport Patterns and Property Rights Approaches

As was noted in Chapter 2, closely related to the issue of dwelling densities is the question of transport patterns and the environmental consequences of urban form. A major effect of urban containment in Britain and even more so the practice of large lot zoning in the United States, has been to increase the length of commuting distances as suburban developments have been pushed further and further out from the major urban centres. An important cause of such patterns has again been the political power exerted by nimby lobbies. For the reasons outlined in the previous sections, a property rights approach is likely to result in more development taking place on the immediate urban fringe because the demand for planning controls such as Green Belts is likely to be lower in a market system where individuals are required to purchase the rights to control other peoples' property. There are thus strong theoretical reasons to believe that a free market in land would reduce the tendency for people to live further from their place of work and would thus reduce the incidence of long distance commuting.

In order for this approach to have a significant effect, however, would require a still more radical extension of market forces. The major externalities associated with long distance commuting are vehicular emissions and the air pollution that results. In addition to the problems created by planning, the major cause of long distance commuting is the continued provision of road space – 'free at the point of delivery' (ASI, 1988; Anderson and Leal, 1991; Gordan and Richardson, 1997). Consumers of the road network do not pay directly for the use of roads and as a consequence do not face the full opportunity cost of their actions. Because the provision of road space is not priced in the market, consumers have no incentive to reduce their consumption rates or to search for other less costly forms of travel. The property rights solution to this problem would be to privatise the trunk road network itself, (or at the very least to introduce some form of government road pricing) allowing road owning companies to charge for the use of road space through tolls or similar devices and thus to discourage over-use (Anderson and Leal, 1991, p. 165).[5] Seen in this context, it is ironic that many environmentalists blame traffic problems on the free market when roads are supplied by the public sector, railways have until recently been nationalised and commuting distances have been lengthened by one of the most comprehensive systems of land use planning in the western world.

Of itself, the privatisation of the trunk road network and the introduction of market pricing might reduce the incentive for people to live further away from their place of work. This is not to say, however, that the resultant market prices would reflect *all* of the relevant externalities. Road owning companies may set road charges at levels that reflect road construction and maintenance costs but which do not necessarily take into account the major externalities of road use such as the emission of air borne pollutants. Automobile emissions are a difficult problem because the mobile source makes it costly to track polluters and to charge them for damages (Anderson and Leal, 1991, p. 165). These costs could, however, be reduced substantially by considering highways themselves as the source of pollution and by *making the road owner liable for environmental damages*. If road owners were fined or charged for excessive levels of air pollution then they would in turn charge road users a higher price, which would be reflective of these costs. Higher prices for road use would then provide incentives for people to switch to less polluting cars or to the use of privately provided public transit (Anderson and Leal, 1991, p.165).[6] This is an area where there may remain an important role for the state. At present, the transaction costs for private individuals to monitor pollution levels associated with major roads are insurmountable. By setting basic pollution limits, there-fore, and by imposing fines on road owners who exceed these limits, government action could help to lower transaction costs and to facilitate the development of a more effective transport market.

There continues to be considerable uncertainty about the relationship between transport patterns and the connected issue of dwelling densities and urban form. Land use planners are simply not in a position to know what the 'optimum' dwelling densities are in terms of reducing the need for auto-travel and the related air pollution. There is so much 'expert' disagreement about the likely effect of urban form on pollution levels because there are so many interconnected variables that are difficult to predict or model. What, for example, would be the optimum urban form in terms of air pollution, if technological change results in the widespread adoption of the electric car? The greater degree of experimenta-tion in urban form brought about by a market driven approach may thus provide important informational advantages over government planning procedures. Competition between proprietary developments exhibiting a variety of urban densities would generate more information on the environmental costs and benefits of different forms of development. Combined with a system of private road pricing and a basic framework of pollution control provided by the state, consumers would have more scope to make their own subjective trade-offs between communities according to travel costs and other such environmental parameters. Not all of the relevant costs and benefits would be known in advance but market competition would allow more of the relevant environmental and economic trade-offs to be revealed through a process of trial and error discovery. Institutional sclerosis in land use planning, by contrast, has thwarted the development of such experiments in living and has, in the British case, forced the land use system into a blanket emphasis on urban containment.

Urban Regeneration and Property Rights Approaches

The property rights approaches to planning outlined in this chapter do not provide any guarantees that economic and environmental problems will be solved in some optimal sense, but they do offer an institutional foundation which may be *more likely* to provide such solutions through the discovery of information and the internalisation of external costs. In the specific case of urban regeneration, a free market system of land use control cannot guarantee that the decline of inner urban areas brought about by wider processes of economic and technological change will be reversed. From the perspective of Virginia public choice theory, however, it may offer a better institutional environment in which cities are able to adapt to such trends than the continuation of statutory planning.

As Chapter 6 argued, the structure of incentives within the political market of planning has continually pushed in the direction of high profile, 'quick fix' solutions to urban decline. Such approaches have, however, failed to address some of the fundamental institutional sources of these problems. Planning bureaucrats, in particular, have little incentive to encourage the development of self-sustaining economic activity because their budgets are largely dependent on regulation and the receipt of grants and subsidies to 'regenerate' urban areas. It is largely as a result of such incentive structures that some of the most depressed urban areas supposedly committed to pro-growth policies, often face the full gamut of regulatory controls that are deployed in the more affluent suburbs and the countryside. Correspondingly, high levels of public sector land ownership have often prevented access to land for small businesses and developers. Local authorities have been reluctant to sell land at low prices in a declining market and have sought instead to lobby for additional central government aid in order to engage in subsidised land redevelopment projects with politically favoured developers. In the meantime, inner urban areas continue to be characterised by high taxes and poor service provision. The result has often been a 'cycle of interventionism' as yet more resources are sought from the taxpayer to repair the subsequent decline (Gordan and Richardson, 1997; Woodlief, 1998a, 1998b).

From a public choice perspective, therefore, urban areas may have much to gain from the adoption of a property rights approach and a market system of land use control. A primary benefit might flow from the removal of much of the planning bureaucracy and regulation that thwarts new development especially from small developers. Small-scale developments and changes of land use would no longer have to proceed through complex planning procedures under such a system. It is likely that in those areas suffering the most severe problems in terms of unemployment, the demand for restrictive covenants or their equivalents would be relatively low and their requirements minimal. This would help to facilitate a greater level of new development than is the case under statutory land use planning. Correspondingly, removing government planning controls is also likely to reduce the bias towards monopolistic local authority landowners and corporatist interests that have been important features of urban policy.

A property rights approach would imply that public sector land banks should be broken up and sold off to the private sector and that all subsidies and grants for urban redevelopment should be phased out. This is not to say that large-scale redevelopment schemes have no part to play in urban re-generation, but that in so far as they do they should not be based on the *subsidisation* of corporatist interests.

Fragmented ownership patterns in urban areas often do present obstacles to private redevelopment projects because the transaction costs of acquiring property from a large number of smaller owners can be very high. There are also collective action problems associated with the so-called 'hold-out' phenomena. In this case, an individual owner may keep her land off the market if the property concerned is the last parcel of a much larger package, in order to obtain a much higher price. A developer may be willing to pay an extraordinary price for such parcels, because if the sale does not take place, then all previous purchases will have been wasted. There are, however, private contractual means that can reduce if not eliminate the incidence of such problems. Contingent contracts, for example, may be used to overcome this particular version of the free-rider problem. These arrangements specify to each individual seller in advance that the contract will not be activated until all of the other contracting parties have agreed to sign. As a consequence, individual owners *do not know* whether they are the first or the last prospective seller and the collective action problem may be resolved (Buchanan, 1965; Ostrom, 1988, 1990). Such approaches are far from perfect, but from a Virginia public choice perspective they may offer a more reliable institutional environment than the subsidised land acquisition and corporatist, rent seeking policies that have tended to characterise government-led urban renewal schemes.

The relaxation of blanket urban containment policies under a market system may also have a part to play in providing a stimulus to urban businesses and landlords to improve the quality and range of services provided. To the extent that urban containment policies have prevented a proportion of the population from leaving the older cities they have also granted urban local authorities and businesses a semi-monopolistic market. As a consequence, incentives to improve service provision and to make urban areas more attractive places in which to live have been reduced, a position that has been made substantially worse in the British case by the central government financing of local authority services. Shifting to a model of private proprietary development, therefore, is likely to have considerable advantages, as private communities/common property regimes would have to compete to attract residents in order to raise the value of their assets and to avoid the possibility of community bankruptcy (Foldvary, 1994).

In urban areas that are already developed and where collective goods, such as street cleaning, environmental health, road maintenance etc., are provided by local authorities rather than by proprietary communities or their equivalents, it would be difficult to set up the arrangements for private community governance from scratch. There may, therefore, be an important role for the state in helping to set up proprietary associations and to transfer control over collective services to such bodies. In so far as local authorities do continue to play a role in service provision, meanwhile, a market system of land use control would provide these authorities with a stimulus to seek more innovative ways of improving the quality of life in the cities. If the local tax base is no longer protected by the planning system and if local authorities have to compete to attract residents for fear of losing revenue, then there will be a much greater incentive to seek out new ways of improving service provision and the quality of urban life. Correspondingly, shifting to a local, rather than a centrally based system of taxation would place a greater competitive discipline on local authorities to minimise un-necessary regulation and to improve the quality of services provided (V. Ostrom et al., 1988).

It is, of course, still possible that wider forces of social and economic change may lead people to vacate the major cities. If this were indeed to be the case, however, a property rights approach may offer a wider variety of options in seeking to adapt to such changes than is currently the case under land use planning. The greater flexibility and diversity of land use controls that would emerge under a market system and the reduction of nimbyist behaviour as discussed previously would offer more opportunities for people to leave declining areas and to seek employment elsewhere. A welfare safety net would still be required to help those most disadvantaged in markets, but if the aim is to redistribute resources to low income people then it may be better to do so directly through the tax system. From a public choice perspective, giving poorer people the resources to spend *themselves* in the market place to access housing and other such goods may prove a far more effective means of empowerment than continuing to rely on special interest politics and the bureaucracy of land use planning.

Countryside Protection and Property Rights Approaches

Many defenders of land use planning often support continued government intervention on the grounds that market forces would result in the destruction of valuable habitats and landscapes under a tide of urban development. For the reasons outlined earlier in this chapter, it is certainly the case that in Britain at least, more green-field development is likely to result from a property rights approach. This does not, however, necessarily imply that the aesthetic and other environmental qualities of the countryside will be sacrificed under such a regime.

The major cause of environmental damage to the countryside has been the continued subsidisation of modern agri-business through government programmes such as the Common Agricultural Policy. Huge agricultural subsidy programmes have been defining features of rural policies in Britain, Western Europe and the United States and these have been responsible for considerably more habitat loss than can be attributed to urban developments such as house-building. Under a property rights approach there would be no place for the continuation of such policies, which are often the product of special interest rent seeking. As the recent experience of New Zealand has shown, the abolition of farm subsidies may well be the most beneficial course of action. In this case, marginal, environmentally sensitive tracts of land have been taken out of agricultural production altogether and there has been a decline in the use of chemical pesticides and fertilisers (Ridley, 1996, 1998). Such an approach would seem to be more desirable than the alternative of introducing yet another set of 'agri-environment' subsidies to counteract the effect of production subsidies or the possibility of introducing regulation over agricultural land uses. Regulation, in particular, is likely to be manipulated by the larger farmers (as it has been in the United States – see Pasour, 1983) in much the way that urban planning controls have been by corporate developers, in order to reduce competition. In this case, external costs might be pushed onto consumers in much the way that occurs by way of direct subsidies. The major beneficiaries of a property rights approach, therefore, would be the taxpayers (lower taxes), food consumers (lower prices) and all those members of the population who wish to see a greater emphasis on habitat conservation (less intensification).

Whilst it must be accepted that some rural land and open spaces are likely to be lost to urban development it is also likely that under a property rights approach a greater number of ways of combining new developments in rural areas with high levels of environmental quality will emerge. Proprietary communities of the sort documented by Foldvary (1994), which included the provision of country parks, thickly wooded zones separating residential districts and the provision of nature reserves, might provide an environmentally acceptable way of accommodating housing development in rural areas by allowing the transfer of land out of agricultural uses. As incomes rise with economic growth, the demand for environmental amenity is also likely to rise and with it the incentives for developers to devise all manner of contractual devices to maintain aesthetic quality. Anderson and Leal (1997) cite numerous examples of private condominium developments, which specify an array of contractual restrictions to ensure the provision of amenities and open spaces. In parts of the Rocky Mountains and the Appalachian chain, developers have supplied contractual arrangements to preserve the appearance of scenic views. Stroup (1990, p. 176), for example, notes that at Big Sky Valley in Montana, developers bought up an entire mountain valley, which they then subdivided, selling tracts with restrictive covenants allowing only aesthetically acceptable development. Under a property rights alternative there would be considerable potential for such schemes, which could combine high environmental quality with new housing development.

More important, however, the removal of farm subsidies is likely to encourage farmers to seek alternative ways of earning a living, which would include the marketing of valued environmental characteristics. The growing demand for recreational use of the countryside, for walking and other leisure activities has been thwarted by the continued subsidisation of agricultural practices. As the ongoing debate over the so called 'Right to Roam' in Britain has demonstrated, many farmers have actively sought to prevent recreational users and walkers from entering their property for fear of damage to crops and for more general breaches of property rights (Ridley, 1996, 1998). If agricultural subsidies were removed, however, farmers would have a positive incentive to *attract recreational users onto their land so long as they could charge a market price for doing so*. Alternatively, farmers and other rural landowners might sell their holdings to specialised nature conservation companies, which would be likely to develop as a response to the changed incentive structures resulting from a property rights approach (Pennington, 1996).

In the United States, the North Maine Woods, a private company formed through an association of 20 farmers and landowners provides an illustration of the type of institutional arrangement that may emerge more frequently under a property rights approach. The company manages recreational activities in a 2.8 million acre park – *an area half the size of Wales*. Entrance to the park is controlled through 17 checkpoints and access roads situated around the perimeter with fees charged according to the length of stay (Anderson and Leal, 1991). The bird reserves of the Wildfowl Trust, meanwhile, provide a further demonstration of Foldvary's (1994) theory of territorial provision. At places such as Martin Mere (Lancashire) and Slimbridge (Gloucestershire), the Trust holds large tracts of land, which are a haven for migrant ducks and geese. Birdwatchers and other recreational users are charged entrance fees through a turnstile system and a wide range of visitor facilities is provided. Similarly, the Royal Society for the Protection of Birds (RSPB) already acts in a commercial capacity charging entrance fees for visits to its 118 nature reserves (Pennington, 1996).[7]

Within this context, the property rights approach may offer a greater prospect of protecting habitats than contemporary policy developments in Britain, which are based on maintaining the subsidised agricultural regime whilst at the same time facilitating recreational access through a statutory right to roam on uncultivated land. The latter has effectively removed the right of landowners to exclude recreational users from their property and has thus created the possibility of a 'tragedy of the commons' scenario (Ridley, 1996, 1998). In thinly populated countries, such as Sweden, which have a long established tradition of free access rights to uncultivated land, the environmental consequences of such policies have been minimal. Where population densities are low and pressure on resources is relatively light 'open access regimes' may actually be the most appropriate institutional option, because the environmental costs of enforcing private property rights or common property regimes may not be sufficiently outweighed by the relevant benefits (Demsetz, 1967; Libecap, 1989). In Britain, by contrast, with a substantially higher population to land ratio and much greater demand for recreational access, the environmental consequences are potentially far-reaching. Should recreational use begin to exceed a level which is compatible with nature conservation objectives individual users will have little incentive to modify their behaviour because they are not required to pay a price for the environmental services that are being used. Landowners, meanwhile, will continue to have little incentive to enhance environmental quality because they will be unable to capture the returns from so doing (Pennington, 1996; Ridley, 1996, 1998).

Market solutions to countryside protection will not, by any means, be perfect, but it is a contention of this book that they may be more likely to encourage the internalisation of externalities than the present system of rent seeking and bureaucratic control. In the case of countryside protection, the analysis presented above illustrates the potential for the developments that might flourish more widely under a property rights approach, encouraging the transfer of land out of subsidised agricultural uses, to the potential benefit of consumers, taxpayers and the environment at large.

CONCLUSION

The normative agenda outlined in the preceding pages has emphasised the advantages of relying to a far greater extent on property rights and market processes as an alternative to statutory land use planning. In the light of these advantages the analysis suggests that much greater consideration should be given to the potential of liberal market solutions as an alternative to a regulatory state afflicted by government failure. Markets will always rely on an institutional framework of government to enforce contracts and property rights, a role which must predominantly, be provided by the state. Similarly, all but the most radical Libertarians would accept that the state must play an important role in ensuring the provision of an adequate safety net to protect those who might be disadvantaged in markets. The current extent of government intervention in land markets, however, extends well beyond these classically liberal functions and indeed has actively suppressed the emergence of private solutions through a continued adherence to policy prescriptions, which *do not allow* the market system to work.

The approach set out in this book, will not, of course, satisfy those who adopt an absolutist position on environmental matters and who are prepared to impose a vision of the 'good environment' out of moral commitment, irrespective of individual preferences in society at large. For those who hold to a more liberal view of society, however, the property rights agenda set out here may offer a better prospect for individual empowerment and may provide a greater potential to respond to environmental problems than the present system of special interest and bureaucratic control. To a large extent this system is reinforced by the widespread public belief that only government regulation can ensure an appropriate balance between environmental and economic goals. Changing this worldview, therefore, will require a fundamental challenge to the anti-market ideologies of many environmentalists and the new consensus politics of the 'Third Way'. Given the lack of a classically liberal force on the contemporary political scene this will not be an easy task. If, however, people become aware of the deficiencies of the regulatory state and realise that there are more liberal alternatives to it, then there may be some hope for constructive institutional reform. For too long the case for planning has been sustained by nirvana economics. Perhaps this book has gone some way to redress this imbalance.

NOTES

Chapter 1

1   According to Israel Kirzner (1992), an economic process is efficient to the extent that it harmonizes the plans of individuals in pursuit of their goals. This definition is particularly appropriate to a 'comparative institutions' approach. It does not require that a process is 'perfect' as in many neo-classical welfare economics and equilibrium theories, but that it facilitates co-ordination in a superior way to alternative institutional frameworks. The significance of this approach will become apparent when comparing the 'efficiency' of government and market decision-making later in the chapter.

2   It should be noted that some public choice theorists do not use all the components of this critique. The Chicago school of public choice, following Stigler (1975) is, for example, much closer to orthodox neo-classical economics and its notions of perfect information and certainty over the effects of decisions. Whilst accepting much of the *incentives* based critique of government planning presented by the Virginia school (see pp. 22–6 below), it does not draw on the *informational* critique provided by the Hayekians.

3   The historical evidence of the changing composition of firms strongly refutes the Marxian inspired notion that market competition is a self-eliminating process (see Brozen, 1982 and Steele, 1992 for reviews of this material). Evidence suggests that overall rates of industrial concentration have remained static or have even declined in the last 100 years. Many of the corporate giants who 'dominated' their particular markets in yesteryear have subsequently seen their market share whittled away by new entrants, so that they are no longer the market leaders today. Moreover, even in industries that *do* continue to exhibit high levels of concentration, the composition of the relevant firms has itself often changed. The thirty or so companies that 'dominate' industries such as tobacco production today, are in many cases not the same thirty companies that also 'dominated' such industries 50 years ago – the majority are in fact new market entrants or previously smaller firms that have grown in the intervening years (Brozen, 1982, pp. 1–21). Such evidence would appear to offer considerable support for Austrian or Schumpeterian conceptions of how markets work (Kirzner, 1997).

4   Suppose, for example, that an individual is motivated by an altruistic concern to reduce her individual water consumption to 'socially efficient' levels'. As Steele (1992, p. 205) points out, in the absence of market prices for water there is no easy way for the individual concerned to know the 'right' or 'socially efficient' amount of water she should actually consume. In this situation, even the most altruistically inclined person with only a tiny streak of self interest is likely to consume as much water as she personally wants, because at least she *knows* that, whereas the social costs are highly uncertain. An altruistic person could attempt to guess the appropriate social trade off, but in the absence of market prices will make mistakes and inefficiency will be the result (Steele, 1992, p. 205).

5   This is not the case in Chicago school public choice theory. Chicagoans persist with the rigid and unrealistic assumption that nearly *all* individual behaviour is driven by pecuniary maximisation (see, for example, Stigler and Becker, 1977 and Posner, 1986).

6   This would be the condition required in order to meet the so-called Kaldor/Hicks 'efficiency test'. Where, for a policy to be 'efficient' the gainers could in theory fully compensate the losers – even if no such transaction should actually take place.

7   Accepting the significance of 'structure', it is far from clear that many versions of structuralism and especially Marxism, have an appropriate understanding of what the relevant structures are. This is reflected, perhaps most clearly, by the clinging of many neo-Marxists to theories based on the 'laws of capitalist motion', notwithstanding the manifest shortcomings of the labour theory of value and falling rate of profit thesis on which they are based, (Bohm-Bawerk, 1937; Steedman, 1977), – critiques which have been accepted by most contemporary socialists (see Dunleavy and O'Leary, 1987).

Chapter 2

1   A number of authors have suggested that the primary goal was to maximise revenue for the Treasury – hence the failure of the government to break up public monopolies prior to sale – rather than to maximise competition (Marsh, 1991).

2   Gordan and Richardson (1997) quote cost/benefit studies, which appear to suggest that even when taking into account the non-financial environmental benefits, public transport subsidies are *still* in excess of those directed at the private car. Others will doubtless disagree with such pronouncements. Whether one believes that public transport subsidies have been 'too high' or 'too low' appears to be a matter for personal value judgement. If nothing else, these disputes do throw very clearly into light the subjective nature of attempts to second guess public preferences by attempting to perform supposedly value 'neutral' cost/benefit analyses (see also note 3 below).

3   The fundamental difficulty with cost/ benefit analysis is the assumption that money is a unit of measurement when in fact it is a *medium of exchange*. When an individual exchanges money for a good or service, she does so because she values the good concerned more than the money – it is not possible, however, to say *how much more*, because the opportunity cost is subjective. Because money is a medium of exchange rather than a precise measure of value, attempts to measure the value of goods which are not actually traded are of little if any use (Formaini, 1991).

Chapter 3

1   This figure is a rough approximation derived from the author's own interviews and from previous empirical work. Short et al. (1986), for example, found from an analysis of local amenity societies in Central Berkshire that 47 per cent had a membership of less than 200, 20 per cent had between 200 and 400 members, 11 per cent between 400 and 800 and 6 per cent over 2,000. Assuming the average local CPRE has about 200 members, then the total membership covered by CPRE affiliation is probably about 560,000, i.e. $200 \times 2,574 + 46,000$.

2   Chapter 4 provides an analysis of bureaucratic incentives in this regard.

3   I borrow this phrase from Olson (1965, p. 165).

4   In the Kaldor/Hicks sense.

Chapter 4

1   A different version of this chapter was printed in *Environmental Politics*, Vol. 6, No.4 pp. 76-107. The author wishes to thank Frank Cass Publishing for the right to reprint some of this material and especially the data contained in Tables 4.1–4.9.

2   Niskanen (1991) appears to accept the implications of Dunleavy's more disaggregated approach, but does not himself set out a fully developed model.

3   Dunleavy (1991) suggests that the relative absence of budget maximising incentives in such agencies calls into question what he describes as 'New Right' notions of government failure. Even on Dunleavy's own terms, however, no such conclusion follows. That social security or education bureau are not necessarily budget maximisers in terms of their total budget, says nothing about the organisational efficiency of these agencies. Dunleavy's account of education bureaux, for example, suggests that central agencies will maximise core funding on their own administration costs and starve local authorities of funding for direct education expenditures. Local authorities themselves will also attempt to keep as much of the budget that they do receive from the DoE for their own administrative funding, rather than transfer the whole of the budget to individual schools. On these grounds one would expect a progressively higher proportion of education expenditures to be taken by administrative costs rather than service delivery by individual schools. This is, by any standards, hardly a model that suggests public sector efficiency in the delivery of education services.

4   Central government grants to local authorities are based on the so called Standard Spending Assessment (SSA) in which central government estimates what local authorities should spend on the provision of various local services such as Education, Social Services, Planning etc. The block grant which central government provides to local authorities - Revenue Support Grant (RSG), is based on these spending estimates. Once local authorities receive this grant, however, they still have considerable discretion in how they choose to allocate the block grant between different local departments. Even though central government control over *total* local authority spending has increased substantially in recent years, councils still retain discretion concerning how that money is actually used. Only 23 per cent of central government grants are earmarked for specific projects and services (Wilson and Game, 1994).

5   'Quango' is the term used for quasi-autonomous non-governmental organizations. These bodies are state appointed boards employed to implement elements of government policy. They are nominally separate from the agencies of central government, but still constitute an arm of the state bureaucracy with discretionary decision-making powers.

6   Social Services must be distinguished from the Department of Social Security (DSS). Social services at the local authority level is in a delivery bureau format – most of its budget is devoted to professional social service provision including the management of children's homes, supervision of child adoption and foster care, services for the elderly and disabled and various health related services. The DSS at the national level is a transfer bureau – most of its budget is devoted to transfer payments for the unemployed and old aged pensioners. Local social services is predicted to have a tendency towards budget maximisation but the DSS is not.
     Some of the enormous rise in social service spending may well be accounted for by the four fold increase in unemployment since the mid 1970s - greater unemployment may have led to more family breakdown, child delinquency etc. and hence a demand for more social workers. However, it is difficult to believe that the increase spending on social services, from 1.9 to 8.8 per cent of a tripled local authority budget, can be explained solely by this trend. A more plausible explanation would point to budget maximisation by the professional social workers who administer these services – see for example Lait (1980).

7   Apart from social services and administration of justice only planning saw a consistent year on year pattern of growth. The other agencies which saw a net gain between 1960/61–1990/91, Police and Housing – displayed a more erratic pattern – Police spending fell as a percentage during the 1960s and early 1970s before rising quickly during the 1980s. Housing increased during the 1960s, fell back in the mid 1970s, increased in the early 1980s before falling back again later in the decade.

8   The development control data should be treated with some caution because they do not weight applications in any way to take into account the size and complexity of the development being proposed. Even accepting this limitation, however, there is little

evidence to suggest that the scale of the planning permissions put forward can account for the low level of productivity suggested by these figures. For a more detailed elaboration of this point see Pennington (1997a, pp. 122–3).

9   With the introduction of budget holding by individual schools following the 1988 Education Act, education bureaux shifted into a control agency format. It might be argued that teachers should be classed as professionals in the same way as town planners and should therefore have secured greater levels of growth and resisted the introduction of individual budget holding. It is not to denigrate teachers that I do not include them in the same professional category as town planners – what is important for the theory of professionalization and bureaucracy offered here, is the organization within these bureaux and in particular the status gap between high grade policy staff and low grade implementation staff. In education bureaux policy is developed by high grade professionals in the local authority, with a considerable status gap between these bureaucrats and the many hundreds of teachers implementing policy in the individual schools. There appears little incentive for high grade bureaucrats to be concerned about expanding opportunities for promotion in the lower ranks and so these bureaucrats are less likely to maximize the overall budget. In planning bureaux by contrast there is less gradation between ranks of bureaucrats. In the case of planning senior bureaucrats will often work in the same office and on the same policy documents as the rest of the staff. Increases in the budget and promotion prospects for top bureaucrats will trigger similar opportunities for most if not all of the other bureaucrats in the agency.

10   Housing Corporation spending was flat throughout the 1980s until the 1988 Housing Act, through which the Conservative government greatly expanded the role of housing associations in the provision of social housing. Since then spending increased from £0.8 billion to £2 billion in 1993, before falling back to £1.4 billion in 1996 (Housing Corporation *Fact File*, 1996).

11   There are numerous examples of government enterprises or government supported enterprises operating without the constraints imposed on the wider population. Consider the enforcement of anti-trust laws in the US. or the actions of the Monopolies and Mergers Commission in the UK. Industrial mergers in the private sector or co-operative arrangements between firms are often subject to rigorous scrutiny, supposedly to avoid actions which will reduce competition. Government enterprises on the other hand are often granted monopoly status, with all or most forms of competition outlawed, as was the case with telephones and other 'public utilities' before privatisation. In many cases government provision of utilities is given the justification that these are public goods where competition in supply is not possible. But, if competition is impossible, why the need to outlaw the entry of private competitors?

     In the case of UK planning laws, is it merely coincidental that the two forms of land use where the state itself is an active player – agriculture through the enormous post war subsidy programmes and forestry where the state owns a high percentage of commercial plantations through the Forestry Commission, are also the two forms of land use excluded from statutory planning control (Pennington, 1996)?

Chapter 5

1   A different version of this chapter is due to be published in *Environment and Planning C: Government and Policy* (forthcoming 2000). The author wishes to thank Pion Press for permission to reprint some of this material and especially the data presented in Tables 5.1–5.3 and Table 5.5.

2   It ignores the possibility of 'extremist' abstention if a party moves too far away from its more 'extreme' supporters and also the possible loss of support from party workers should a moderate position be adopted. Party activists on whom most politicians rely to 'get the voters out' – through campaigning, canvassing etc. have a tendency to be more

'extreme' in their opinions than the general electorate. Thus, if a moderate position is adopted and party activists lose the incentive to work for their party this may reduce the party's ability to fight an effective election campaign (McLean, 1982).

3   In a market context where consumers are faced directly with the consequences of their purchasing decisions there might be an incentive to purchase 'expert' advise, but few such incentives exist for voters in the sphere of representative politics. As Kuran argues (1991, p. 78) 'The individual who buys a slickly advertised automobile is in a position to judge how well the automobile really runs. And, if something goes wrong with it has an incentive to find out why. By contrast, an ordinary person cannot easily determine the effects of trade protection. In any case, since most of the costs and benefits would accrue to others, and since his ability to affect the outcome is minuscule, he has little incentive to find out.'

4   Likewise, it is difficult for voters to attribute the source of higher import prices and higher unemployment to the impact of quotas and minimum wage laws respectively. In these cases, benefits are concentrated on readily identifiable groups – e.g. trade union members employed in a minimum wage industry, whereas costs are dispersed invisibly on consumers – through higher prices and higher unemployment. In many cases, losers in the rent-seeking game will not even know that they are losers – as in the case of workers who are employed in one industry when a minimum wage is introduced, but in future years are not able to find jobs in an alternative industry because of its existence. For a empirical analyses of the costs of regulation and the lobbying activities of the beneficiaries, see Stigler (1975), Block and Olsen (1982) and Tucker (1990).

5   The distinction between Metropolitan seats – defined by the *Times Guide to the House of Commons* as those falling within the boundaries of the old metropolitan counties – does not provide a perfect urban-rural distinction. There are actually about 30 seats within the metropolitan category, which are on the suburban – rural fringe and are likely to exhibit more rural characteristics, including local amenity interests. Equally, however, there are a similar number of seats within the non-metropolitan shires which are predominantly urban and are likely to have a relative lack of such interests – so the distinction drawn here does not bias the analysis.

6   Amenity interests affiliated to the CPRE must be distinguished from those affiliated to the Civic Trust. The latter are found predominantly within central urban areas and are not the focus of the argument here. The groups affiliated to CPRE are predominantly village residents associations in rural areas or on the urban fringe (Short et al., 1986). It is this type of organisation, which has a direct amenity interest in the preservation of green field sites. In the absence of data, which indicate the exact proportion of CPRE members living in these areas, however, it is not possible to establish precisely the extent to which CPRE affiliations are of the 'nimbyist' variety. If anything, the figures presented here may underestimate the potential significance of the amenity lobby because if the theoretical argument is correct one would expect membership to be more concentrated in Green Belt and other designated areas, rather than evenly spread throughout all of the non-metropolitan areas.

7   These figures may, to an extent, underestimate the current significance of the agricultural vote. Under more inclusive definitions – those that take account of employment in food processing and agri-chemicals, for example, – the agricultural vote may be rather higher.

8   Scottish members are not represented on this committee, because environmental affairs in Scotland are dealt with through the Scottish Office and now through the new Scottish parliament. Welsh members are rarely represented because of the role played by the Welsh Office/Welsh Assembly – although there is occasionally some overlap with the DETR.

9   This position may now be changing somewhat. The new Labour government, unlike its Conservative predecessor, has very few farming representatives within its ranks and with a huge parliamentary majority may be able to afford to ignore the demands of farming and land owning interests. This may have been a key factor in the recent introduction of

a statutory 'right to roam' in the countryside, a policy vigorously opposed by the farm lobby.

Chapter 7

1   Coase himself was one of the first authors to follow such an approach. In an article entitled, 'The Lighthouse in Economics', Coase showed that Lighthouses – often considered a collective good by many welfare economists and therefore unlikely to be provided by the private sector, were actually supplied privately in Britain before nationalization. Neo-classical analysis assumed that vessels could benefit from the lighthouse facility irrespective of payment. In fact, lighthouses were provided by harbour companies with fees charged on entrance to harbour. Those refusing to pay were simply excluded from the port (Coase, 1989).

2   As is now widely recognised in the property rights literature, 'common property' regimes are radically different from the 'open access' regimes that are associated with the 'tragedy of the commons'. The latter refers to a situation where a resource or asset lacks any form of organisational structure to manage the resource in question (Ostrom, 1990). 'Common property' regimes, however, refer to a position where a resource is managed by some form of co-operative organisation. McKean and Ostrom (1995) have described 'common property' regimes as approximating a model of shared private ownership.

3   There is of course, a possibility that such rules could be used for purposes, such as the creation of racist or homophobic communities the worst excesses of which might not wish to be tolerated by a liberal state.

4   It should be noted that the Houston system was not totally privatized – there were for example some minimum standards building regulations. What does make Houston distinctive and thus a good example of what might happen under a privatized system, is that unlike any other major American city there was no statutory planning/zoning ordinance. As late as the mid 1980s, the population of Houston voted down proposals to introduce zoning controls by way of referendums. I am not, however, aware of the precise situation at the present time.

5   The environmental economist Herman Daly (1993 p.175) has criticised the proposal by Anderson and Leal (1991) that highways should be privatised. 'More important, one might have expected "free market" economists to be a bit more sensitive to the problems of monopoly ownership - or are we to envision many parallel highways competing for the motorist.' In making these remarks Daly is clearly sticking to a narrowly neo-classical conception of the way markets work and does not appear aware of the Hayekian approach to competition outlined in Chapter 1. The fact there may be only one supplier of roads between two places on a map *does not* mean that the competitive market process has ceased. If, for example, there is only sufficient demand for one road to exist then it makes no sense to speak of 'monopoly power'. What is required for market competition to be effective is *freedom of entry* into the relevant market. Within this context the principal source of competition in road travel need not come from 'parallel highways', but from other modes of transport such as rail. Whilst the transport market is never likely to approach conditions of 'perfect competition' there is plenty of scope to increase the level of competition above the levels that are witnessed today.

6   There is not, in this perspective, a case for subsidising buses and other forms of public transit any more than there is a case for subsidising roads. Both buses and cars would be charged by road companies, according to the pollution that they produce. If buses are less polluting, road owners would have an incentive to increase charges on cars and to encourage buses in order to avoid paying additional fines for the breach of pollution limits.

7   Contrary to welfare economic analysis, the charging of entrance fees where consumption is potentially non-rival does not detract from efficiency. When deciding how to use a

resource, the relevant cost is its value in alternative uses and not the marginal cost of admitting additional consumers. Thus, the only way to discover whether consumers prefer the preservation of a country park to a new housing development is to charge a fee for entrance to the park (Baden and Leal, 1990; Anderson and Leal, 1991).

BIBLIOGRAPHY

Adam Smith Institute (1988) *The Green Quadratic*, London: Adam Smith Institute.

Adams, D. (1994) *Land for Industrial Development*, London: E and F Spon.

Adams, D. (1995) *The Urban Development Process*, London: Methuen.

Adams, W. (1993) 'Places for Nature: Protected Areas in British Nature Conservation', in F.B. Goldsmith and A. Warren (eds) *Conservation in Progress*. Chichester; Wiley.

Alchian, A. and Demsetz, H. (1973) 'The Property Rights Paradigm', *Journal of Economic History*, Vol. 3, No. 1, pp. 16–27.

Allmendinger, P. (1997) *Thatcherism and Planning: The Case of Simplified Planning Zones*, Aldershot: Ashgate

Alston, L.J. and Spiller, P.T. (1992) 'A Congressional Theory of Indian Property Rights: The Cherokee Outlet', Chapter 6, in T. Anderson (ed.), *Property Rights and Indian Economies*, MD: Rowman and Littlechild.

Altshuler, A.A. and Gomez Ibanez, J.A. (1993) *Regulation for Revenue: The Political Economy of Land Use Exactions*, Washington, DC: Brookings Institution.

Ambrose, P. (1986) *Whatever Happened to Planning?* London: Methuen.

Anderson, T. (ed.) (1983*) Water Rights: Scarce Resource Allocation, Bureaucracy and the Environment*, San Francisco: Pacific Research Institute for Public Policy.

Anderson, T. and Leal, D. (1991) *Free Market Environmentalism*, San Francisco: Pacific Research Institute for Public Policy.

Aranson, P. (1990) 'Rational Ignorance in Politics, Economics and Law', *Journal des Economistes et des Etudes Humaines*, Vol. 1, No. 1, pp 25–42.

Arrow, K. (1951) *Social Choice and Individual Values*, New York: Wiley

Ascher, K. (1987) *The Politics of Privatization*, London: Macmillan.

Ashworth, G.J. and Voogd, A.H. (1990) *Selling the City: Marketing Approaches in Public Sector Urban Planning*, London: Belhaven.

Axelrod, R. (1984) *The Evolution of Co-operation*, New York: Basic Books.

Bachratz, A.P and Baratz, S.R (1970) *Power and Poverty: Theory and Practice*, New York: Oxford University Press.

Baden, J. and Leal, D. (eds) (1990): *The Yellowstone Primer*, San Francisco: Pacific Research Institute for Public Policy.

Baden, J. and Stroup, R. (1979) 'Property Rights and Natural Resource Management', *Literature of Liberty*, Vol. 2, No.4, pp. 5–44.

Baden, J. and Stroup, R. (1981) *Bureaucracy versus the Environment*, Ann Arbor: University of Michigan Press.

Bagguley, P., Mark-Lawson, J., Shapiro, D., Urry, J., Walby, S. and Warde, A. (1990) *Restructuring, Place, Class and Gender*, London: Sage.

Bailey, S. (1999) *Local Government Economics*, London: Macmillan

Ball, M. (1983*) Housing Policy and Economic Power*, London: Methuen.

Banister, D. (1997) 'Sustainable Development and Transport', Interim Report to the Bundes forschungsandstalt fur Landeskunde und Raumordung (Mimeo).

Barde, J.P. and Button, K.J. (1990) *Transport Policy and the Environment: Six Case Studies*, London: Earthscan.

Barlow, J. and Duncan, S. (1992) 'Markets, States and Housing Provision: Four European Growth Regions Compared', *Progress in Planning*, Vol. 38, Part 2, pp. 94–177.

Bartel, A.P. and Thomas, L.G. (1987) 'Predation Through Regulation', *Journal of Law and Economics*, Vol. 30, pp. 239–64.

Basset, K. and Harloe, M. (1990) 'Swindon: The Rise and Decline of a Growth Coalition', in M. Harloe, C. Pickvance and J. Urry (eds) *Place, Politics and Policy: Do Localities Matter?* London: Unwin Hyman.

Becker, G.S. (1983) 'A Theory of Competition Among Pressure Groups for Political Influence', *Quarterly Journal of Economics*, Vol. 98, No. 3, pp. 371–400.

Becker, G.S. (1985) 'Public Policies, Pressure Groups and Dead-Weight Costs', *Journal of Public Economics*, Vol. 28, No. 2, pp. 329–47.

Beito, D. and Smith, B. (1990) 'The Formation of Urban Infrastructure Through Non-Governmental Means', *Journal of Urban History*, Vol. 16, No. 3, pp. 263–303.

Bennie, L.G. and Rudig,W. (1993) 'Youth and Environment: Attitudes and Action in the 1990s', *Youth and Policy*, Vol. 42, No. 1 pp. 6–21.

Benson, B. (1990) *The Enterprise of Law*, San Francisco: Pacific Research Institute for Public Policy.

Black, D. (1958) *The Theory of Committees and Elections*, Cambridge: Cambridge University Press.

Blais, A. and Dion, S. (eds) (1991) *The Budget Maximising Bureaucrat: Appraisals and Evidence*, Pittsburgh: University of Pittsburgh Press.

Block, W. and Olsen, E. (1982) *Rent Control: Myths and Realities*, Vancouver: Fraser Institute.

Blowers, A. (ed.) (1994) *Planning for a Sustainable Environment*, London: Town and Country Planning Association/ Earthscan.

Body, R. (1984) *Farming in the Clouds*, Aldershot: Temple/Smith/Gower.

Bohm-Bawerk, E. von (1937) *Karl Marx and the Close of his System*, Indianapolis: Liberty Press.

Borcherding, T.E. (ed.) (1977) *Budgets and Bureaucrats: The Sources of Government Growth*, Durham, NC: Duke University Press.

Bowers, J.K. and Cheshire, P. (1983) *Agriculture, the Countryside and Landuse*, London: University Paperbacks, Methuen.

Bramley, G. Bartlett, W. and Lambert, C. (1995) *Planning, the Market and Private House Building*, London: UCL Press.

Breheny, M., Gordan, I. and Archer, S. (1998) 'Building Densities and Sustainable Cities', *Engineering and Physical Sciences Research Council* (EPSRC), Sustainable Cities Programme, Project Outline, No.5.

Breton, A. and Wintrobe, R. (1975) 'The Equilibrium Size of a Budget Maximising Bureau: A Note on Niskanen's Theory of Bureaucracy', *Journal of Political Economy*, No. 83, pp. 195–207

Brindley, T., Rydin, Y. and Stoker, G. (1989) *Remaking Planning*, London: Unwin Hyman.

Brownhill, S. (1990) *Developing London's Docklands: Another Great Planning Disaster?* London: Paul Chapman.

Brozen, Y. (1982) *Concentration, Mergers and Public Policy*, New York: Macmillan.

Brubaker, E.R. (1975) 'Free Ride, Free Revelation or Golden Rule?' *Journal of Law and Economics*, Vol. 18, April, pp. 147–61.

Bruce Johnson, M. (ed.) (1982) *Resolving the Housing Crisis*, San Francisco: Pacific Institute for Public Policy Research.

Buchanan, J.M. (1965) 'An Economic Theory of Clubs', *Economica*, Vol. 32, pp. 1–14

Buchanan, J.M. (1969) *Cost and Choice*, Chicago: Chicago University Press.

Buchanan, J.M. (1975) *The Limits of Liberty*, Chicago: Chicago University Press.

Buchanan, J.M. (1986) *Liberty, Market and State*, Brighton: Harvester Press.

Buchanan, J.M. (1987) *What Should Economists Do?* Indianapolis: Liberty Press.

Buchanan, J.M. and Stubblebine, W.C. (1962), 'Externality', *Economica*, Vol. 29, November, pp. 371–84.

Buchanan, J.M. and Tullock ,G. (1962) *The Calculus of Consent*, Ann Arbor: University of Michigan Press.

Buchanan, J.M. and Tullock, G. (eds) (1982) *Towards a Theory of the Rent Seeking Society*, Austin: Texas A&M Press.

Buller, H. and Lowe, P.D. (1982) 'Politics and Class in Rural Preservation', in M. Moseley (ed.) *Power, Planning and People in Rural East Anglia*, Norwich: Centre of East Anglia Studies.

Burke, T. and Shackleton, J.R. (1996) *Trouble in Store: UK Retailing in the 1990s*, Hobart Paper 130, London: Institute of Economic Affairs.

Burton, T. (1991)·'The Planning and Compensation Bill', *Ecos*.

Butler, D.E. and Stokes, D. (1974) *Political Change in Britain*, London: Macmillan

Button, K. (1995) 'UK Environmental Policy and Transport', in T.S Gray (ed.) *UK Environmental Policy in the 1990s*, London, Macmillan.

Caldwell, B. (1994) *Beyond Positivism*, (2nd edition), London: Routledge.

Campbell, A., Converse, P., Stokes, D. and Miller, W. (1960) *The American Voter*, New York: John Wiley.

Castells, M. (1977) *The Urban Question*, London: Edward Arnold.

Cervero, R. (1993) *Transit Villages: From Ideas to Implementation*, Access 5, Berkeley, University of California, Transportation Centre.

Cervero, R. (1994) *Transit Focused Development: Does It Draw People Into Transit and Buses?* Institute of Urban and Regional Development, Universe 4, Berkeley, University of California.

Cherry, G. (1996) *Town Planning in Britain Since 1900*, Oxford: Blackwell.

Cheshire, P. and Gordon, I. (1996) 'Territorial Competition and The Predictability of Collective (In) Action', *Urban Studies*, Vol. 33, pp. 383–99.

Cheshire, P. and Sheppard, S. (1989) 'British Planning Policy and Access to Housing: Some Empirical Estimates', *Urban Studies*, Vol. 26, pp. 469–85.

Cheshire, P. and Sheppard, S. (1997) 'The Welfare Economics of Land Use Regulation', *Research Papers in Environmental and Spatial Analysis* No.42, Department of Geography: London School of Economics and Political Science.

Chisholm, M. and Kivell, P. (1987) *Inner City Wasteland*, London: Institute of Economic Affairs.

Chong, D. (1991) *Collective Action and the Civil Rights Movement*, Chicago: University of Chicago Press.

Chong, D. (1995) 'Rational Choice Theory's Mysterious Rivals', *Critical Review*, Vol. 9, Nos. 1–2, pp. 37–57.

Clark, S. and Gaile, G. (1994) 'Globalism and the New Work of Cities'. Paper presented to the conference, *Shaping the Urban Future*, School for Advanced Urban Studies, University of Bristol (July).

Clark, T. and Goetz, E. (1994) 'The Anti-Growth Machine: Can City Governments Control, Limit or Manage Growth?' in T. Clark (ed.) *Urban Innovation: Creative Strategies for Turbulent Times*, London: Sage.

Coase, R.H. (1960) 'The Problem of Social Cost', *Journal of Law and Economics*, Vol. 3, pp. 1–44.

Coase, R.H. (1989) *The Firm, the Market and the Law*, Chicago: Chicago University Press.

Connell, J. (1972) 'Amenity Societies: The Preservation of Central Surrey', *Town and Country Planning*, Vol. 40, pp. 63–81.

Converse, P. (1964) 'The Nature of Belief Systems in Mass Publics', in D. Apter (ed.) *Ideology and Discontent*, New York: Free Press.

Converse, P. and Pierce, R. (1986) *Political Representation in France*, Cambridge, Mass: Harvard University Press.

Cooke, P. (ed.) (1986) *Localities*, London: Unwin Hyman.

Cordato, R.E. (1992) *Welfare Economics and Externalities in an Open-Ended Universe: A Modern Austrian Perspective*, London: Kluwer Academic Press.

Cowen, T. (1985) 'Public Goods and Their Institutional Context: A Critique of Public Goods Theory', *Review of Social Economy*, Vol. 43, pp. 53–63.

Cowen, T. (ed.) (1988) *The Theory of Market Failure*, Fairfax, VA. : George Mason University Press.

Crane, R. (1996) 'Cars and Drivers in the New Suburbs: Linking Access to Travel in Neotraditional Planning', *Journal of the American Planning Association*, Vol. 62, No. 1, pp. 51–65.

Cullingworth, J.M. (1988) *Town and Country Planning in Britain*, (10th Edition), London: Routledge.

Cullingworth, J.M. and Nadin, V. (1994) *Town and Country Planning in Britain*, London: Routledge.

Dahl, R.A. (1961) *Who Governs?* New Haven: Yale University Press.

Dahlman, K. (1979) 'The Problem of Externality', *Journal of Legal Studies*, Vol. 22, No. 1, pp. 141–62.

Daly, H. (1993) 'Free Market Environmentalism: Turning a Good Servant into a Bad Master', *Critical Review*, Vol. 6, Nos 2–3, pp. 171–84.

Danielson, M.N. (1976) *The Politics of Exclusion*, New York: Columbia University Press.

Deakin, N. (1985) 'Vanishing Utopias: The Changing Nature of Planning and Participation in Twentieth Century Britain', *Regional Studies*, Vol. 19, No. 4, pp. 291–300.

De Alessi, L. (1974) 'An Economic Analysis of Government Ownership and Regulation: Theory and Evidence from the Electric Power Industry', *Public Choice*, 19. Fall, pp. 1–42.

Delli Carpini, M.X. and Keeter, S. (1996) *What Americans Know About Politics and Why It Matters*, New Haven: Yale University Press.

Demsetz, H. (1964) 'The Exchange and Enforcement of Property Rights', *Journal of Law and Economics*, Vol. 7, October, pp. 127–46.

Demsetz, H. (1967) 'Towards a Theory of Property Rights', *American Economic Review*, Vol. 57, pp. 347–59.

Demsetz, H. (1969) 'Information and Efficiency: Another Viewpoint', *Journal of Law and Economics*, Vol. 12, No. 1, pp. 1–22.

Denman, D. and Goodchild, R. (1989) *Planning Fails the Inner Cities*, London: Social Affairs Unit.

Derkowski, A. (1975) 'Costs in the Land Development Process'. Report for the Housing and Urban Development Association of Canada, Toronto: HUDAC.

DETR (1997) *Planning News Bulletin*, September, London: Department of the Environment, Transport and the Regions.

DETR (1998) *Modernising Planning*, London: HMSO.

Di Lorenzo, T. (1987) 'Competition and Political Entrepreneurship: Austrian Insights into Public Choice Theory', *Review of Austrian Economics*, Vol. 2, pp. 59–72.

Di Zerega, G. (1993) 'Social Ecology, Deep Ecology and Liberalism', *Critical Review*, Vol. 6, Nos 2–3, pp. 305–70.

DoE. (1992b) *Planning Policy Guidance Note 12: Development Plans and Regional Planning Guidance*, London: HMSO.

DoE. (1993a) *Green Belts*, London: HMSO.

DoE. (1993b) *Planning Policy Guidance Note 13: Transport*, London: HMSO.

DoE. (1994a) *Planning Policy Guidance Note 2: Green Belts*, London: HMSO.

DoE. (1994b) *Planning Policy Guidance Note 6: Major Retail Development*, London: HMSO.

DoE. (1994c) *Sustainable Development: The UK Strategy*, London: HMSO

DoE (1994d) *Statistics of Planning Applications*, London: DoE.

DoE. (1996) *Household Growth: Where Should We Live?* London: HMSO

Dowall, D.E. (1984) *The Suburban Squeeze: Land Conversion and Regulation in the San Francisco Bay Area*, Berkeley: University of California Press.

Dowding, K. (1991) *Rational Choice and Political Power*, Aldershot: Edward Elgar.

Dowding, K. (1995) *The Civil Service*, London: Routledge.

Dowding, K., John, P. and Biggs, S. (1994) 'Tiebout: A Survey of the Empirical Literature', *Urban Studies*, Vol. 31, Nos 4–5, pp. 767–97.

Downs, A. (1957) *An Economic Theory of Democracy*, New York: Harper and Row.

Downs, A. (1967) *Inside Bureaucracy*, Boston: Little Brown.

Downs, A. (1992) *Stuck in Traffic*, Washington DC: Brookings Institution/ Lincoln Institute for Land Policy.

Drewry, G. (ed.) (1985) *The New Select Committees*, Oxford: Clarendon Press.

Dryzek, J. (1996) 'Foundations for Environmental Political Economy: The Search for Homo Ecologicus', *New Political Economy*, Vol. 1, pp. 27–40.

Dunleavy, P. (1981) *The Politics of Mass Housing in Britain, 1945–1975*, Oxford: Clarendon Press.

Dunleavy, P. (1991) *Democracy, Bureaucracy and Public Choice*, London: Harvester/Wheatsheaf.

Dunleavy, P. and Biggs, S. (1995) 'Changing Organisational Patterns in Local Government: A Bureau Shaping Analysis', *Paper Presented at the 1995 Annual Conference of the British Political Studies Association*, University of York.

Dunleavy, P. and O'Leary, B. (1987) *Theories of the State*, London: Macmillan.

Dunleavy, P. and Ward, H. (1981) 'Exogenous Voter Preferences and Parties with State Power: Some Internal Problems of Economic Models of Party Competition', *British Journal of Political Science*, Vol. 11, No. 3, pp. 351–80.

Dunsire, A. (1991) 'Bureaucrats and Conservative Governments', in A. Blais and S. Dion (eds) *The Budget Maximising Bureaucrat: Appraisals and Evidence*, Pittsburgh: University of Pittsburgh Press.

Dwyer, C. and Hodge, I. (1996) *The Countryside in Trust*, Chichester: Wiley.

Eggertsson, T. (1990) *Economic Behaviour and Institutions*, Cambridge: Cambridge University Press.

Ehrman, R. (1988) *Planning, Planning*, London: Centre for Policy Studies.

Ehrman, R. (1990) Nimbyism: The Disease and the Cure, London: Centre for Policy Studies.

Ellickson, R. (1973) 'Alternatives to Zoning: Covenants, Nuisance Rules and Fines as Land Use Controls', *University of Chicago Law Review*, Vol. 40, pp. 681–782.

Ellickson, R. (1991) *Order Without Law*, Cambridge, MA: Harvard University Press.

Elson, M. (1986) *Green Belts*, London: Heinemann.

Enelow, J.M. and Hinich, M.J. (1984) *The Spatial Theory of Voting: An Introduction*, Cambridge: Cambridge University Press.

Evans, A.W. (1985) *Urban Economics*, Oxford: Blackwell.

Evans, A.W. (1987) *House Pruces and Land Prices in the South East: A Review*, London: House Builders Federation.

Evans, A.W. (1988) *No Room, No Room!* Occasional Paper No.79, London: Institute of Economic Affairs.

Evans, A.W. (1991) 'Rabbit Hutches on Postage Stamps: Planning, Development and Political Economy', *Urban Studies*, Vol. 28, No. 6, pp. 853–70.

Evans, A.W. (1996) 'Foreword', in M. Pennington (ed.) *Conservation and the Countryside: By Quango or Market?* Studies on the Environment No. 6, London: Institute of Economic Affairs.

Faludi, A. (1973) *A Reader in Planning Theory*, Oxford: Pergamon.
Ferejohn, J. and Satz, D. (1995) 'Rational Choice Universalism', *Critical Review*, Vol. 9, Nos 1–2, pp. 71–84.
Fiorina, M.P. (1995) 'Rational Choice, Empirical Contributions and the Scientific Enterprise', *Critical Review*, Vol. 9, Nos 1–2, pp. 85–94.
Fischel, W. (1985) *The Economics of Zoning Laws*, Baltimore: John Hopkins University Press.
Fischel, W. (1995) *Regulatory Takings*, Cambridge MA: Harvard University Press.
Foldvary, F. (1994) *Public Goods and Private Communities*, London: Edward Elgar.
Forester, J. (1989) *Planning in the Face of Power*, Berkeley: University of California Press.
Formaini, R. (1991) *The Myth of Scientific Public Policy*, New York: Transaction Books.
Forman, F. (1985) *Mastering British Politics*, London: Macmillan.
Frech, H.E. and Lafferty, R.N. (1976) 'The Economic Impact of the California Coastal Zone Commission: Land Use and Land Values', in M. Bruce Johnson (ed.) *The California Coastal Plain: A Critique*, San Francisco: Institute for Contemporary Studies.
Frech, H.E. and Lafferty, R.N. (1984) 'The Effect of the Californian Coastal Commission on Housing Prices', *Journal of Urban Economics*, Vol. 16, pp. 105–23.
Frieden, B. J. (1979) *The Environment Protection Hustle*, Cambridge: MIT Press.
Frieden, B.J. (1982) 'The Exclusionary Effect of Growth Controls', in M. Bruce Johnson (ed.) *Resolving the Housing Crisis*, San Francisco: Pacific Institute for Public Policy Research.
Frieden, B. and Sagalyn, L.B. (1989) *Downtown Inc: How America Rebuilds Cities*, Cambridge: MIT Press.
Fry, J.A. (ed.) (1979) *Limits of the Welfare State: Critical Views on Post War Sweden*, Westmead: Saxon House.

Gamble, A. (1988) *The Free Economy and The Strong State*, London: Macmillan.
Ganzs, G. (1985) 'The Transport Select Committee', in G. Drewry (ed.) *The New Select Committees*, Oxford: Clarendon Press.
Gerald Eve and Cambridge Department of Land Economy (1992) The Relationship Between House Prices and Land Supply, Department of the Environment Planning Research Programme, London: HMSO.
Goldsmith, F.B. and Warren, A. (eds) (1993) *Conservation in Progress*, Chichester: Wiley.
Goodchild, R. and Denman, D. (1989) *Planning Fails the Inner Cities*, London: Social Affairs Unit.
Goodchild, R. and Munton, R. (1985) *Development and the Landowner*, London: Allen and Unwin.
Goodin, R. and Le Grand, J. (1987) *Not Only The Poor*, London: Allen and Unwin.
Gordan, P. and Richardson, H.W. (1997) 'Are Compact Cities a Desirable Planning Goal?' *Journal of the American Planning Association*, Vol. 63, No. 1, pp. 95–107.
Gouldson, A. and Murphy, J. (1998) *Regulatory Realities*, London: Earthscan.
Graham, T. (1988) 'The Pattern and Importance of Public Knowledge in the Nuclear Age', *Journal of Conflict Resolution*, Vol. 32, pp. 319–34.
Grant, M. and Heap, D. (1991) *Encyclopaedia of Planning Law and Practice*, London: Sweet and Maxwell.
Gray, J. (1993) *Beyond the New Right: Markets, Governments and the Common Environment*, London: Routledge.
Gray, T.S. (ed.) (1995) *UK Environmental Policy in the 1990s*, London: Macmillan.
Green, D. and Shapiro, I. (1995) *Pathologies of Rational Choice Theory*, New Haven: Yale University Press.
Grigson, W. (1986) *House Prices in Perspective: A Review of South-East Evidence*, London: SERPLAN.

Hall, P. (1975) *Urban and Regional Planning*, London: Allen and Unwin.
Hall, P. (1998) *Sustainable Cities or Town Cramming?* Town and Country Planning Association, London: TCPA/Entec.
Hall, P., Gracey, H., Drewett, R. and Thomas and R. (1973) *The Containment of Urban England*, London: Allen and Unwin.
Hardin, R. (1982) *Collective Action*, Baltimore: Resources for the Future and John Hopkins University Press.
Harding, A. (1991) 'The Rise of Urban Growth Coalitions, UK Style?' *Environment and Planning C, Government and Policy*, Vol. 9, pp. 295–317.
Harding, A. (1994) 'Urban Regimes and Growth Machines: Towards a Cross-National Research Agenda', *Urban Affairs Quarterly*, Vol. 29, No. 3, pp. 356–82.

Harding, A. (1995) 'Elite Theory and Growth Machines', in D. Judge, G. Stoker and H. Wolman (eds) *Theories of Urban Politics*, London: Sage.

Hardy, D. and Ward, C. (1990) *Arcadia: Legacy of a Lost Landscape*, London: Mansell Press.

Harrison, A. (1977) *Economics and Land Use Planning*, Newbury: Policy Journals.

Harvey, D. (1973) *Social Justice and the City*, London: Edward Arnold.

Harvey, D. (1985) *The Urbanisation of Capital*, Oxford: Blackwell.

Hayek, F.A. (1945) 'The Use of Knowledge in Society', *American Economic Review*, Vol. 35, No. 4, pp. 519–30.

Hayek, F.A. (1948) *Individualism and Economic Order*, Chicago: Chicago University Press.

Hayek, F.A. (1959) *The Counter-Revolution of Science*, Indianapolis: Liberty Press.

Hayek, F.A. (1960) *The Constitution of Liberty*, London: Routledge.

Hayek, F.A. (1982) *Law, Legislation and Liberty*, London: Routledge.

Hayek, F.A. (1988) *The Fatal Conceit*, London: Routledge.

Healey, P. (1990) 'Policy Processes in Planning', *Policy and Politics*, Vol. 18, No. 1, pp. 91–103.

Healey, P. (1992) 'The Reorganisation of State and Market in Planning', *Urban Studies*, Vol. 29, Nos. 3/4, pp. 411–34.

Healey, P. (1997) *Collaborative Planning*, London: Macmillan.

Healey, P., Macnamara, P., Elson, M. and Doak, A. (1988) *Land Use Planning and the Mediation of Urban Change: The British Planning System in Practice*, Cambridge: Cambridge University Press.

Healey, P., Davoudi, S., O'Toole, M., Tavsanoglu, S. and Usher, D. (1992) *Property-Led Urban Regeneration*, London: E and F Spon.

Herington, J.M. (1984) *The Outer City*, London: Paul Chapman.

Herington, J.M. (1990) *Green Belts*, London: Regional Studies Association.

Hibbs, J. (1992) *On the Move*, London: Institute of Economic Affairs.

Hill, M. and Bramley, G. (1986) *Analysing Social Policy*, Oxford: Blackwell.

Hirschman, A. (1970) *Exit, Voice and Loyalty*, Cambridge, MA: Harvard University Press.

Hirschman, A. (1982) *Shifting Involvements*, Oxford: Martin Robertson.

HMSO (1997) *Attitudes to the Environment Survey, DETR*, London: HMSO.

Holbrook, T. and Garand, J. (1996) 'Homo Economicus: Economic Information and Economic Voting', *Political Research Quarterly*, Vol. 49, pp. 351–75.

Housing Corporation (1996) *Fact File*, London: Housing Corporation.

Howarth, R.W. (1990) *Farming for Farmers*, Hobart Paperback No. 20 (2nd Edition), London: Institute of Economic Affairs.

Imrie, I. and Thomas, H. (1993) *British Urban Policy*, London: Sage.

Jacobs, M. (1992) *The Green Economy*, London: Pluto Press.

Jones, R. (1982) *Town and Country Chaos*, London: Adam Smith Institute.

Jordan, A. (1993) 'Integrated Pollution Control and the Evolving Style and Structure of Environmental Regulation in the UK', *Environmental Politics*, Vol. 2, pp. 405–27.

Jordan, G. and Maloney, W. (1997) *The Protest Business*, Manchester: Manchester University Press.

Jordan, G. and Richardson, J. (1987) *British Politics and the Policy Process*, London: Allen and Unwin.

Judge, D. (1991) *Parliament and Industry*, Aldershot: Dartmouth.

Kasper, W. and Streit, M. (1998) *Institutional Economics: Social Order and Public Policy*, London: Edward Elgar.

Keating, W.D. and Krumholtz, N. (1991) 'Downtown Plans for the 1980s: The Case for More Equity in the 1990s', *Journal of the American Planning Association*, Vol. 57, No. 2, pp. 136–52.

Kirzner, I. (1973) *Competition and Entrepreneurship*, Chicago: University of Chicago Press.

Kirzner, I. (1985) *Discovery and the Capitalist Process*, Chicago: University of Chicago Press.

Kirzner, I. (1992) *The Meaning of Market Process*, London: Routledge.

Kirzner, I. (1997) 'Entrepreneurial Discovery and the Competitive Market Process: An Austrian Approach', *Journal of Economic Literature*, Vol. 35, pp. 66–85.

Klosterman, R.E. (1985) 'Arguments For and Against Planning', *Town Planning Review*, Vol. 56, pp. 5–20.

Kneisel, R. (1979) *Economic Impacts of Land Use Control: The California Coastal Zone Conservation Commission*, Environmental Quality Series, No.30, Institute of Government Affairs and Institute of Ecology: University of California.

Komesar, H.K. (1978) 'Housing, Zoning and the Public Interest', in B. Weisrod (ed.) *Public Interest Law*, Berkeley: University of California Press.

Kuran, T. (1991) 'The Role of Deception in Political Competition', in A. Breton (ed.) *The Competitive State*, London: Kluwer Academic Press.

Kuran, T. (1995) *Private Truths, Public Lies*, Cambridge, Mass: Harvard University Press.

Kwong, J. (1990) *Market Environmentalism*, Hong Kong Centre for Economic Research, Hong Kong: China University Press.

Lai, L. (1997) 'Property Rights Justifications for Planning and a Theory of Zoning', *Progress in Planning*, Vol. 48, pp. 161–246.

Lait, J. (1980) 'Government Ineptitude in Monitoring Local Welfare', in A. Seldon (ed.) *Town Hall Power or Whitehall Pawn?* Readings 25, London: Institute of Economic Affairs.

Landis, J.D. (1986) 'Land Regulation and the Price of New Housing', *Journal of the American Planning Association*, Vol. 52, (Winter), pp. 9–21.

Larkham, P. (1993) 'Conservation in Action', *Town Planning Review*, Vol. 64, No. 4, pp. 351–7.

Latham, E. (1952) 'The Group Basis of Politics', *American Political Science Review*, Vol. 46, No. 2, pp. 376–97.

Lavoie, D. (1985) *Rivalry and Central Planning*, New York: Cambridge University Press.

Libecap, G. (1981) *Locking Up the Range*, San Francisco: Pacific Research Institute for Public Policy.

Libecap, G. (1989) *Contracting for Property Rights*, Cambridge: Cambridge University Press.

Lindblom, C. (1977) *Politics and Markets*, New York: Basic Books.

Littlechild, S. (1986) *The Fallacy of the Mixed Economy: A Neo-Austrian Critique of Recent Economic Thinking*, London: Institute of Economic Affairs.

Logan, J. and Molotch, H. (1987) *Urban Fortunes: The Political Economy of Place*, Berkeley: University of California Press.

Loveless, J. (1983) *The Waste Land: A Critique of Urban Land Policy*, London: Adam Smith Institute.

Loveless, J. (1987) *Why Wasteland?* London: Adam Smith Institute

Lowe, P. (1977) 'Amenity and Equity: A Review of Local Environmental Pressure Groups in Britain', *Environment and Planning A*, Vol. 9, pp. 39–58.

Lowe, P. and Goyder, J. (1983) *Environmental Groups in Politics*, Resource Management Series, Vol. 6, London: Allen and Unwin.

Lowe, P. Cox, G., MacEwen, M., O'Riordan, T. and Winter, M. (1986) *Countryside Conflicts*, Aldershot: Temple/Smith/Gower.

MacAvoy, P.W. (1965) *The Economic Effects of Regulation*, Cambridge: MIT Press.

McCormick, J. (1991) *British Politics and the Environment*, London: Earthscan.

Marren, P. (1993) 'The Siege of the NCC', in F.B. Goldsmith and A. Warren (eds) *Conservation in Progress*, Chichester: Wiley.

Marsden, T., Murdoch, J., Lowe, P., Munton, R. and Flynn, A. (1993) *Constructing the Countryside*, London: UCL Press.

Marsh, D. (1991) 'Privatisation Under Mrs Thatcher', *Public Administration*, Vol. 69, pp. 459–80.

Marsh, D. and Rhodes, R.A.W. (eds) (1992) *Implementing Thatcherite Policies: Audit of an Era*, Buckingham: Open University Press.

Martin, L. (1975) *Land Use Dynamics on the Toronto Urban Fringe*. Ottawa: Information Canada for Environment Canada.

McKean, M. and Ostrom, E. (1995) 'Common Property Regions in the Forest: Just a Relic from the Past?' *Unasylva*, Vol. 46, No. 180, pp. 3–15.

McLean, I. (1982) *Dealing in Votes*, New York: St Martins Press.

McLean, I. (1985) *Public Choice*, Oxford: Blackwell.

Mercer, L.J. and Morgan, D.W. (1982) 'An Estimate of Residential Growth Controls' Impact on House Prices', in M. Bruce Johnson (ed.) *Resolving the Housing Crisis*, San Francisco: Pacific Institute for Public Policy Research.

Miller, B. (1992) 'Collective Action and Rational Choice: Place, Community and the Limits of Individual Self-Interest', *Economic Geography*, Vol. 68, pp. 27–42.

Mills, E.S. (1991) *Should Governments Own Convention Centres?* Palatine, Illinois: Heartland Institute.

Minford, P., Peel, M. and Ashton, P. (1987) *The Housing Morass*, London: Institute of Economic Affairs.

Mitchell, W.C. (1988) *Government as It Is*, Hobart Paper 109, London: Institute of Economic Affairs.

Mitchell, N. and Bretting, J.G. (1991) 'Business and Political Finance in the United Kingdom', *Department of Political Science Working Paper*, University of New Mexico.

Mitchell, W.C. and Simmons, R.T. (1995) *Beyond Politics*, San Francisco: Westview.

Moe, T. (1981) 'Toward a Broader View of Interest Groups', *Journal of Politics*, Vol. 43, pp. 531–43.

Mollenkopf, J. (1983) *The Contested City*, New Jersey: Princeton University Press.
Molotch, H. (1976) 'The City as a Growth Machine', *America Journal of Sociology*, Vol. 82, No. 2, pp. 309–55.
Montgomery, J. and Thornley, A. (eds) (1990) *Radical Planning Initiatives*, Aldershot: Gower.
Munton, R. (1983) 'Agriculture and Conservation: What Room for Compromise?' in A. Warren and F.B. Goldsmith *Conservation in Perspective*, Chichester: Wiley.
Murdoch, J. and Marsden, T. (1994) *Reconstituting Rurality*, London: UCL Press.
Musgrave, R. and Musgrave, P. (1980) *Public Finance in Theory and Practice*, New York: McGraw Hill.

Nelson, R.H (1977) *Zoning and Property Rights*, Cambridge: MIT Press.
Neuberger, H. and Nichol, B. (1975) *The Recent Course of Land and Property Prices and the Factors Underlying It*, London: Department of the Environment.
Newby, H. (1985) *Green and Pleasant Land*, London: Hutchinson.
Newman, P. and Kenworthy, J.R. (1989) *Cities and Automobile Dependence: A Sourcebook*, Aldershot: Gower.
Newman, P. and Thornley, A. (1996) *Urban Planning in Europe*, London: Routledge.
NFU (1993) *National Farmers Union Annual Report*, London: NFU.
Niskanen, W.A. (1971) *Bureaucracy and Representative Government*, Chicago: Aldine Atherton.
Niskanen, W.A. (1975) 'Bureaucrats and Politicians', *Journal of Law and Economics*, Vol. 18, No. 4, pp. 617–43.
Niskanen, W.A. (1991) 'Introduction', in A. Blais and S. Dion (eds) *The Budget Maximising Bureaucrat: Appraisals and Evidence*, Pittsburgh: University of Pittsburgh Press.
Niskanen, W.A. (1995) *Bureaucracy and Public Economics*, London: Edward Elgar.
Norten, P. and Aughey, A. (1981) *Conservatives and Conservatism*, London: Temple Smith.
North, D. (1990) *Institutions, Institutional Change and Economic Performance*, Cambridge: Cambridge University Press.
Nozick, R. (1974) *Anarchy, State and Utopia*, Oxford: Blackwell.

Olson. M. (1965) *The Logic of Collective Action*, Cambridge, MA: Harvard University Press.
Olson, M. (1982) *The Rise and Decline of Nations*, New Haven: Yale University Press.
Opp, K.-D. (1986) 'Soft Incentives and Collective Action', *British Journal of Political Science*, Vol. 16, pp. 87–112.
Ostrom, E. (1988) 'Institutional Arrangements and the Commons Dilemma', in V.Ostrom, D. Feeny and H. Picht (eds) *Rethinking Institutional Analysis and Development*, San Francisco: Institute for Contemporary Studies.
Ostrom, E. (1990) *Governing the Commons: The Evolution of Institutions for Collective Action*, Cambridge: Cambridge University Press.
Ostrom, V., Bish, R. and Ostrom, E. (1988) *Local Government in the United States*, San Francisco: Institute for Contemporary Studies.

Page, B.I. and Shapiro, R.Y. (1992) *The Rational Public*, Chicago: University of Chicago Press.
Pahl, R.E. (1975) *Whose City?* Harmondsworth: Penguin.
Pasour, E.C. (1983) *Agriculture and the State*, San Francisco: Boulder.
Peacock, A.T. (1983) 'X-Inefficiency: Informational and Institutional Constraints', in H. Hanusch (ed.) *Anatomy of Government Deficiencies*, Berlin: Springer.
Peacock, A.T. (ed.) (1984) *The Regulation Game*, Oxford: Blackwell.
Pearce, D., Marandya, A. and Barbier, E. (1989) *Blue Print for a Green Economy*, London: Earthscan.
Pennington, M. (1996) *Conservation and the Countryside: By Quango or Market?* Studies on the Environment No. 6, London: Institute of Economic Affairs.
Pennington, M. (1997a) *Property Rights, Public Choice and the Containment of Urban England*, Unpublished PhD Thesis, London School of Economics and Political Science, University of London.
Pennington, M. (1997b) 'Budgets, Bureaucrats and the Containment of Urban England', *Environmental Politics*, Vol. 6, No. 4, pp. 76–107.
Pennington, M. (1999) 'Free Market Environmentalism and the Limits of Land Use Planning', *Journal of Environmental Policy and Planning*, Vol. 1, No.1, pp. 43–59.
Pennington, M. (2000) 'Public Choice Theory and the Politics of Urban Containment: Voter-Centred versus Special Interest Explanations', *Environment and Planning C, Government and Policy*, forthcoming.
Pennington, M. and Rydin, Y. (2000) 'Researching Social Capital in Local Environmental Policy Contexts', *Policy and Politics*, forthcoming.

Peters, B.G. (1989) *Comparing Public Bureaucracies: Problems of Theory and Method*, Tuscaloosa: University of Alabama Press.
Pigou, A.C. (1920) *The Economics of Welfare*, London: Macmillan.
Polanyi, M. (1951) *The Logic of Liberty*, Chicago: University of Chicago Press.
Poole, K.P. (1975) *The Local Government Service*, London: Allen and Unwin.
Poole, R. (1985) *Unnatural Monopoly*, Lexington, Mass: Lexington Books.
Posner, R.A. (1986) *Economic Analysis of Law*, Boston: Littlebrown.

Raco, M. (1997) 'Business Associations and the Politics of Urban Renewal: The Case of the Lower Don Valley, Sheffield', *Urban Studies*, Vol. 34, No. 3, pp. 383–402.
Rawcliffe, P. (1998) *Environmental Pressure Groups in Transition*, Manchester: Manchester University Press.
Reade, E. (1987) *British Town and Country Planning*, Milton Keynes: Open University Press.
Ridley, M. (1996) *Down to Earth*, London: Institute of Economic Affairs.
Ridley, M. (1998) *Down to Earth 2*, London: Institute of Economic Affairs.
Riker, W.H. (1982) *Liberalism Against Populism: A Confrontation Between the Theory of Democracy and the Theory of Social Choice*, San Francisco: W.H Freeman.
Riker, W.H. (1984) 'The Heresthetics of Constitution-Making', *American Political Science Review*, Vol.78, pp. 1–16.
Riker, W. and Ordeshook, P.C. (1968) 'A Theory of the Calculus of Voting', *American Political Science Review*, Vol. 62, pp. 25–42.
Riker, W.H. and Ordeshook, P.C. (1973) *An Introduction to Positive Political Theory*, Englewood Cliffs, NJ: Prentice Hall.
Robinson, A. (1985) 'The Financial Work of the New Select Committees', in G. Drewry (ed.) *The New Select Commitees*, Oxford: Clarendon Press.
Robinson, C. (1993) *Energy Policy: Errors Ilusions and Market Realities*, Occasional Paper No. 90, London: Institute of Economic Affairs.
Robinson, M. (1992) *The Greening of British Party Politics*, Manchester: Manchester University Press.
Roemer, J. (1994) *A Future for Socialism*, Cambridge, MA: Harvard University Press.
Rojas, M. (1998) *The Rise and Fall of the Swedish Model*, London: Social Market Foundation.
Rosen, K.T. and Katz, L.F. (1981) 'Growth Management and Land Use Controls: The San Francisco Bay Area Experience', *American Real Estate and Urban Economics Association Journal*, Vol. 9, pp. 321–44.
Rowley, C. (1992) *The Political Economy of Legal Services*, London: Edward Elgar.
Royal Town Planning Institute (1992) *Planning Staffs Survey*, London: RTPI.
Rydin, Y. (1986) *Housing Land Policy*, Aldershot: Gower.
Rydin, Y. (1995) 'Sustainable Development and the Role of Land Use Planning', *Area*, Vol. 27, No. 2, pp. 369–77.
Rydin, Y. (1998a) 'Managing Urban Air Quality: Language and Rational Choice in Metropolitan Governance', *Environment and Planning A*, Vol. 30, pp. 1429–44.
Rydin, Y. (1998b) *Urban and Environmental Planning in the UK*, London: Macmillan.
Sadler, D. (1993) 'Place Marketing, Competitive Places and the Construction of Hegemony in Britain in the 1980s', in G. Kearns and C. Philo (eds) *Selling Places: The City as Cultural Capital Past and Present*, Oxford: Pergamon.
Sagoff, M. (1994) 'Environmentalism vs Value Subjectivism: Rejoinder to Anderson and Leal', *Critical Review*, Vol. 8, No. 3, pp. 457–73.
Salins, P.D. (1994) 'Metropolitan Visions', *Reason*, (December), pp. 60–3.
Salisbury, R.H. (1969) 'An Exchange Theory of Interest Groups', *Midwest Journal of Political Science*, Vol. 13, pp. 1–32.
Schattschneider, E. (1960) *The Semi-Sovereign People*, New York: Holt, Reinhart and Winston.
Schmidtz. D. (1994) 'Market Failure?' *Critical Review*, Vol. 7, No. 4, pp. 525–37.
Schumpeter, J.A. (1962) *Capitalism, Socialism and Democracy*, Third Edition, New York: Harper Torchbooks.
Schwartz, S., Hansen, D. and Green, R. (1981) 'Suburban Growth Controls and the Price of New Housing', *Journal of Environmental Economics and Management*, Vol. 8, pp. 303–20.
Schwartz, S., Hansen, D. and Green, R. (1984) 'The Effect of Growth Control on the Production of Moderate Priced Housing', *Land Economics*, Vol. 60, pp. 110–14.
Seldon, A. (ed.) (1980) *Town Hall Power or Whitehall Pawn*, Institute of Economic Affairs, London: IEA.
Self, P. (1989) *Government by the Market: The Politics of Public Choice*, London: Macmillan.

Shaw, J. (1994) 'Real People Prefer Free Market Environmentalism: Reply to Jeffrey Friedman', *Critical Review*, Vol. 8, No. 3, pp. 475–82.

Shaw, K. (1993) 'The Development of a New Urban Corporatism: The Politics of Urban Regeneration in the North east of England', *Regional Studies*, Vol. 27, No. 3, pp. 251–9.

Shepsle, K.A. (1995) 'Statistical Political Philosophy and Positive Political Economy', *Critical Review*, Vol. 9, Nos 1–2, pp. 213–22.

Shepsle, K.A. and Weingast, B.R. (1987) 'The Institutional Foundations of Committee Power', *American Political Science Review*, Vol. 81, pp. 85–104.

Short, J.R. (1982) *Housing in Britain: The Post War Experience*, London: Methuen.

Short, J.R., Fleming, S. and Witt, S. (1986) *House Building, Planning and Community Action*, London: Routledge and Kegan Paul.

Shucksmith, M. (1990) *House Building in Britain's Countryside*, London: Routledge.

Siegan, B. (1974) *Land Use Without Zoning*, Mass: Lexington Books.

Simmie, J. (1981) *Power, Property and Corporatism: The Political Sociology of Planning*, London: Macmillan.

Simmie, J. (1993) *Planning at the Crossroads*, London: UCL Press.

Simon, H. (1957) *Models of Man*, New York: Wiley.

Skea, J. (1995) 'Acid Rain: A Business as Usual Scenario', in T.S. Gray (ed.) *UK Environmental Policy in the 1990s*, London: Macmillan.

Smith, A. (1997) *Integrated Pollution Control*, Aldershot: Gower.

Somin, I. (1998) 'Voter Ignorance and the Democratic Ideal', *Critical Review*, Vol. 12, No. 4, pp. 413–58.

Spiers, M. (1976) *Victoria Park: A Nineteenth Century Suburb in its Social and Adminstrative Context*, Manchester: Cletham Society.

Spiller, P.T. (1990) 'Politicians, Regulators and Interest Groups: A Multiple Principles Theory of Regulation', *Journal of Law and Economics*, Vol. 33, pp. 65–101.

Staley, S. (1994) *Planning Rules and Urban Economic Performance: The Case of Hong Kong*, Hong Kong: The Chinese University Press.

Steedman, I. (1977) *Marx After Sraffa*, London: New Left Books.

Steele, D.R. (1992) *From Marx to Mises: Post Capitalist Society and the Challenge of Economic Calculation*, Chicago: La Salle, Open Court.

Stein, P. (1982) 'Sweden: Failure of the Welfare State', *Journal of Economic Growth*, Vol. 2, No. 4.

Stewart, P. (1987) *Growing Against the Grain*, London: Council for the Protection of Rural England.

Stigler, G. (1975) *The Citizen and the State*, Chicago: Chicago University Press.

Stigler, G. and Becker, G. (1977) *De Gustus non est disputandum*, *American Economic Review*, Vol. 67, No. 1, pp. 76–90.

Stoker, G. and Mossberger, K. (1994) 'Urban Regime Theory in Comparative Perspective', *Environment and Planning C, Government and Policy*, Vol. 12, pp. 195–212.

Stroup, R. (1990) 'Rescuing Yellowstone from Politics: Expanding Parks While Reducing Conflicts', in J. Baden and D. Leal (eds) *The Yellowstone Primer*, San Francisco: Pacific Research Institute for Public Policy.

Taylor, M. (1987) *The Possibility of Co-operation*, Cambridge: Cambridge University Press.

Taylor, M. and Ward, H. (1982) 'Chickens, Whales and Lumpy Goods: Alternative Models of Public Goods Provision', *Political Studies*, Vol. 30, pp. 350–70.

Tiebout, C.M. (1956) 'A Pure Theory of Local Expenditure', *Journal of Political Economy*, Vol. 64, pp. 416–24.

Thornley, A. (1991) *Urban Planning Under Thatcherism*, London: Routledge.

Thornley, A. (1994) *Urban Planning Under Thatcherism*, (2nd edition), London: Routledge.

Times Guide (1983–1995) *Times Guide to Parliament*, London: Times Publishing Company.

Truman, D. (1951) *The Governmental Process*, New York: Alfred A. Knopf.

Tucker, R. (1990) *Zoning, Rent Control and Affordable Housing*, Washington DC: Cato Institute.

Tullock, G. (1977) *The Vote Motive*, London: Institute of Economic Affairs.

Tullock, G. (1989) *The Economics of Special Privilege and Rent Seeking*, London: Kluwer Academic Press.

Tullock, G. (1993) *Rent Seeking*, London: Edward Elgar.

Turner, D.K., Pearce, D. and Bateman, I. (1994) *Environmental Economics: An Elementary Introduction*, Brighton: Harvester.

Urban Task Force (1999) *Towards an Urban Renaissance*, London: HMSO and E and F Spon.

Varian, H. (1994) 'Markets for Public Goods?' *Critical Review*, Vol. 7, No. 4, pp. 539–56.

Veljanowski, C. (1988) 'Foreword', in A.W. Evans (ed.) *No Room! No Room!* Occasional Paper No. 79, London Institute of Economic Affairs.

Walters, A.A., Pennance, F.G., West, W.A. Denman, D.R. and Bracewell-Milnes, B.(1974) *Government and the Land*, London: Institute of Economic Affairs.

Ward, H. (1995) 'Rational Choice', in D. Marsh and G. Stoker (eds) *Theory and Methods in Political Science*, London: Macmillan.

Warren, A. and Goldsmith, F.B. (1983) *Conservation in Perspective*, Chichester: Wiley.

Weale, A. (1992) *The New Politics of Pollution*, Manchester: Manchester University Press.

Weale, A. (1993) 'Nature versus the State: Markets, States and Environmental Protection', *Critical Review*, Vol. 6, Nos. 2–3, pp. 153–70.

Webster, C. (1998) 'Public Choice, Pigouvian and Coasian Planning Theory', *Urban Studies*, Vol. 35, pp. 53–76.

Weingast, B.R. and Marshall, W.J. (1988) 'The Industrial Organisation of Congress', *Journal of Political Economy*, Vol. 96, pp. 132–63.

West, W.A. (1969) *Private Capital for New Towns*, Occasional Paper No.28, London: Institute of Economic Affairs.

Wilson, D. and Game, C. (1994) *Local Government in the United Kingdom*, London: Macmillan.

Wilson, J.Q. (1989) *Bureaucracy: What Government Agencies Do and Why They Do It*, New York: Basic Books.

Winter, M. (1996) *Rural Politics*, London: Routledge.

Woodlief, A. (1998a) 'Unforeseen Consequences and Pathological Self-Reinforcement: Why Cities Decline', *Critical Review*, Vol. 12, Nos. 1–2, pp. 13–34.

Woodlief, A. (1998b) 'The Path Dependent City', *Urban Affairs Review*, Vol. 33, No. 3, pp. 405–37.

Young, S. (1995) 'Running Up the Down Escalator: Developments in British Wildlife Policies After Mrs Thatcher's 1988 Speeches', in T.S. Gray (ed.) *UK Environmental Policy in the 1990s*, London: Macmillan.

INDEX